CLIFFORD ODETS:
THE THIRTIES
AND AFTER

EDWARD MURRAY

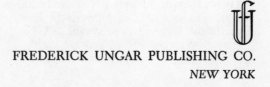

FREDERICK UNGAR PUBLISHING CO.
NEW YORK

For my mother and father

I read in a book the other day that the Germans are intellectually complex, emotionally simple. We are just the opposite. Our future will have to come out of our emotional complexes—but we have that unshakable moralistic sense as a stabilizer and come hell or high water it will pull us through.

Clifford Odets,
Los Angeles Times, May 14, 1944

The form [of a play] is always dictated by the material; there can be nothing ready-made about it. It will use certain dramatic laws because, after all, you have to relate this material to an audience, and a form is the quickest way to get your content to an audience. That's all form is. Form is viability.

Clifford Odets to Arthur Wagner, 1961
(*Harper's*, September 1966)

PREFACE

It is not unusual today to meet young people—occasionally even graduate students of American literature—who have never heard the name Clifford Odets. Thirty years ago it was a different matter. As William Gibson has rightly pointed out: "In the late thirties Odets was the playwright most of my generation wanted to be." Even twenty years ago James Agee said that Odets was "obviously one of the very few genuine dramatic poets alive." Although there has been a revival of interest in the thirties there has been as yet no rediscovery of the most famous dramatist of that decade. Not that Odets is merely of historical concern now, or that his significance is restricted to the thirties. For three of Odets' plays written after the thirties have as much intrinsic importance, and thus as much claim on our attention, as the best plays he presented during the Great Depression. Indeed, it is my belief that Clifford Odets is the only American dramatist, with the possible exception of Edward Albee, worthy to be considered in the same class with Eugene O'Neill, Arthur Miller, and Tennessee Williams.

The chapters of this book which are devoted to an analytical study of Odets' best plays attempt to offer substantial evidence in support of my claim for Odets' relevance and durable achievement. Two chapters—the first and the fifth—deal for the most part with the public life of Odets and the historical background of his work. I have not attempted to write a biography, nor have I sought to present a formal chronicle of the times. This book is a critical study. Nevertheless, I feel that some knowledge of Odets' life and the age that shaped him—and by "the age"

I mean not only the thirties but the later years too—is desirable
for a full appreciation of his contribution to our theater and
literature. But my chief emphasis, as I have suggested, is on the
form of Odets' work; that is, on each play as a separate work of
art. Hence, the analytical chapters of the book focus on the parts
of each play—namely, structure, character, language and theme—
in an attempt to evaluate their complexity and coherence. By
close analysis of each play, I try to reveal Odets' mastery of form
and stimulate appreciation of him as an artist. Although the
historical significance of *Waiting for Lefty* (1935) is discussed
in Chapter One, I have not devoted an analytical chapter to this
crude early effort. Similarly, I have ignored *Till the Day I Die*
(1935) and *Paradise Lost* (1935), neither of which, in my view,
can add any luster to Odets' critical reputation. *Night Music*
(1940) and *Clash by Night* (1941), though relative failures in
the Odets canon, do justify analysis, I believe, for reasons given
in the chapters bearing on these transitional pieces.

   Clifford Odets was distinguished by his gift for verbal expression; therefore, in the pages that follow I have not prevented
him from speaking as much as possible for himself. In other
words, I have quoted generously from Odets' plays, articles, and
press interviews. It is time, I think, for a new generation to hear
the words of "one of the very few genuine dramatic poets" of
the modern theater.

Brockport, New York   E.M.
July 1968

EDITIONS CITED

Six Plays of Clifford Odets. New York: Random House, 1939 (includes *Waiting for Lefty, Awake and Sing! Till the Day I Die, Paradise Lost, Golden Boy* and *Rocket to the Moon*).

Night Music. New York: Random House, 1940.

Clash by Night. New York: Random House, 1942.

The Big Knife. New York: Dramatists' Play Service, 1949.

The Country Girl. New York: Viking, 1951.

The Flowering Peach. This play is presently available only in typescript. (See Acknowledgments.)

Odets' "Introduction" to Gogol's *Dead Souls* appears in the Modern Library (New York: Random House, 1936).

A bibliography of secondary sources—with the exception of newspaper pieces, which are cited in the text—appears at the end of the book. This bibliography is restricted to sources actually quoted or referred to in the course of my study.

CONTENTS

CLIFFORD ODETS: THE THIRTIES

CLIFFORD ODETS: AFTER THE THIRTIES

CLIFFORD ODETS: THE THIRTIES

CHAPTER ONE

Odets and the Thirties

To hell with the last century! This is a wonderful time to write. Hart Crane jumped off a boat crying: "This is no time for poets!" He was wrong. This is no time for weakness, but it is certainly a time for poets.

—Clifford Odets, *Time,*
December 5, 1938

In *The God That Failed* Arthur Koestler says: "The case-history of most revolutionaries and reformers reveals a neurotic conflict with family or society. But this only proves, to paraphrase Marx, that a moribund society creates its own morbid gravediggers." Perhaps Koestler's analysis of the relationship between the individual and society makes the interaction between the two seem much neater than it is in reality. However that may be, one might fairly argue that a distinguishing mark of the thirties was an inclination on the part of many reformers to use Marx as an answer to *all* the problems of life. If the men of the thirties were a Found Generation, it seems to us in the sixties that most of them found themselves much too quickly, much too easily. Clifford Odets, who claimed to have discovered himself in the crucible of the Great Depression, is typical in this respect. Odets' interviews with the press during the thirties reveal a bumptious, glib, positive-thinking "proletarian dramatist." However, his plays of the period—the goods ones, I mean, like *Awake and Sing!*, *Golden Boy* and *Rocket to the Moon*—tell a different story: They reflect the complex personal tensions of the artist, while they also underscore the dark side of the Found Generation's cocky assertiveness. It is interesting to note that some early critics of Odets referred to him as an optimistic writer, but others were equally convinced that he was pessimistic. "I would say that I have a *belief* in man and his possibilities as the measure of things," Odets told Michael J. Mendelsohn in 1963, "but I would not say that I was an optimistic writer. I would say that I have shown as much of the seamy side of life as any other playwright of the twentieth century, if not more." Actually, Odets' plays are both optimistic and pessimistic, the degree of each attitude varying from play to play; and it is the conflict between the two moods within a specific play that contributes to the density and complexity of the piece.

It was characteristic of the early Odets, however, to give what he himself called an "ideological direction" to his work. In 1961 he informed Arthur Wagner: "When I started to write *Awake and Sing!* I didn't have a mission in life; I wasn't going to change society. When I came to rewriting it I was going to change the world—or help change it." Marxism seemed to provide a cure-all for whatever pained Odets and his society. Today, as I have said, it is easy to see that Marxism was a spurious solution to the problem of human existence. To Odets' credit as a playwright, though, it can be affirmed that his work did not suffer for long from the Communist delusion. Speaking of his early plays, Odets told Mendelsohn: "Frequently, the simplicity of some of my endings comes from the fact that I did not say at the same time, 'This is a beginning; this will give you the right to begin in a clean and simple way.' But these things are not ends in themselves. A strike and a better wage is not an end in itself. It will give you the chance to begin." If Odets' plays of 1935 tend to offer smooth answers to thorny questions, the explanation lies in the heady quality of the social reform that Odets, among others, imbibed rather too freely in those hectic days. "I per-

sonally did not do too much [reading of Marxist literature] because it was a little beyond me, and my interest was going toward
writing plays," Odets told the House Committee on Un-American Activities in 1952. "To study these matters required really
months of very serious study which I did not give them." Marxism, far from being a "scientific" explanation of the laws of
history, was merely an opiate for Odets. "Everything was extremely heightened," the dramatist explained to Wagner. "You
didn't know whether it was real or mystic. Were these real
human beings? Where was this happening?"

Which provides a cue for two key questions: What kind of
man was Odets *before* he had a "mission in life"? And what is
the "truth" behind our stereotype of the thirties? Naturally,
both questions are extremely difficult to answer.

A *New Yorker* profile by John McCarten in 1938 reports
Odets as saying: "This boy was a very ordinary middle-class boy,
unconsciously ambitious, but with a kind of purity and unselfish-
ness. He did typical things, for everything about him was typical,
typical, so typical." Twenty-three years later Odets, speaking
of his new-found sense of direction in 1935, informed Wagner:
"It's surprising how very important a small satisfaction can be
in the life of one who is moving away from what I can only
call illness to some kind of health or strength. (You must remember . . . that before I was twenty-five I had tried to commit
suicide three times; once I stopped it myself and twice my life
was saved by perfect strangers.)" The bald facts of Odets' early
life give no clear insight into the nature of the conflict which
drove an "ordinary middle-class boy" into three attempted sui-
cides. Childhood and the first years of manhood are pivotal
points in an individual's life. Until we possess a definitive biography of Odets, however, the origin of his neurotic illness will
remain largely concealed behind the few well-established facts
of his early years.

Why, for example, did Odets tell Mendelsohn: "I've always
felt homeless. I have never felt that I had a home"? What we

know about Odets' early years does not provide an easy answer to this problem. Odets was the eldest child and only son of Louis and Pearl Geisinger Odets, both of whom were Jewish. Clifford was born in Philadelphia on July 18, 1906. Until the age of twelve, Odets aggressively proclaimed in 1938, he "was a worker's son." Louis Odets sold newspapers and peddled salt in Philadelphia; he also worked as a printer there for the Curtis Publishing Company. Pearl Odets was born in Rumania. Years later the playwright told the Un-American Activities Committee: "If I were moved by certain situations of poverty . . . this would be because my mother worked in a stocking factory in Philadelphia at the age of eleven and died a broken woman and an old woman at the age of forty-eight, and when I wrote, sir, it was out of central, personal things. I did not learn my hatred of poverty, sir, out of Communism." Nevertheless, the social and economic situation of the Odets family vastly improved over the years. They moved to New York City in 1912 where the elder Odets, beginning as a feeder in a printing shop, prospered and ended by being the capitalist who owned the plant. In the *New Yorker* article mentioned above McCarten notes: "The Bronx that Odets depicted in *Awake and Sing!* was one of the gloomiest places in the world, but the Bronx he actually lived in was quite pleasant, full of trees and open fields, and his family got along fine there." In *The New York Times* on February 20, 1949, Seymour Peck quoted Odets as follows:

> It has been implied that the only play I ever wrote out of personal experience was *Awake and Sing!* . . . As a matter of fact, *Awake and Sing!* was not a personal experience of mine at all. I never came from such a family, there was never a Yiddish word spoken in my family. I never lived such a life. My mother was a strange and nunlike woman who had to live with two brawling, trigger-tempered men in the house—my father and myself. She couldn't take it, with that nunlike quality. When she died, I came back to

the house and burned every piece of writing I had done before *Awake and Sing!* and *Waiting for Lefty*. This was the end of a whole period in my life. Was that in *Awake and Sing!*?

Odets appears to have been strongly attached to his mother. He dedicated *Six Plays* to "Pearl Geisinger, My Mother"; inscribed *Paradise Lost* to "My Dead Mother"; and named the daughter in that play, a pianist who refuses to marry and who withdraws from reality, "Pearl." When Odets came to the Group Theater in 1930, Harold Clurman recalls in *The Fervent Years*, he was still "rather shy" around girls. The playwright was thirty-one when he married Luise Rainer—two years after his mother's death—in 1937. The marriage ended in divorce. Odets' marriage to a second actress, Betty Grayson, in 1943 was also terminated in Reno.

The dramatist's relations with his father were often extremely difficult. "I was a melancholy kid," Odets said in 1938. Why was Odets "melancholy"? Economically, as noted, Louis Odets was able to provide a more than comfortable home for his family. The father was able to send his wife on long and expensive trips to California for her health. In 1927 he took a position as vice-president and general sales manager of a boiler company in Philadelphia. At the same time he continued as a merchandising counsellor and retained ownership of an advertising agency. When Louis Odets retired in 1936 he sold the agency for two hundred thousand dollars. Although money was hardly scarce in the Odets household, young Clifford was both melancholy and rebellious.

For example, Odets found Morris High School in New York "a waste of time," and promptly quit after two years. It was the hope of the elder Odets that his son would join the advertising business and become a copywriter. Instead Clifford wrote poetry. On one occasion Louis Odets furiously exploded and smashed his son's typewriter. "Believe me," Odets said once, "there were some very gloomy evenings." Indeed there must have been. In Odets' plays the family generally plays a conspicuous role; and in the early work, as Mendelsohn has noted, rebellion against a repressive family is in the forefront. Although Mendelsohn believes that Odets' attitude is fairly common in our culture, he nevertheless concludes that the playwright "carries the idea to an extreme that is surprising, especially when viewed in the light of the traditional Jewish pattern of close family ties." After one of their discords Odets told his father: "You can't harness me to a truck—can't you see I'm not a truck horse?" Finally Louis Odets compromised and gave his son permission to become an actor.

Odets had been stagestruck since his sixth year at Public School 52, where he played Prince Charming in a first grade production of *Cinderella*. After the elder Odets gave his son permission to become an actor, Clifford joined a small group of amateurs called the Drawing Room Players, who performed at the Heckscher Theater; and from there he went with Harry Kemp's Poets' Theater. Finally Odets formed his own group, which acted on radio; the group also appeared in vaudeville and summer stock. More important, Odets gained valuable experience writing radio plays. Unfortunately, Odets made little money. One year, for example, he earned the munificent sum of twenty dollars. Stranded in Hawley, Pennsylvania on one occasion, Odets had to wire his father for money. When he was twenty-one the future revolutionary playwright of American drama returned home for two years. Mr. and Mrs. Odets were beginning to speculate whether Clifford would be a dependent forever. "Their son," Odets told McCarten, "was not industrious." It is not difficult to see where at least some of the conflict between father and son originated.

Whatever the explanation for Odets' neurotic personality, the progress of his morbid illness was not self-limiting. In 1929, when Odets went to New York to understudy Spencer Tracy in *Conflict*, he lived in a ratty hotel on Sixtieth Street.

Probably the place became a model for the "unsavory" Hotel Algiers which appears in *Rocket to the Moon* and *Night Music*. During periods of unemployment the management allowed Odets to live on credit. His room was on the ground floor, and he was thus in an excellent position to overhear the dialogue of the other boarders ("amazing conversation," Odets said of the Hotel Algiers in *Night Music*, "obscene and amatory, often pitiful . . ." [p. 67]). In such an environment Odets grew increasingly introspective and moody. Years later he told McCarten that the feeling possessed him that he was a character in a Dostoevski novel. "Try to be happy," says the protagonist of *The Big Knife*, "this isn't a Russian novel" (p. 55). Although William Dean Howells felt that Russian novels were poor models for American writers—that "the more smiling aspects of life . . . are the more American"—Odets was struck by the tragi-comic queerness of urban life in the United States. By the winter of 1930 the Depression had darkened the lives of millions of Americans, and Howells' view of things seemed less relevant than ever. Odets moved to a dingy furnished room on West Eighty-Second Street. "By then he was so steeped in melancholy," McCarten reported, "that he wanted to make himself as unattractive as possible in order to keep life at arm's length." Consequently, Odets shaved off all his hair, grew a beard and wore turtleneck sweaters. Frequently he stayed locked inside his room for several days, "trying," as McCarten put it, "to find out what was the matter with him." Although he wanted desperately to write, he could not mold his confused thoughts and feelings into a coherent form. Instead Odets jotted down his morbid ruminations in a diary. He was in this "state of being" (an expression Odets often used) when his association with the Theater Guild led him to join the Group Theater in 1930. This was a major turning point in Odets' life.

Although Odets spent most of his time absorbing the philosophy of the Group and learning to act, he also continued in his efforts to write. One play written during this period, called 910

Eden Street, dealt with Philadelphia intellectuals. Odets later explained to Mendelsohn his motives for writing such pieces:

> They were very painful attempts to not only find my identity—not only to locate myself—but to write down the nature of neurotic illness, to try to come to some clear, objective sense of myself and my inability to handle and deal with life. They also had in them considerable ambition, which simply means a desire to be *a* playwright, to be a significant writer. They were very sad affairs, and I think they have no value whatsoever as plays or even scenes....

Odets showed 910 *Eden Street* to Harold Clurman. The play, says Clurman, was "full of confused and unhappy young people. ... It gave evidence of an internal injury in the writer. ... Something in his past life had hurt him. He was doubled up in pain now, and in his pain he appeared to be shutting out the world. His perception was disturbed because everything was seen in relation to his hurt. He had to learn to stand up straight and see the world more objectively." Odets, Clurman concluded, was a "peculiar duck" who had a "tendency to nurse his own oddities." Whether Odets learned to "see the world more objectively" in the next few years is certainly arguable. He did learn, however, to sublimate his inner conflicts in the form of plays; to feel that he had some semblance of a "home" with the Group Theater; to identify his private suffering with the pain of millions of other people; and to vent his hostility against the forces which he conceived to be responsible for the Depression.

In 1961 Odets told Wagner that the Group Theater made him a playwright, that "the so-called 'method' forced you to face yourself and really function out of the kind of person you are ... using your own materials." He had been writing a play about Beethoven before the discovery that changed the course of his development. "Now I see again in myself flight always flight," Odets noted at the time in his diary. "Why not write something about the Greenberg family, something I know better, something that is closer to me?" The play about the Greenberg family was entitled *I've Got the Blues*; it later appeared as *Awake and Sing!*, with the Greenbergs changed into the Berger family. The shift in emphasis from the personal to the social gave Odets a sense of direction, but the individual did not disappear into the mass. "The best procedure is to take your own subjective experience and self and break that up to bits," Odets told a New York *Daily Mirror* reporter in 1935. "Dostoevski is a marvellous example of this principle of creative construction. Writers should not cancel their own life experiences, but use them wherever possible." The *New York World-Telegram* on March 19, 1935, however, carried the following self-analysis by Odets:

> I was sore; that's why I wrote [*Awake and Sing!*]. I was sore at my whole life. Getting nothing done. . . . A young man in America tries to get away from himself—tries to cancel his own experience until it resembles more the general patterns. . . . I began wrong. But now . . . I saw where my own experience was richest. . . . When I looked it over I saw I hadn't wanted to write exactly the play that came out. But it satisfied me. . . .

Although Odets tried to express material closer to his own experience in his plays, he did not, as his statement to Peck in 1949 suggests, write straight autobiography. Indeed, the playwright's remarks in 1935 are somewhat misleading. While drawing on his own experience of life, Odets also attempted to make the personal drama symbolic of "the general patterns." In short, Odets aimed to have it both ways. The endeavor to fuse personal and social motivation—never an easy task for a dramatist—accounts for both the strength of Odets and his occasional weakness. "Theater in its profoundest sense," Odets told Mendelsohn, ". . . has come in periods when the plight or problem expressed by the actors was completely at one with the plight and problems and values or even moralities of the audience." It was Odets' attempt to make the problems of his characters "completely at one" with the audience, however, that sometimes led him to falsify his plays. He told Wagner: "The form . . . is always dictated by the material; there can be nothing ready-made about it"; later in the same interview, though, he admitted the following about his early writing: "I tried to press it into an ideological mold. . . . I used to try many ways to make the materials of my plays say something that they really were not saying . . . but I couldn't have done otherwise in that period. It's the one thing that really disturbs me about the early plays. . . ." It disturbs most critics, too.

In spite of the fact that Odets confessed that he had "always *felt* homeless," the Group Theater gave him a sense of belonging that he was never to enjoy again after leaving that organization in 1940. Since the Group was perhaps the greatest single influence on Odets' development as a dramatist something needs to be said about it. Both Harold Clurman and Lee Strasberg, who founded the organization in 1931, aimed for a theater of human relevance. The Group was a response to the cynicism and disillusionment of the twenties. Where Clurman emphasized theme, Strasberg stressed form. Apparently Clurman was the more messianic of the two men, for he saw theater as a "temple" and drama as a form of "communion." The Group Theater offered its people an escape from what a sociologist was later to call "the lonely crowd." There had to be a vital relationship between the creative individual and the audience viewed as a "community." According to Clurman: "The criterion of judgment for what is good or bad in the theater . . . does not derive from some abstract standard of artistic or literary excellence, but from a judgment of what is fitting—that is, humanly desirable—for a particular audience." There was a strong belief among members of the Group in the perfectibility of man.

The Group Theater clearly shaped Odets' theory of the drama. Much of what is best in Odets—his hope for man, his love for humanity, his attempt to address as wide an audience as possible

—was nourished in the years he spent working with Clurman. At the same time, though, the Group Theater would seem to have had a less beneficial influence on the playwright. Throughout his career Odets tended, like Clurman, to *over*emphasize the importance of theme in a play. It was this tendency that was perhaps partly responsible for the large number of bad plays produced by the Group. The stress on theme was a common failing during the thirties. (One can see this tendency clearly, for example, in John Howard Lawson's *Theory and Technique of Playwriting* [1936], which was intended to be a manual for revolutionary dramatists.) The belief that man could exercise a measure of control over his environment and the circumstances of his life was a healthy corrective to the despair and drift of the twenties. But the belief that man was capable of being *perfected*—well, that was another matter. Such naïve innocence made the postwar period all the harder to bear for those, like Odets, whose intellectual conscience and emotional commitments were fashioned in the previous decade.

"In our exchange Clifford Odets and I contributed much to each other," says Clurman, "but we both received most of our nurture at this time from the world around us. . . ." And that world, misshaped by a great economic depression and rapidly proliferating competing ideologies, was a menacing spectacle that sent many confused men and women in search of a home. Clurman admits that the Group "attracted the unbalanced," the obviously neurotic; yet he insists that the organization "represented a drive toward wholeness." It was the burden of the Group "to provide what society itself failed to provide." Says Clurman:

> If one wished to take a patronizing attitude, one might say of many of the Group that they were crying for a new papa and mamma to take care of them. . . . They were seeking moral guidance as much as economic stability; they were seeking something they could truly respect,

believe in, and devote themselves to. . . . What lent our people certain attributes of eccentricity was their inability to accept the anarchy of our times as their norm, and their demand that the Group by itself supply what the rest of the world could not.

It is difficult to determine, as Clurman seems to suggest, where infantile neuroticism ends and where "the central needs of the healthy person" begin. Odets was very much caught up in the conflict between, on the one hand, morbid dependence and compulsive revolt, and, on the other, a healthy need to experience "the safety that comes from feeling oneself part of a whole community." Success as a playwright gradually lured Odets away from the Group Theater. In any case that organization could not, even had Odets been spared his private demons, provide him with a lasting or wholly satisfactory sanctuary in a world bent on self-destruction. The Group Theater finally failed, Clurman concludes, because it was "isolated" from the rest of society. This basic problem of the modern theater has not, of course, disappeared.

While the thirties lasted, though, Odets was able to derive a sense of power and purpose from the social reform that was in the air. He was able to forget his personal conflicts, whatever their origin, in the social struggle of the masses. After a time it was not enough for Odets to make a home of sorts in the Group Theater; he had to feel at one with those outside the Group who suffered from social dislocation. Perhaps Odets felt that what had driven him to attempted suicide three times in the past was merely the sick response of a pampered ego functioning in a void; perhaps he perceived the common man as one who was faced with "real" problems. At any rate, ideology was beckoning to Odets. Of the thirty-five or so members of the Group only four or five joined the Communist Party. Odets was one of them. It was an extremely dangerous move—not because it would later look like treason to a generation in the grip of McCarthyism—

but because it was so terribly self-deceptive. There was a manifest
religious intensity about it; the converted ones were secular
priests proclaiming a new gospel. What made this new faith especially attractive, it seems, is the fact that little or no self-reforma-
tion was urgently required; indeed, one need not even know
precisely what one believed—it was quite enough merely to feel
intensely and to utter dogmatic, oracular pronouncements. The
theologian calls this form of religious intoxication the "heresy of
action." It is a "heresy" because the deluded one seeks to purify
the world before purifying himself. "I wondered about the habit
that Communists had of devoting little time or thought or
kindness to their personal relations," Malcolm Cowley remarks
in "A Remembrance of the Red Romance." "Was it the right
foundation for a new society?" Clurman warned Odets of his
folly: "One may belie oneself through ill-considered boldness
or through false humility. But none of my homilies could have
the slightest effect on him. He was driven by a powerful emotional impetus, like a lover on the threshold of an elopment."
Odets' failure in self-knowledge—a failure, by the way, that is
by no means unique with Odets or with other men of his time—
was to plague him throughout his life.

It would be a serious mistake, however, to suggest that Odets
and others were simply self-deluded, were merely neurotic
sleight-of-hand artists. Some of their response was honestly
prompted by revulsion at the ravages of an evil that could not be
entirely attributed to the metaphysical absurdity of life. "We
know now," as Murray Kempton says, "that it was a very complicated time and that they were more complicated people than
they knew." In 1952 Odets tried to explain his feelings in the
thirties to the Un-American Activities Committee:

> Literature was passed around, and in a time of great
> social unrest many people found themselves reaching
> out for new ideas, new ways of solving depressions or
> making a better living, fighting for one's rights. . . . The

rights to be steadily employed, for instance. I believe at that time there were perhaps fifteen or sixteen million unemployed people in the United States, and I myself was living on ten cents a day. . . . They were horrendous days that none of us would like to go through again. . . .[I] finally joined the Communist Party, in the belief, in the honest and real belief, that this was some way out of the dilemma in which we found ourselves.

At the conclusion of *Writers on the Left,* Daniel Aaron, reflecting on the men of the thirties, says: "We who precariously survive in the sixties can regret their inadequacies and failures, their romanticism, their capacity for self-deception, their shrillness, their self-righteousness. It is less easy to scorn their efforts, however blundering and ineffective, to change the world." Is this a fair view of the thirties? Or is it evidence, as Richard Kostelanetz maintains, of "sentimental piety"? In order to fully understand Odets it is necessary to understand the period—be it the thirties or after—in which he wrote. Consequently, something needs to be said here about that first decade.

The affluent sixties have witnessed a remarkable revival of interest in the Great Depression. Recently Edna Ferber said: "We're so frantic today it's like living the thirties all over again. So much apprehension. There's a curious feeling of waiting for that snowball to hit you in the back of the neck" (*The New York Times,* September 25, 1966). Malcolm Cowley accounts for this situation in terms of "arithmetical sequence": "The 1920's looked back to the 1890's, and the 1950's looked back to the 1920's." Every thirty years, it would seem, literary moods repeat themselves. According to William Phillips the men of the sixties are again searching for radical solutions; hence the return to the mood of the thirties. As yet, however, the thirties—some excellent studies notwithstanding—have not been adequately explained. After thirty years we are still too close to that turbulent decade; too many people who write about it remain emotionally involved in its struggles and disappointments. As Leslie Fiedler says: "We do not have finally any shared myth of the age. The thirties do not yet exist in our common imagination—as do, for instance, the twenties, securely fixed in a single continuous legend from John Held, Jr. to Scott Fitzgerald." Nevertheless, some points seem to have been rather clearly established: Daniel Aaron, for example, has presented evidence that the Communists "failed to attract more than a minority of writers or, more significantly, to hold very many of its intellectual supporters"; Walter Rideout's conclusion on the period in his *The Radical Novel in the United States* is: "to charge that the American writers were *in uniform,* in the necessary sense that they all wrote exactly alike and obediently to whatever arbitrary command is to exaggerate for the sake of polemics," and the author adds that seventy "proletarian" novels out of a total of nineteen thousand published in the decade hardly constitute a Red takeover; finally, Morgan Y. Himelstein's researches lead him to conclude that the Communists, in spite of determined attempts, failed to win control of the American theater during the Depression. Yet there is more to the problem of understanding the thirties than a mere demonstration of the fact that both the Marxists and McCarthyites made excessive claims "for the sake of polemics."

One might adopt any number of attitudes toward the thirties. The young might view the period, for example, with a sense of nostalgia: "Why wasn't I living then," Cowley reports a young writer as saying, "when the world was more interesting?" In his review of George Plimpton's *Paper Lion,* Mordecai Richler strikes a more serious note:

> Much as I enjoyed Plimpton's book, I can't help feeling guilty, like having been to a movie on a fine summer's afternoon. An earlier generation of American writers had to test themselves not against Bart Starr and Archie Moore, but the Spanish Civil War and the Moscow trials.

... This is not meant to be an attack on Plimpton, but on all of us, Plimpton's generation and mine. One day, I fear, we will be put down as a trivial, peripheral bunch. Crazy about bad old movies, nostalgic for comic books. Our Gods don't fail. At worst, they grow infirm. They suffer pinched nerves, like Paul Hornung, or arthritic arms, like Sandy Koufax.

Many veterans of the thirties seem to look back on their younger days with something like the nostalgia of Cowley's young writer. In his "Introduction" to *Famous American Plays of the 1930's* (1959) Harold Clurman—perhaps in response to the reaction against the thirties during the forties and fifties—remarks: "The lean days and hungry nights of the thirties were a brave time. Aren't we a little torpid now?" Murray Kempton, who for a time was a member of the Young Communist League, leans to the opposite extreme in *Part of Our Time* and appears to be overly apologetic for the radicalism of the thirties: "We represented an island of guilt surrounded by a sea of innocence. . . . There remain some today who would tell us that we were the most important part of our time. If a nation of the healthy chooses to believe that its history was made by a little group of the sick, then it is in peril of the mistake only a few made in the thirties, trading the real for the malignant unreal." Kempton seems to forget that the number unemployed ranged during the Depression, according to Frederick Lewis Allen's figures, from eight and a half to seventeen million. Hitler was real—not a neurotic fantasy—and only the Communists were wholly committed to an anti-Fascist policy. Until the signs were so clear that even a blind man could discern their meaning, the democracies attempted to appease Hitler. Kempton's book was written in 1955, and that might account in part for his inclination to view the thirties as composed of the wholly "healthy" and the wholly "sick"—a melodramatic vision in which the usual moral conflict between the "good guys" and the "bad guys" is translated into equally oversimple psychological terms.

If some men of the thirties now seem to assume one or another extreme posture toward the period of their youth, some younger critics of today are led into similar exaggerated attitudes. Thus, Richard Kostelanetz is at pains to dismiss the thirties *totally* "as a cultural entity." But can *any* period in history be so sweepingly banished from serious consideration? Without offering a shred of evidence for his evaluations Kostelanetz roundly declares that the creative writers who "emerged" in the twenties and forties "are superior, in both achievement and development, to the best of the thirties." This business of matching the writers of one decade with the current favorites of another period is extremely suspect. And how can one, except arbitrarily, limit a writer to one decade? Why is it of overriding importance when a writer "emerged"? Isn't it equally significant where the writer goes *after* his emergence? "We live in a time where you say something in one decade, and a decade later you're old-fashioned," Odets exploded to Mendelsohn. "They talk about me as *a* playwright, or *the* playwright of the thirties. I've set down some of my best plays outside of the thirties. . . ." Faulkner "emerged" in the twenties— with such gems as *Soldiers' Pay* and *Mosquitoes*, it should be added—but *Light in August* appeared in 1932 and *Absalom, Absalom!* was published in 1936. Fitzgerald "emerged" in the twenties—indolent critics, in fact, continue to identify him solely with the Jazz Age—but he wrote "Babylon Revisited," *Tender Is the Night* and *The Last Tycoon* in the thirties. Kostelanetz praises Edmund Wilson as "consistently excellent and prolific" —but he arrives at this judgment because Wilson, like the other "good guys," "came of age in the twenties"! How can one identify the man who wrote *The American Jitters* (1932) and *To the Finland Station* (1940) wholly with the twenties? Kostelanetz is riding a hobbyhorse and hence, like so many others who revisit the thirties, he oversimplifies an extremely complex situation for the sake of a thesis.

Even the sympathetic Harvey Swados—who was, like the present writer, too young to have been really a part of the thirties— is an unsteady guide to the age. In his recent anthology *The*

American Writer and the Great Depression, Swados attempts
to steer a middle course between those who, like Kostelanetz,
mindlessly and totally reject the decade and those who, like
Cowley's young writer, romanticize it. Yet one might find much
to quarrel with in both Swados' introduction to the anthology
and in the selections themselves. Being a novelist and short story
writer, Swados tends to underrate dramatists of the thirties. For
the same reason he is inclined to overestimate the worth of, say,
James T. Farrell ("*Studs Lanigan* [is] a book that will not
die . . .") and John Dos Passos ("*USA* . . . continues to resist oblivion"). James Agee, Erskine Caldwell, Nelson Algren, Sher-
wood Anderson and Kenneth Fearing are treated in a manner
generally reserved for the immortals. Clifford Odets is not represented in Swados' collection of significant writing of the
thirties. Indeed, the author of *Awake and Sing!, Golden Boy* and
Rocket to the Moon is placed in the same category as Grace
Lumpkin, Michael Gold and Fielding Burke, "excluded because
it was felt that the areas of social concern with which they deal
are more memorably described by others." What others? Jack
Conroy, Stanley Burnshaw, Meridel Le Sueur, Weldon Kees,
Edward Newhouse, Jack Douglas, Ruth McKenney, Kenneth
Patchen—but why go on? For the most part it is a dreary collection of writings. It is for the likes of Marc Blitzstein, whose *The
Cradle Will Rock* is the one play represented in an anthology
devoted to the thirties, that Swados would have us ditch Odets.
Swados concludes his introduction on a note which suggests why
he was the wrong man for the job: "The Depression was in
truth not just a tragic era but in many ways a triumphant one
for American literary artists, one which . . . may be an inspiration
to those who are yet to create, with their hands and their spirits,
a greater society." This is an exhortation in favor of uplift which
resembles the dialogue that Swados rightly faults in *Waiting for
Lefty.*

Obviously, scholarship is still a long way from a fair and balanced perspective on the thirties. Unless the student of the

period realizes that the men of the thirties were complex in motivation, and that the times were enormously difficult, glib simplifications will continue to distort efforts at understanding. In "The 1930's Were An Age of Faith" Malcolm Cowley says of the faithful: "They were not trinitarians but dualists and Manicheans. They bisected and bifurcated; they dichotomized; they either-ored: either light or darkness, but nothing between; either Socialism or Fascism, our side or their side, Russia or Germany, the glorious future or a reversion to the Middle Ages." There is some truth to Cowley's picture of the age. Murray Kempton, for instance, continues to be trapped in "either-or" modes of thought: "All the noise of the thirties," he says, ". . . was surface; what beat beneath, as it has always beaten, was a chorus of the hearts of so many different men. And man is a private and not a social animal." Leslie Fiedler takes Kempton to task for his "utterly misleading" view of the age. Fiedler, justly impatient with "doctrinaire and artificial definition[s] of the Proletarian Novel out of the *New Masses*," says: "Books as different in commitment as Wyndham Lewis's *Revenge for Love*, R. P. Warren's *At Heaven's Gate*, Hemingway's *To Have and Have Not*, Fitzgerald's *The Last Tycoon*, reflect what is essential: a vision of the world so desperate that it breaks through the lyrical self-pity characteristic of the twenties to a kind of impersonal rage and nausea." The essence of the thirties, according to Fiedler, is in *Sanctuary* (which, says Fiedler in "John Peale Bishop and the Other Thirties," "rocked the world of the mid-30's"—an odd circumstance, since *Sanctuary* was published in 1931) and Nathanael West's *A Cool Million*: "Here," says Fiedler, ". . . is the true 'myth' of the thirties: the sense of sterility, the despair, the outrage before the senseless waste of the human turned crazy laughter and at last art; but for most people this is too strong, too 'morbid,' too *real* a vision to be endured." (Presumably, Fiedler advances the publication date of *Sanctuary* to 1935 in order to make that dreadful novel—Faulkner himself disparaged it—a comment on the Popular Front, which eventually, together with other factors, obliterated the revolutionary dream of the early thirties.) Although Fiedler is an influential critic—he is one of Kostelanetz's heroes who "emerged" in the forties—his vision of the thirties is tendentious. Fiedler simply *prefers* one "vision" to another, that is all.

Tom Kromer's *Waiting for Nothing* (1935) and Clifford Odets' *Waiting for Lefty* (1935), though both works are far from being examples of great writing, represent two poles of the imagination in the thirties. It was precisely the vision of sterility and waste that inspired the hope for something positive. If significant achievement in literature on the thematic level is the result of the writer's ability to "hold in balance," as Fitzgerald put it, "the sense of the futility of effort and the sense of the necessity to struggle, the conviction of the inevitability of failure and still the determination to 'succeed'—and, more than these, the contradiction between the dead hand of the past and the high intentions of the future"—then one might argue that in his best work Odets manages to project both the horror and the faith that characterized the "vision" of the thirties.

Cowley, Kempton and Fiedler are, in one way or another, much too one-sided in their approaches to the thirties. Although the rhetoric of the faithful suggests, as Cowley argues, that they "either-ored," their personal actions speak louder across the years to us than their public utterances. "Mostly," says William Phillips, "the thirties was a period of contradictions. It was a time of sense and nonsense, idealism and cynicism, morality and immorality, disinterestedness and power drive, and it was a time when it was possible to believe simultaneously in democracy and dictatorship, in an anti-human abstraction called History and in a moral idea of man usually regarded as unhistorical. It seemed possible to believe in everything and its opposite. . . ."

It is within such a context of "contradictions," then, that the reader today must view Odets' appearance as a radical playwright of the thirties. For *Waiting for Lefty* was an extreme solution to that "rage and nausea" Fiedler speaks of, to that "sense of sterility" and "despair" and "the senseless waste of the human" which marked the mood of the decade. The audience at the Civic Repertory Theater on Fourteenth Street that Sunday night in January 1935 greeted Odets' short play with wild religious fervor. "The actors no longer performed," says Clurman, "they were being carried along as if by an exultancy of communication such as I had never witnessed before. Audience and actors had become one." Neither Odets nor Clurman seem to have ever fully recovered from this too fervent experience. They had seen the face of the Living God—and all else was straw. But drama is not religion; the theater is not a temple. The ecstacy that attended performances of *Waiting for Lefty* had nothing to do with dramatic art. "To recapture the effect of its first performance," Cowley says in "While They Waited for Lefty," "either one would have to rewrite [the play] in terms of a new age or else one would have to reconstitute the audience that remembered five years of depression, the banks closing, the landlord at the door, and that shouted 'Strike!' with a sense of release—then again, louder, 'Strike! Strike!!'—as it raised a thousand clenched fists." Even Cowley is too indulgent toward Odets' propaganda piece to satisfy the demands of any reader who did not personally experience the Depression. *Waiting for Lefty* has often been called "the definitive specimen of the whole proletarian drama in America." But is that something to shout about? It does nothing for the intrinsic worth of the play, and little for the reader's enjoyment of it today, for scholars to trace its antecedents to naturalism and expressionism; to see the influence of vaudeville and the movies on its techniques; to compare the committee on stage to a Greek chorus; to regard it as a fusion of the older minstrel show and the newer agitprop play—for no amount of historical criticism can redeem the artistic crudity of the piece. Himelstein says: "By adding realistic characters, situations, and dialogue to the nonrealistic structure of the agitprop, Odets completed the agitprop's movement toward realistic human drama and, because this new realism made the agitation and propaganda seem comparatively unobtrusive, he continued the trend toward political subtlety." *Waiting for Lefty* is about as subtle and unobtrusive in theme as a machinegun—in fact, that is exactly the word Odets used to describe his play: "It was at one time a kind of light machinegun," he told the Un-American Activities Committee, "that you wheeled in to use whenever there was any kind of strike trouble."

Unhappily, Odets has been tagged with *Waiting for Lefty*, while his best work has largely been forgotten. Odets was too often applauded for the wrong things in the thirties—"it was for his message," Kempton notes, "that [Odets] was worshipped by his candlebearers in those days"—and ignored today chiefly for the same reasons. Students of American drama have little to hope for when a recent historian, Walter J. Meserve, declares that *Waiting for Lefty* is the best Odets play of 1935, and adds: "Although [Odets] wrote three plays after World War II, he never reached his earlier success in the theater." It is difficult to know in this context what is meant by "success." Even in the newspaper meaning of the word, *The Country Girl* (1951) was a "success." Our historian, by the way, neglects to mention the existence of either *Golden Boy* or *Rocket to the Moon*. He does devote, however, two hundred and twelve of his three hundred and sixty-one pages of text to the American drama before ONeill, allowing "Plot" and "Discussion" to such memorable pieces as *Charles the Second; or, The Merry Monarch* and *The Sentinels; or, The Two Sergeants*.

According to Harold Clurman, *Waiting for Lefty* "was the birth cry of the thirties." It would be more accurate to say that the play expresses the revolutionary mood of 1930 to 1935; for, as Malcolm Cowley points out, *Waiting for Lefty* was not followed by similar pieces. Due to the Communist shift from an emphasis on class war to the Popular Front alignment against Fascism, "proletarian literature" passed off the scene. "At the moment," Granville Hicks confidently asserted in 1935, "the revolutionary drama is gratifyingly healthy." The following year

the finest writer of "revolutionary drama"—Clifford Odets—
headed for Hollywood. Indeed, Odets' relationship to the working class was always a tenuous one. Although *Waiting for Lefty*
was inspired by the New York taxi strike of February 1934,
Odets—according to his testimony in Washington—had "never
been near a strike" when he wrote the play. In 1939 Philip Rahv
argued that "proletarian literature" had died a quick death because, among other reasons, it was "the literature of a party disguised as the literature of a class." Odets joined the Communist
Party in 1934, but he quit the following year because the Left
press attacked his work and tried to dictate to him his subject
matter. "I have a great deal of work to do," he later reported
telling himself at the time; "I have enough to say out of my own
mind and heart, and I had better leave."

But another Communist action that prompted Odets to exit
from the Party was his unfortunate trip to Cuba in July 1935.
Along with fourteen other members of a commission whose
stated aim was to investigate social and economic conditions in
the Mendieta government—which the group saw as supported
by American financial and industrial interests—Odets was immediately arrested upon arrival as a Communist agitator, tossed
into a naval police station for a day and a night, and shipped
back to New York. At the time Odets denied being a member
of the Party: "A man making a thousand dollars a week has no
reason to be a Communist," he told newsmen in 1935. "I'm
doing pretty well by myself and my fellow men. Everything that
I've got I'll share with people who are not so fortunate. If that
is Communism, then I'm a Communist." In 1952 Odets admitted before the Washington committee that he had been a
member of the Party in 1935. Odets added, however, that he
went to Cuba, not as a Communist, but as a citizen of the United
States. When Odets returned from Cuba, he was, as usual, very
angry. He said the American Ambassador to Cuba, Jefferson
Caffrey, had a "heart of sugar"; he called the Cuban officials and
their secret police—who aimed real machineguns at the author of

Waiting for Lefty—"greasy people who use a knife to eat peas," and added: "They don't know what existence means." But Odets' chief anger was directed at the Party, for he felt that the Communists had deliberately exploited him for propaganda purposes. "I was politically extremely naïve," Odets said afterward in Washington. Disillusioned by the Party's cynical lack of idealism, then, the dramatist was encouraged to make a break with the Reds.

Other forces were also at work, however, to alter the course of Odets' development. "A new Odets has come to town," the dramatist informed reporters after the opening of Awake and Sing!. "I see him as a suit of my clothes with some utter stranger inside them who is known as 'Odets, the successful playwright,' and who receives fantastic offers from Hollywood, invitations to address ladies' clubs, one hundred and fifty telephone calls a day and a lot of solemn consideration from guys who write pieces for the dramatic page. Meanwhile I follow along behind him, exactly the same as I was six months ago. . . ." Exactly the same? Years later Odets told Wagner:

> All I wanted then in 1935 were some of the things that were mentioned in Waiting for Lefty—a room of my own, a girl of my own, a phonograph and some records. And I got 'em. Nothing more I wanted. Then I ran into a nerve-racking period where I thought I was going to go to pieces, just out of emotional exhaustion. I understood in this period of my life how van Gogh felt. I understood the kind of insanity and frenzy of his painting. I almost couldn't stop writing. The hand kept going. It began to frighten me. With all this set in the matrix of an American success—nothing is more noisy and clamorous than that. There are enormous tensions and strains within it, because you don't want to change, you want to hold on. You want time to digest, but you're just kind of swept off your feet, with wire services and interviews and people

telephoning you; the parties you're invited to, the people who just take you up. You want to savor these things, flavor them, but you'd like it on your own terms. You'd like the time to establish forms with which to deal with it, or else it will drive you cuckoo.

In 1935 Odets had four plays produced—*Waiting for Lefty, Awake and Sing!, Till the Day I Die* and *Paradise Lost*—but when the last one faltered at the box office Odets was finally left in peace. The telephone stopped ringing; the invitations to parties ceased. Hollywood, whose offers Odets had previously refused, now looked attractive to him. In order to save *Paradise Lost*, Odets signed a movie contract for twenty-five hundred dollars a week; and once in California he sent four thousand dollars to the Group Theater in an effort to sustain his failing play. While in Hollywood Lewis Milestone, the director, met Odets at a party and interested him in writing *The General Died at Dawn* for Gary Cooper and Madeleine Carroll. Odets received twenty thousand dollars for the film. In order to ease his conscience, however, he felt constrained to declare that writers who are "clever" can say anything in pictures they may wish to say: "One doesn't have to be gloomy about it either," he insisted to journalists. "People can be given a sense of problems, a heightened perception of life, and at the same time be entertained and even gripped. . . . I tried to produce a bang-up interesting action story." Later, though, Odets admitted to the congressman in Washington that even a "clever" writer could not, due to the vigilance of the screen moguls, propagandize in films. It was *The General Died at Dawn* that occasioned the now well-worn observation of Frank Nugent: "Odets, where is thy sting?"

In spite of his cocky statements to newspapermen about Hollywood in 1935, however, it seems likely that Odets had little real desire to propagandize in either film or drama. For one thing, as I hope to show in my chapters devoted to analysis of specific plays, Odets was growing in artistry and subtlety after 1935, and "messages" were to remain largely unsent. For another thing, as Clurman points out, Odets "did not want to remain a Left playwright. He wanted to be at the very center of standard playwrights of quality. He wanted to be inside, not outside that circle which the mass of Americans might regard as their own. In this center was safety—not simply crude economic safety, since in one way or another he would do very well, but the safety that comes from feeling oneself part of a whole community." Although the movies reached eighty-five million people a week during the Depression, as opposed to some thousands who might witness a Broadway play, the films, with few exceptions, gave no hint of the economic and social misery of the country. Consequently, Hollywood would remain—save on the pecuniary side—distinctly unsatisfactory for a serious writer. I shall return to Odets' complex feelings about Hollywood in Chapter Five. Suffice it here to remark that Odets' ambivalent attitude toward the motion picture capital was not an isolated conflict in his total personality.

Now, as I have tried to suggest, it is not difficult to see how Odets is a man of the thirties. What the dramatist said of Gogol can also be said of Odets: "With all important artists, he shares the ability to express in a single work an entire epoch, thus fusing forever history and art." Dixon Wecter notes: "In the middle 1930's more than a quarter of the youths in their late 'teens and early twenties had never had regular work. . . . Four out of five were still living with parents, including nearly half of those married." This historical situation is mirrored by Florence and Sid in *Waiting for Lefty*—"We got the blues, Babe," Sid remarks, "—the 1935 blues" (p. 22)—and Ralph and Blanche in *Awake and Sing!*. In both plays Odets also reflects the willingness of increasing numbers of intellectuals to view Marxism as a possible alternative to the chaos of the Depression. In *The Communist Manifesto*, Marx and Engels say: "The bourgeoisie has torn away from the family its sentimental veil, and has reduced the family relation to a mere money relation." The situation de-

scribed in the *Manifesto* is symbolized by Odets through the
Berger family in *Awake and Sing!*. Jacob, the grandfather, says:
"In a house like this [Ralph] don't realize even the possibilities
of life. Economics comes down like a ton of coal on the head"
(p. 71). "You know Mom's not letting my sixteen bucks out of
the house if she can help it," Ralph informs Jacob. "She'd take
one look at Blanche and insult her in a minute—a kid who's
got nothing" (p. 47). "Why won't Mom let us live here?"
Ralph asks later, and Jacob replies: "Why? Why? Because in a
society like this today people don't love. Hate!" (p. 77). Money
is the single yardstick to measure human worth. "Ralph should
only be a success like you, Morty," Bessie tells her brother. "I
could die happy, believe me"; to which Jacob snaps: "Don't
live, just make success" (p. 66). Morty declares: "Business don't
stop for personal life" (p. 89).

Bessie Berger is a destructive force because she thinks only
of the family, and for the Odets of 1935 the family is a moribund
institution. Through Bessie's actions her daughter, Hennie, is
compelled into a loveless marriage, which later prompts the
girl to take flight with another man, Moe Axelrod, and to
abandon her baby; Ralph is blocked from marrying his girl; and
Jacob is driven to self-destruction. At the end of the play Bessie
even seeks to defraud her son out of Jacob's insurance money:
"A family needs for a rainy day," she asserts (p. 95). Although
the soul of the family is corrupt, Bessie insists on keeping up
appearances. The pregnant Hennie must marry Sam for the sake
of "the neighbors' opinion" (p. 55). At one point Bessie complains about the windowshade being up: "I like my house to
look respectable" (p. 59). When Blanche calls Ralph on the
telephone, Bessie goes to it in an effort to end her son's love affair
with the girl; as she does so she snaps: "Don't forget the shade"
(p. 61).

In 1938 Louis Adamic pointed out that during the Depression the father in the family frequently lost not only his economic power but his potency within the household as well.

One sees this situation enacted in *Awake and Sing!*, together with a number of other imaginative works of the thirties, most notably in Steinbeck's *The Grapes of Wrath* (1939). The answer to the selfishness of the family, many writers during the thirties felt, was the brotherhood of man. Thus, Ralph says near the end of Odets' play: "It's a team down the warehouse. . . . Get teams together all over. . . . And with enough teams together maybe we'll get steam in the warehouse so our fingers don't freeze off. Maybe we'll fix it so life won't be printed on dollar bills" (p. 97). Although Rose of Sharon in *The Grapes of Wrath* loses her baby, she gives her milk to a starving old man; while Tom, in the same novel, takes leave of his family saying: "A fella ain't got a soul of his own, but on'y a piece of a big one. . . ." "As long as there is one of us there is both of us," Robert Jordan tells Maria in Hemingway's *For Whom the Bell Tolls* (1940). Lesser works of the decade also reflect the same preoccupations and themes.

Perhaps it is less easy to see, though, how Odets is *not* like the typical writer of the thirties at all. "Proletarian" writing, as Cowley notes, possessed a very narrow range of emotion: anger, the desire for comradeship, the need for the masses to unite for a better world—that was pretty much the limit; "there was not much place," says Cowley, "for gentler feelings like sorrow and romantic love." Kempton makes an even stronger point: the thirties were a time "blighted more than anything else by the absence of pity and mercy." Certainly the work of Odets is an exception to the general run of work written during the decade, and this is one reason why it is absurd to restrict his significance to "proletarian drama." True, Odets is an angry playwright and his work expresses a hunger for union with others. Aside from the obvious fact that neither anger nor passion for identification with others need necessarily pass out of style, Odets' plays are distinguished by their emphasis on "gentler feelings like sorrow" (consider, for example, that scene in *Awake and Sing!* where Jacob and Ralph weep and embrace, while outside in the kitchen Morty howls with laughter [p. 75]) and "romantic love" (consider almost *every* play Odets wrote). There is power and vitality in Odets' plays, but there is also a quality that is "young, lyrical, yearning," as Clurman puts it, "—as of someone on the threshold of life." Nor is this the end of Odets' uniqueness in an age when, according to the playwright himself, new art works were expected to "shoot bullets" ("Preface" to *Six Plays*, p. ix). In *The Angry Decade*, Leo Gurko says that *Awake and Sing!*, "though full of passion [is] humorless and heavy as lead." Which tells us more about Gurko than Odets. Perhaps more than any other Odets play *Awake and Sing!* is noteworthy for its blend of tragedy and comedy. Moe Axelrod, for instance, is an unforgettable character largely because of his bitterly humorous dialogue. And this kind of writing is *not* characteristic of "proletarian literature."

When Joseph Wood Krutch reviewed *Golden Boy* in 1937 he said:

> No one that I know can more powerfully suggest the essential loneliness of men and women, their inability to explain the varied forms assumed by the symbols of their desire, and the powerlessness of any one of them to help the other. His dialogue is often brilliantly suggestive, especially when he puts it into the mouths of ignorant or uncultivated people; even the vulgarest of his villains rises to the dignity of the tortured; and he involves the spectator in the agonies of his characters until the palms sweat and one goes out of the theater tense with emotion which the author has been unwilling or unable to resolve.

Could Krutch have been so wrong in 1937? I doubt it. Odets is both *of his time* and *for*—if not *all* time (only the future can tell about that)—*our time*. And in the analytical portions of my study this is the Odets I want to emphasize, namely, the Odets who reveals "the *essential* loneliness of men and women," the Odets who still speaks to us. But I am also concerned with the *form* in which Odets "speaks" to us, and for that reason I wish to focus on the dramatist *qua* dramatist. For Odets is too good a playwright—too skillful in technique, too relevant in his themes, too human in his approach, too important in the relatively impoverished American drama—merely to be labeled "*a* playwright, or *the* playwright of the thirties" . . . and then forgotten.

When the thirties came to an end Odets also had reached a turning point in his life. The Nazi-Soviet pact in 1939 had disillusioned all but the most gullible and perverse radicals. A decade that had begun with the chiliastic dream of Michael Gold: "O workers' Revolution, you brought hope to me, a lonely, suicidal boy. You are the true Messiah . . . O Revolution, that forced me to think, to struggle and to live. O great Beginning!"— had ended with the lament of Richard Wright: "I knew in my heart that I should never be able to write that way again, should never be able to feel with that simple sharpness about life, should never again express such passionate hope, should never again make so total a commitment of faith." Like Gold, Odets had been a "lonely, suicidal boy" in the late twenties. Like Wright, Odets—now at the end of the Angry Decade—would try "to keep alive in our hearts a sense of the inexpressibly human." It would not be easy. The war in Europe had spurred the American economy out of the Depression. Although Odets had broken with the Communist Party in 1935 he remained a "radical" in his emotional attachments—which is to say (in his own words) he remained "politically extremely naïve." In the prosperous years to come, Odets, with many others, would come to seem a rebel without a cause. With the collapse of the Group Theater in 1941, furthermore, the one "home" Odets had known was gone forever. The challenge of the future—both to Odets the man and Odets the playwright—was enormous. Facing the forties, with so much of the past in shambles about him, Odets must have wondered whether it was possible, or even desirable, for him to make another "great Beginning."

CHAPTER TWO

Awake and Sing!

> When I was a kid I laid awake at nights and heard the
> sounds of trains . . . far-away lonesome sounds . . . boats
> going up and down the river. I used to think of all kinds
> of things I wanted to do. What was it, Jake? Just a bunch
> of noise in my head?
>
> —Ralph Berger in *Awake and Sing!*,
> p. 76

The structure of Odets' plays has been misinterpreted. To
some extent the playwright himself is responsible for this critical
confusion. "I was influenced a little by Chekhov," Odets told
Mendelsohn in 1963. "Not by Ibsen, because you see my forms
are not Ibsen's. But my chief influence as a playwright was the
Group Theater acting company. . . ." Invariably, critics and
scholars of the drama refer to Odets' plays as Chekhovian in structure. The truth of the matter, however, is that the basic structure
of an Odets play is Ibsenite; that is, one can perceive in it a single
rising line of action which can be analyzed in terms of a point
of attack, a turning point, and a resolution composed of a crisis,
climax and conclusion. Chekhov's plays do not have this single-
action structure. Odets also admitted to Mendelsohn that he was
not "really acquainted with Greek drama." Although Malcolm
Goldstein discerns that the basic structure of an Odets play is
not Chekhovian, he errs in designating it as "the form of the

33

well-made play." This is a common error. There are, however,
important differences between Ibsenite structure and the well-
made play. (See Eric Bentley's essay "Ibsen, Pro and Con" and
"The Well-Made Play and the Modern Theater" by Stephen S.
Stanton.) "These early plays," Odets informed Wagner, "were
made for the collective acting company technique. They're
written for eight characters, with six or seven of the characters of
equal importance. Well, this is purely from the Group Theater
ideal of a stage ensemble, and this so fetched me and so took me
over that this was how I wrote." Writing for a "collective acting
company" led Odets to use contrapuntal patterns, and such
Chekhovian surface techniques as cross-purpose dialogue. It was
Odets' achievement to integrate a basic Ibsenite action with
certain structural techniques of a Chekhov play, and thus assure
his work a rising line of tension while simultaneously enriching
the piece by counterpoint and the indirect expression of emotion
and feeling. In short, Odets avoided, on the one hand, reducing
the Ibsenite structure to a bald, straight-forward thesis play, and,
on the other, fashioning a static genre study in the alleged Russian manner. It is necessary to add, however, that Odets' recourse
to Chekhovian devices is much more apparent in *Awake and
Sing!* than in his other plays. Finally, Odets has sometimes been
dubbed a "scenewright" by critics; but as I hope to show throughout this study the structure of an Odets play is generally much
more unified than some critics have allowed. In short, Odets is
very much a "playwright."

Awake and Sing! was first presented by the Group at the
Belasco Theater on February 19, 1935. The action of the play,
which covers about one year, takes place in a single setting: the
Berger apartment in the Bronx. In the introduction, Odets
carefully prepares the audience for the point of attack. Indeed,
the first line spoken in *Awake and Sing!* starts the conflict and the
forward motion of the action toward the revelation of the theme:
"Where's advancement down the place?" Ralph Berger, the
young man of the family and the central actor in the piece, ex-

plodes: "Work like crazy. Think they see it? You'd drop dead
first" (p. 41). The basic motivation in the play is Ralph's conflict between marrying his girl, Blanche, and making "advancement" in society, or sacrificing his girl in favor of group action
which will alter the commercial foundations of modern society.
Jacob, the grandfather, is the catalyst, or pivotal character, in
the play:

JACOB. Boys like you could fix it some day. Look on the world,
    not on yourself so much. . . . Everybody hates, nobody loves.
RALPH. I don't get all that.
JACOB. For years, I watched you grow up. Wait! You'll graduate
    from my university!

(p. 45)

Immediately following Jacob's exhortation to Ralph, Bessie
enters and reminds her father to take the dog on the roof. Her
entrance is significant here because it is Bessie, and not Blanche,
that is the chief obstacle facing Ralph in his quest for self-realization. Furthermore, Bessie's dominant role in the family, and
her dictatorial attitude toward her father, underlines the play's
theme that modern society, with its overemphasis on money,
perverts natural family relationships. And when Bessie mentions
the roof to Jacob, Odets not only suggests the degradation of the
old man, but he also foreshadows the turning point of the play.
When Ralph sarcastically informs his mother that he is "flying
to Hollywood by plane" (p. 45), the boy's idealism is stressed—
for the plane becomes a gathering metaphor for his romantic
aspirations—and the audience is prepared, in an ironic manner,
for his crucial decision in Act Three. Schlosser, the janitor, then
follows on stage and his appearance is prophetic because he
appears again at the turning point to announce Jacob's death.
Schlosser's ghost is also evoked at the end of the play when Moe
Axelrod persuades Hennie to desert her husband, Sam Feinschreiber, for the janitor's wife ran away with another man, too.
Odets says: "[Schlosser] has lost his identity twenty years before"

(p. 39)—as Sam, placed in a similar situation at the conclusion of the play, is to lose *his* identity.

When Ralph, speaking of Blanche later in the opening act, says: "Boy, I could sing when I think about it! Her and me together—that's a new life!," Jacob initiates the point of attack:

JACOB. Don't make a mistake! A new death!

RALPH. What's the idea?

JACOB. Me, I'm the idea! Once I had in *my* heart a dream, a vision, but come marriage and then you forget. Children come and you forget because—

RALPH. Don't worry, Jake.

JACOB. Remember, a woman insults a man's soul like no other thing in the whole world!

RALPH. Why get so excited? No one—

JACOB. Boychick, wake up! Be something! Make your life something good. For the love of an old man who sees in your young days his new life, for such love take the world in your two hands and make it like new. Go out and fight so life shouldn't be printed on dollar bills. A woman waits.

RALPH. Say, I'm no fool!

JACOB. From my heart I hope not.

(p. 48, italics in original)

Thus the major dramatic question of the play is focused. At this stage in his development, however, Ralph chooses Blanche instead of social idealism. Worth noting is Odets' skillful play on the word "sing"—here applied to romantic love, later employed in the biblical sense: "Awake and sing, ye that dwell in dust." Which also suggests, as I hope to show later, the musical motif that is thematically linked with Jacob's idealism. Furthermore, the juxtaposition of "a new life" with "a new death" is also part of an intricate pattern woven throughout the play. Before the ending of Act One, Bessie quarrels with Jacob and tells him: "Go in the room!"; to which Jacob replies: "Some day I'll come out I'll . . . Bessie, some day you'll talk to me so fresh . . . I'll leave

the house for good!" (p. 56). Once again, then, Odets prepares
the audience for the turning point of the play.

In Act Two the conflict of values in the play is sharpened, with
the result that Ralph and Jacob are drawn closer together
against the other members of the family. This character alignment is effectively realized in the Chekhovian counterpoint that
ends Scene One. Jacob has been humiliated by the family because
of his Marxist slogans and Ralph has been increasingly at odds
with his mother over Blanche. For a moment Jacob and Ralph
are alone in the front room:

JACOB. Don't cry, boychick. (*Goes over to* RALPH.) Why should
   you make like this? Tell me why you should cry, just tell me.
   . . . (JACOB *takes* RALPH *in his arms and both, trying to keep
   back the tears, trying fearfully not to be heard by the others in
   the dining room, begin crying.*) You musn't cry. . . .
   (*The tango twists on. Inside the clatter of dishes and the clash
   of cutlery sound.* MORTY *begins to howl with laughter.*)
                                                              (p. 75)

In the following scene Ralph and Jacob again focus the main
issue of the play. Odets underlines the fact that Ralph's aims in
life have been selfish and individualistic. Repeatedly, Jacob
endeavors to make his nephew see the revolutionary light:

JACOB. Look on me and learn what to do, boychick. . . . Look
   on this failure and see for seventy years he talked, with good
   ideas, but only in the head . . . This is why I tell you—DO! . . .
RALPH (*listening*). Hear it? The Boston air mail plane. Ten
   minutes late. I get a kick the way it cuts across the Bronx every
   night.
                                                              (p. 78)

Jacob's use of "boychick" as a form of address stresses the Isaiah,
or resurrection, motif in the play. Before Ralph can be moved
to act on Jacob's gospel, however, he must be forced to see the
utter corruption of the family and the futility of his present life.

Again it is the old man who shows Ralph the way. When Ralph learns that Bessie forced the pregnant Hennie to marry innocent Sam Feinschreiber he recoils from the family—including his beloved but weak grandfather—in disgust. In a rage over the sudden turn of events, Bessie thunders into her father's room and destroys his phonograph records. This, in effect, signals the end of Jacob's dream for himself, for music has been his one tie with a finer life. In order to provide Ralph with insurance money that will enable the boy to escape the dominance of the family and its mean, necessitous existence, Jacob commits suicide. The old man is probably further motivated by a desire to prove his worth by taking, for once in his life, a decisive action ("DO!"), and also to expiate the guilt he feels over his acquiescence in Hennie's marriage to Sam. When Jacob jumps off the roof at the turning point in the play—which occurs in the conventional manner at the end of Act Two—he prepares the way for the resolution of the action. Since the insurance money will also allow Ralph to marry Blanche and pursue his individual development the crisis of the play is made inevitable, for the protagonist must decide: self or society? Blanche or revolution?

In Act Three the family tries to cheat Ralph out of his legacy, but the young man, supported by Moe, asserts his rights. It becomes increasingly manifest that Jacob's insistence that Ralph "DO" has had, finally, an influence on him. The crisis of the play occurs when Ralph wins his right to Jacob's money, and is then compelled to demonstrate his real values:

BESSIE. Ralphie, I worked too hard all my years to be treated like dirt. . . . Here I'm not only the mother, but also the father. The first two years I worked in a stocking factory for six dollars while Myron Berger went to law school. If I didn't worry about the family who would? . . . [H]ere without a dollar you don't look the world in the eye . . . this is life in America.

RALPH. Then it's wrong. It don't make sense. If life made you this way, then it's wrong! . . . I see every house lousy with lies and hate. He said it, Grandpa—Brooklyn hates the Bronx. Smacked on the nose twice a day. But boys and girls can get ahead like that, Mom. We don't want life printed on dollar bills, Mom!

BESSIE. So go out and change the world if you don't like it.

RALPH. I will! And why? 'Cause life's different in my head. Gimme the earth in two hands. I'm strong. There . . . hear him? The air mail off to Boston. Day or night, he flies away, a job to do. That's us and it's no time to die.

(p. 95)

This is the climax of the play. Ralph decides to renounce Blanche and to organize his fellow workers in order to erect a better world for love and labor:

RALPH. No girl means anything to me until . . .

MOE. Till when?

RALPH. Till I can take care of her.

(p. 96)

Odets suggests that Ralph will be more successful than the "sentimental idealist" Jacob (p. 38) when the boy discovers that half the pages in his grandfather's Marxist books have not been cut: "A ten-cent nailfile cuts them," he says. "Uptown, down-town, I'll read them on the way" (pp. 96–97).

At the conclusion of the play, Moe urges Hennie to desert Sam, and Ralph joins in the escape plans: "I didn't hear a word," Ralph says, "but do it, Hennie, do it!" (p. 100). While the curtain descends on the fleeing lovers, Ralph "stands full and strong in the doorway" and declares:

> My days won't be for nothing. Let Mom have the dough. I'm twenty-two and kickin'! I'll get along. Did Jake die for us to fight about nickels? No! "Awake and sing," he said. Right here he stood and said it. The night he died, I saw it like a thunderbolt! I saw he was dead and I was born! I swear to God, I'm one week old! I want the whole

city to hear it—fresh blood, arms. We've got 'em. We're
glad we're living.

(pp. 100–101)

These lines underscore the resurrection theme once again,
and they also echo Jacob's earlier lament: "Give me back my
young days . . . give me fresh blood . . . arms . . . give me—"
(p. 74).

My description and analysis of the structure of *Awake and
Sing!* should indicate that the play is far more unified than
critics generally allow. John Howard Lawson was one of the
first critics to attack the structure of Odets' play. According to
the author of *Theory and Technique of Playwriting* the turning
point in the piece looks back to the scene in Act One in which
Jacob entertains Moe by playing Caruso records (pp. 50–51);
but, says Lawson, Jacob's death "has no organic connection with
the play as a whole." Lawson misses the point of attack—his
analytical approach fails to include such a point—and hence
he does not account for the total action of the play. Furthermore, contrary to what Lawson maintains, Ralph does show signs
of development as a result of Jacob's death: he is able to choose
social idealism in favor of Blanche—something he was not able,
or willing, to do before—and, moreover, this change is dramatized
when Ralph breaks with his girl, when he reads Jacob's books,
and when he asserts himself with Bessie. True, Ralph will remain
at home, but his situation will not be the same as it had been
with the family. Finally, Ralph's motivation is clear because the
basic dramatic conflict was focused at the point of attack and
logically developed throughout the action of the play.

Nevertheless, there *is* a structural defect in *Awake and Sing!*.
Lawson says that Jacob's death does not make Hennie's flight
with Moe "inevitable." One should add that the grandfather's
death does not make Ralph's choice of revolution "inevitable"
either. Nor *should* Jacob's death make either choice "inevitable":
for that way lies contrivance and determinism. What the turning

point in the action makes "inevitable" is a decision of *some* kind: either girl or revolution—either self or society. Jacob's death, however, does not influence Hennie's escape in the same terms, for Hennie has not been involved in the main structure of the play. Yet one might be willing to accept Hennie's action if Odets presented it as a credible response to the situation enacted in the play. Eleanor Flexner argues that Hennie's flight is meaningless, but that such erratic behavior becomes "inevitable" in our society when people lack the revolutionary insights of Jacob and Ralph. (Needless to say, Flexner, like Lawson, is a Marxist critic.) This would be an acceptable explanation for the action if the play itself did not largely refute it. Ralph, who is supposed to be socially "mature" now, announces the dawn of a new world—but how will Hennie's irresponsible behavior usher in that new world? What of her child? Is leaving the child in the keeping of Bessie a wise thing to do? What of Sam? Won't he become another Schlosser? People may act like Hennie in our society, but why the idealistic Marxist Ralph should applaud such action remains a mystery. One might argue that Ralph's new love of action—"DO!"—has gotten the better of him; this would be credible. It would not square entirely, however, with Odets' evident approval of Ralph standing "full and strong in the doorway" as the curtain falls. In his essay on Odets entitled "The Long Journey of a Talent," John Gassner rightly points out that Hennie's flight with Moe is hardly a "well chosen illustration of liberation." Yet Odets, twenty-eight years after having written *Awake and Sing!*, told Mendelsohn: ". . . I believe in the possibilities expressed in the last scene. I do believe that young people can go through an experience and have their eyes opened, and determine from it to live in a different way . . . I do believe that, as the daughter in that family does, she can make a break with the groundling lies of her life, and try to find happiness by walking off with a man who is not her husband." One is forced to conclude that Odets remained somewhat confused about the significance of his play's ending. There is also a suggestion of an agitprop conversion in the last act which runs counter to the more realistic elements in the piece. Furthermore, *Awake and Sing!*, like some other plays and novels of the period, poses an "either-or" dramatic question. But why must it be *either* Blanche *or* the revolution? Wasn't Marx married? Wasn't Lenin? Apparently Odets anticipated such objections, and consequently endeavored to downgrade Blanche by emphasizing her cowardice and lack of sympathy. It is a weakness in the play, however, that the audience is never permitted to see Blanche. After all, she is the counterweight to Jacob's dream and as such she should be palpably on view to sharpen the dramatic conflict. Had she been on stage, though, the logical weakness in Odets' "either-or" construction would have been more clearly manifest. This is not to say, of course, that all "either-or" situations in drama are to be censured. After all, life itself occasionally poses "either-or" questions. It *is* to say, though, that in *Awake and Sing!* the dramatic question seems unrealistic.

The crude Marxist thrust of *Awake and Sing!* makes embarrassing reading today (though it ought to be added that Odets' Marxism as such—technical matters aside—should be no more distracting than the anti-democratic sentiments present in the work of such highly regarded moderns as D. H. Lawrence, T. S. Eliot, Ezra Pound and W. B. Yeats). It is only the warmth of Odets' compassion and characterization that saves his first important play from the oblivion deserved by other less genuinely conceived works. "*Waiting for Lefty* had a functional value," Odets was quoted as saying in the *New York World-Telegram* on March 19, 1935. "This is sometimes called the propaganda angle in writing. But the important thing about *Awake and Sing!* is the fact that the play stems first from real character, life and social background of these people." In his autobiographical account *Starting Out in the Thirties*, Alfred Kazin recalls his response to *Awake and Sing!* in 1935: "In Odets' play there was a lyric uplifting of blunt Jewish speech, boiling over and explosive, that did more to arouse the audience than the political catch-

words that brought the curtain down. Everybody on that stage
was furious, kicking, alive—the words, always real but never flat,
brilliantly authentic like no other theater speech on Broadway,
aroused the audience to such delight that one could feel it bound-
ing back and uniting itself with the mind of the writer." The
years have not diminished the power and realism of *Awake and
Sing!*, qualities which endure in spite of Odets' "ideology." Not
even the romanticism that at the end degenerates into a mind-
less irresponsibility as the lovers escape causes any great harm to
the piece. It would be a mistake, then, to put *Waiting for Lefty*
and *Awake and Sing!* in the same category. As Charles Kaplan recently pointed out, *Awake and Sing!* "is less a play dealing with
the class struggle than one embodying the vague dissatisfactions
of the lower middle class at the thwarting of normal human de-
sires." Indeed, few works in American drama reveal so well what
happens to a family when natural relations are perverted.

Bessie Berger has usurped control in the household, as I
pointed out in my previous chapter, and as a result all the male
characters are warped, impotent and crippled in some way. The
original father figure, Jacob, has been reduced to walking the
dog (p. 45) and washing dishes (p. 50). On at least one occasion, Bessie emasculates her father in a symbolic fashion:

BESSIE. Go lay in your room with Caruso and the books to-
gether.
JACOB. All right!
BESSIE. Go in the room!

(p. 56)

Dependent on Bessie, sleeping with records and books, stripped
of all dignity—Jacob is a sorry figure. Nor does Myron—the second father figure—present a more attractive masculine picture.
He says: "My scalp is impoverished" (p. 85); "The moment I
began losing my hair I just knew I was destined to be a failure
in life . . . and when I grew bald I was" (p. 87). Myron's loss
of hair is a metaphor for spiritual poverty and represents another

symbolic castration. Moe emphasizes Myron's lack of dignity by calling him "our boy friend" (p. 49). Beneath his bland exterior, however, Myron seethes with frustrated rage: "I get so bitter when I take a drink, it just surprises me" (p. 68). Myron Berger has been an underpaid haberdashery clerk for thirty years (p. 41). As compensation for his unhappiness, Myron idolizes Teddy Roosevelt and looks to a strong man to set things right (p. 61). "When I look at him, I'm sad," Ralph says of his father at the end of the play. "Let me die like a dog, if I can't get more from life" (p. 100).

Speaking of *Awake and Sing!*, John Gassner says: "The only thriving individuals [are] the capitalist Uncle Morty and the racketeer Moe Axelrod." Notice, however, that both "thriving individuals" pay a high price in human terms for their monetary well-being. Morty is only half a man, living completely on the sense level and denying whatever is spiritual in his nature. Since Morty is unable to love in a wholesome manner—"He will die unmarried," Odets assures us—the man is reduced to "a fat tomcat" who sleeps with models (p. 38). According to Morty "common sense is thicker than love" (p. 65), but he rationalizes his insensitivity and selfishness by asserting: "I'm a great boy for the practical side" (p. 67). His hatred for the normal and human is evident, however, when he refers to Hennie's baby as "Mickey Louse" (p. 62); and when he utters contradictory statements such as "war is necessary" (p. 62) and "I'm a great boy for live and let live" (p. 65). Although Moe Alexrod is much more sympathetically treated than Uncle Morty, he too is shown as spiritually and physically maimed: "Moe Axelrod lost a leg in the war. He seldom forgets that fact. He has killed two men in extramartial activity. He is mordant, bitter. Life has taught him a disbelief in everything. . . . He seldom shows his feelings: fights against his own sensitivity" (p. 38). Moe is convinced that Hennie rejects him because of his missing leg (p. 58). Like the Depression, the First World War is seen here as a symptom of social sickness. Moe has been emasculated in combat as others have been unmanned by society at large. Odets' gangster, then, resembles the "Wastelanders" of Eliot, Hemingway and Fitzgerald, except for the fact that he is functioning in the thirties instead of the twenties. Hennie, as I shall show later, is Moe's idea of "Paradise"; she is his substitute for the "dead God." Moe's suffering is intense, almost constant. "Hello girls, how's your whiskers?" he greets Jacob and Ralph, for he must always bolster his wounded masculine ego by mocking other men; "Okay, sweetheart," he tells Ralph (p. 48); "It's snowing out, girls," he informs Myron and Ralph, ". . . It's the system, girls" (p. 86).

Sam Feinschreiber is another casualty of the times. It is Sam, not Hennie, who tends the baby's diapers (p. 62). It is Sam, not Hennie, who goes home to Bessie when difficulties arise. Moe asks Hennie: "Does [Sam] sleep with you?" (p. 68). In Russia, under the Czar, Sam's father was attacked by Cossacks and had his beard shaved off; as a result of this indignity the elder Feinschreiber died of shame (p. 79). Odets' meaning seems clear. The father was symbolically castrated by a system similar to the one which has emasculated Sam and the other men in the play. Schlosser—and by the way his name, ironically, means "castle" in German—is the janitor who completes the list of male cripples in *Awake and Sing!*, for his wife deserted him for another man and left him, as noted, without even a sense of identity (p. 39).

The characters in *Awake and Sing!* are extremely frustrated in their social relations, their normal development is blocked, and as a consequence they seem to regress to primitive, or infantile, modes of desire and expression. It is striking how often Odets' characters reveal what the psychoanalyst calls an "oral orientation." "Every other day to sit around," says Ralph, "with the blues and mud in your mouth" (p. 42). "In a minute I'll get up from the table," Bessie declares. "I can't take a bite in my mouth no more" (p. 42). At one point she says of Jacob: "Every job he ever had he lost because he's got a big mouth. He opens his

mouth and the whole Bronx could fall in" (p. 55). "Wait,"
Bessie warns her son, "the day comes when you'll be punished.
When it's too late you'll remember how you sucked away a
mother's life" (p. 85). Uncle Morty "smokes expensive cigars"
(p. 38) and he puts a similarly high regard on food: "Ah, that's life
to a baby. He sleeps—gets it in the mouth—sleeps some more"
(p. 62). "The country's all right," Morty asserts. "A duck quacks
in every pot!" (p. 72); "Everything is peaches and cream. . . .
Everything is hot delicatessen" (p. 89); "I didn't have a piece of
hot pastrami in my mouth for years " (p. 91). Myron Berger is
another oral personality: "I can do anything with my tongue,"
he says. "Make it thick, flat. No fruit in the house lately. Just a
lone apple. . . . Must be something wrong with me—I say I won't
eat but I eat" (p. 100). Even Moe, as I shall show later, conceives
of "Paradise" in oral terms. Clearly, then, Marxist and Freudian
motivation, which for some critics are like oil and water, appear
to mix here, making *Awake and Sing!* one of the most complex
plays in the American drama.

As a result of their pervasive frustration on both the personal
and the social level, the characters in *Awake and Sing!* evince
strong aggressive drives and a preoccupation with death. It is
still another mark of Odets' skill as a playwright that he is able to
fuse the death imagery of his language with the resurrection
motif in the play. Analysis of dialogue reveals an astonishing
number of references to violent action and death. Myron will
"drop dead," remarks Moe, "when I tell him his gentle horse
galloped in fifteen to one. He'll die" (p. 49). When Bessie
informs Moe that Hennie is going to be married, the gangster
asks: "Who's the corpse?" (p. 56); and immediately he adds:
"What I think a women? Take 'em all, cut 'em in little pieces
like a herring in Greek salad. A guy in France had the right idea
—dropped his wife in a bathtub fulla acid. (*Whistles.*) Sss, down
the pipe! Pfft—not even a corset button left!" (p. 56). A moment
later Moe tells Hennie: "Cut your throat, sweetheart. Save time"
(p. 57). When Bessie nags her daughter about the latter's preg-

nancy, Hennie screams: "Shut up! Shut up! I'll jump out the window in a minute" (p. 54). Which line Bessie seems to echo when, speaking to Morty later, she declares: "A woman who don't raise a family—a girl—should jump overboard" (p. 62). Afterward Bessie argues with Ralph over his desire to marry Blanche:

BESSIE. A girl like that he wants to marry. A skinny consumptive-looking . . . six months already she's not working—taking charity from an aunt. You should see her. In a year she's dead on his hands.

RALPH. You'd cut her throat if you could.

BESSIE. That's right! Before she'd ruin a nice boy's life I would first go to prison.

(p. 65)

In Act One Jacob warns Bessie: "Ralph you don't make like you. Before you do it, I'll die first" (p. 55). Later in the play Ralph informs Bessie: "You never in your life bought me a pair of skates even—things I died for when I was a kid" (p. 66). Note how Jacob's line foreshadows the turning point; how Ralph's lament looks back to Jacob's statement and, through its reference to the trivial "pair of skates," prepares the audience for the protagonist's later, more "adult," willingness to renounce Blanche for the cause.

The marriage of Hennie and Sam is repeatedly described in terms of death: "Hennie could kill in bed," says Sam (p. 79); and when Hennie tells her husband about the father of her child Sam moans: "From her own mouth. It went like a knife in my heart. . . . With my bad heart such a remark kills . . . I fell in the chair like a dead" (p. 80). Waving a newspaper Moe tells Hennie: "Here's a dame strangled her hubby with wire. Claimed she didn't like him. Why don't you brain Sam with an axe some night?" (p. 68). In Act Three Moe urges Hennie to take flight with him: "Make a break or spend the rest of your life in a coffin" (p. 99); "The doctor said it—cut off your leg to save your life!" (p. 100). Hennie's "awakening" is prepared for in the first act:

BESSIE. Where are you going?

HENNIE (*crying*). For my beauty nap, Mussolini. Wake me up when it's apple blossom time in Normandy.

(p. 57)

And, it is important to note, Odets fuses Hennie's "awakening" with the "death theme" in the following act:

MORTY. Some day I'll leave you a little nest egg. You like eggs? Ha?

HENNIE. When? When I'm dead and buried?

MORTY. No, when I'm dead and buried. Ha, ha, ha.

HENNIE. You should know what I'm thinking.

MORTY. Ha, ha, ha, I know.

(p. 67)

Thus the resurrection motif, the references to Ralph as "boy-chick," Hennie's name, and lines like the following: "Mom can mind the kid. She'll go on forever, Mom," says Moe. "We'll send money back, and *Easter eggs*" (p. 100, italics mine)—all are part of a thematic pattern of imagery. A study of the language in *Awake and Sing!*, then, reveals a high degree of verbal unity in the play.

Note, furthermore, how subtly Odets integrates structure, imagery and theme in his characterization of Moe. The follow-ing exchange takes place in Act One:

MOE. Didn't I go fight in France for democracy? Didn't I get my goddam leg shot off in that war the day before the armis-tice? Uncle Sam give me the Order of the Purple Heart, didn't he? What'd you mean, a no-good?

JACOB. Excuse me.

MOE. If you got an orange I'll eat an orange.

JACOB. No orange. An apple.

MOE. No oranges, huh?—what a dump!

(p. 49)

Here Odets' "Chekhovian" technique is brilliantly rendered. As Stark Young once said: "[Odets'] theater gift most appears . . . in the dialogue's avoidance of the explicit. The explicit, always to be found in poor writers trying for the serious, is the surest sign of lack of talent. To write in terms of what is not said, of combinations elusive and in detail, perhaps, insignificant, of a hidden stream of sequences, and a resulting air of spontaneity and true pressure—that is quite another matter." The orality that I discussed earlier is also evident in the scene under review, which indicates that Moe's oblique expression of emotion is part of a thematic pattern. Furthermore, the structure of the scene anticipates the end of Act One and the turning point of the play.

Later in the scene just discussed, Odets orchestrates his themes:

MOE. Ever see oranges grow? I know a certain place—One summer I laid under a tree and let them fall right in my mouth.

JACOB. (off, the music is playing; the card game begins). From "L'Africana" . . . a big explorer comes on a new land—"O Paradiso." From act four this piece. Caruso stands on the ship and looks on a Utopia. You hear? "Oh paradise on earth! Oh blue sky, oh fragrant air—"

MOE. Ask him does he see any oranges?

(pp. 50–51)

The counterpoint here is more than merely humorous, for Odets juxtaposes Jacob's Marxist "Utopia" with Moe's version of "Paradise." Jacob says: "In my day the propaganda was for God. Now it's for success" (p. 71). Whereas Jacob opts for the Marxist gospel, Moe seeks a romantic apotheosis. When Hennie remarks: "Oh God, I don't know where I stand," Moe tells her: "Don't look up there. Paradise, you're on a big boat headed south. . . . The whole world's green grass and when you cry it's because you're happy" (p. 99). It is interesting to observe that Moe identifies Hennie with "oranges": "Gone big time, Paradise? Christ, it's suicide! Sure, kids you'll have, gold teeth, get fat, big in the tangerines" (pp. 56–57). Hence, "oranges" equal "tangerines" equal "breasts." If one recalls that Moe has said:

"One summer I laid under a tree and let [oranges] fall right in my mouth" (p. 50), one can see that this imagery in *Awake and Sing!* runs counter to the basic structure of social awakening, for Moe and Hennie, like Myron and Morty, are attempting to solve adult problems in an oral, or infantile, manner. This fact would seem to undercut Odets' confidence in Hennie's attempt to make a new life and appears to be further proof of a certain amount of confusion in the playwright's conception of his material. A search for womb-like security and oral passivity seems plain when Moe informs Hennie: "Come away. A certain place where it's moonlight and roses. We'll lay down, count stars. Hear the big ocean making noise. You lay under the trees. Champagne flows like—" (p. 98). Which contrasts sharply with the image of Ralph at the end of the play: "Spit on your hands and get to work," he says, and Moe remarks of Ralph: "The kid's a fighter!" (p. 97). The tensions within *Awake and Sing!* no doubt spring from polarities in Odets himself.

Finally, I should like to point out how pervasive verbal echoes are in the play and how they knit together its various motifs. Perhaps some of the imagery already discussed was not consciously contrived by Odets, but it seems likely that the greater part of his language, with its various levels of significance, was deliberately wrought. Take, for example, the conclusion of the opening act:

MYRON. I remember that song . . . beautiful. Nora Bayes sang it at the old Proctor's Twenty-third Street—"When It's Apple Blossom Time in Normandy."

MOE. [Hennie] wantsa see me crawl—my head on a plate she wants! A snowball in hell's got a better chance. (*Out of sheer fury he spins the quarter in his fingers.*)

MYRON (*as his eyes slowly fill with tears*). Beautiful . . .

MOE. Match you for a quarter. Match you for any goddam thing you got. (*Spins the coin viciously.*) What the hell kind of house is this it ain't got an orange!!

(p. 58)

Myron's reference to the song, "When It's Apple Blossom Time in Normandy" looks back to Hennie's line, "Wake me up when it's apple blossom time in Normandy" (p. 57), and, what is more important, both lines underscore the resurrection motif. Myron's dialogue also anticipates the end of the play when Hennie escapes with Moe. The repetition of the word "beautiful" in Act One is echoed, along with stressing the resurrection theme again, when Myron tells Hennie as the latter departs with Moe: "Don't wake [mother] up, Beauty. . . . You were a beautiful baby . . ." (p. 100). Observe how artfully Odets associates Bessie and Hennie in his thematic structure. In Act One Myron says: "[Sam's] a very lonely boy"; to which Hennie replies: "So I'll sit down and bust out crying 'cause he's lonely" (p. 43). In Act Two Bessie angrily remarks of Sam: "Maybe [Hennie'll] lay down and die 'cause he makes a living?" (p. 83). Afterward Bessie says: "Me, I don't lay down and die for [Ralph] and Poppa no more. I'll work like a nigger? For what?" (p. 85). This dialogue looks back to Hennie's lament: "I never had anything from life. Sam don't help. . . . Twenty-one a week he brings in—a nigger don't have it so hard" (p. 67). Moe's version of "Paradise"—"We'll lay down, count stars"—suggests, in the present context, that Hennie is merely moving from one "coffin" to another (p. 99). (James T. Farrell unknowingly scored the tension in Odets when he said in a review of *Paradist Lost*: "It should be known to the world as *Lay Down and Die*.")

Equally interesting is Odets' use of language at the turning point in the play. While Myron strives unsuccessfully to be a father to Ralph, and while Jacob is on the roof preparing to make the leap that will father the real man in Ralph, Moe, a kind of antimasque, sings in the background:

> Lights are blinking while you're drinking,
> That's the place where the good fellows go.
> Good-by to all your sorrows,
> You never hear them talk about the war,
> In the land of Yama Yama

Funicalee, funicala, funicalo. . . .

(p. 86)

The irony is sharp here. And Odets maintains his control when, at the end of the act, he reveals, through a sensitive extension of Chekhovian technique, the deeper feelings of Moe after the death of Jacob is announced:

BESSIE. [Jacob] slipped. . . .

MOE (*deeply moved*). Slipped?

BESSIE. I can't see the numbers. Make [the call to Morty], Moe, make it. . . .

MOE. Make it yourself. (*He looks at her and slowly goes back to his game of cards with shaking hands.*)

BESSIE. Riverside 7- . . . (*Unable to talk she dials slowly. The dial whizzes on.*)

MOE. Don't . . . make me laugh. . . . (*He turns over cards.*)

(p. 88)

Moe and Morty have both learned how to exist in the jungle, but Moe "fights against his own sensitivity" while Morty has no sensitivity against which to fight (pp. 38–39). Moe's tag: "Don't make me laugh," contrasts with the hollow, wooden, inhuman tag of Morty: "Ha, ha, ha!"—which suggests that Moe means: "Don't make me laugh *like Morty!*" *Awake and Sing!* is full of such subtle touches of characterization and language.

With all its faults, then, *Awake and Sing!* is a powerful drama and one of the most impressive achievements in the modern theater. An absorbing enactment, told with anger and pity, with humor and love—and above all with verbal brilliance—of people caught in a moment of time, it nevertheless transcends the thirties to reveal the human being in the agony and longing that represents the continuing spiritual plight of man in the twentieth century.

CHAPTER THREE

Golden Boy

> With music I'm never alone when I'm alone—Playing
> music . . . that's like saying, "I am man. I belong here.
> How do you do, World—good evening!" When I play
> music nothing is closed to me. I'm not afraid of people
> and what they say. There's no war in music. It's not like
> the streets.
>
> —Joe Bonaparte in *Golden Boy*,
> p. 263

Golden Boy, which was first presented by the Group Theater
at the Belasco Theater on the evening of November 4, 1937,
has often been cited as an example of cinematic structure in
Odets' work. Having recently completed a stint in Hollywood
Odets, so it is said, fashioned a stage play in filmic terms. Compared to *Awake and Sing!*, it is true, *Golden Boy* does look cinematic. One might point, for example, to the five sets, the twelve
scenes, and the fadeouts that end the scenes. Yet *Waiting for
Letfy,*written before Odets ever saw Hollywood, uses some of the
same techniques employed in *Golden Boy*. Arnold Hauser calls
our period "The Film Age," and for that reason it can be asserted
that Odets did not need to visit Hollywood to be influenced by
the movies: for that influence was in the very air he breathed.
The main point to note about *Golden Boy* in this connection is
that the basic structure of the play is in no way different from the

53

dramatic form of *Awake and Sing!*. Which is to say that the line of action in *Golden Boy*, in spite of its time-sequence covering eighteen months, is in the tradition of classical and Ibsenite structure.

A close analysis of technique in *Golden Boy* reveals its tight causal development. The point of attack occurs in Act One, Scene Two. Although Papa Bonaparte wants his son Joe to be a violinist, the boy has plans to become a prizefighter. Says Joe:

> Papa, I have to tell you—I don't like myself, past, present and future. Do you know there are men who have wonderful things from life? Do you think they're better than me? Do you think I like this feeling of no possessions? Of learning about the world from Carp's encyclopaedia? ... Tomorrow's my birthday! I change my life!
>
> (p. 252)

When Joe's brother Frank, who is a dedicated union organizer, asks: "And what do you do with music?", Joe snaps: "Who says I'm married to music? I take a vacation—the notes won't run away!" (p. 253). The polarities in the play—"self-realization" or "success"—are thus established, and the dramatic question is focused: Will Joe change his life for the better?

Joe's inner struggle is projected outward in the conflict between father and son—a conflict which grows in intensity throughout Act Two. When Joe leaves home for a road tour of bouts, his father urges him to take the violin. Although Joe is visibly moved, he refuses:

JOE. Papa, give me the word—

MR. BONAPARTE. What word?

JOE. Give me the word to go ahead. You're looking at yesterday— I see tomorrow. Maybe you think I ought to spend my whole life here—you and Carp blowing off steam.

MR. BONAPARTE (*holding himself back*). Oh, Joe, shut your mouth!

JOE. Give me the word to go ahead!
MR. BONAPARTE. Be careful fora your hands!
JOE. I want you to give me the word!
MR. BONAPARTE (*crying out*). No! No word! You gonna fight?
  All right! Okay! But I don't gonna give no word! No!

(pp. 271–272)

Later in the same act, preparatory to the turning point,
Joe informs his father: "I'm out for fame and fortune, not to
be different or artistic!"; and Mr. Bonaparte replies: "Now I
know . . . is 'a too late for music. The men musta be free an'
happy for music . . . not like-a you. Now I see whatta you are. . . .
I give-a you every word to fight. . . . I sorry for you" (p. 298). As
the old man departs, Tokio, Joe's trainer, says: "Lay down, Joe.
There's five minutes left to tune you up." And Odets, following
his violin metaphor closely, has Joe reply with pointed irony:
"That's right, tune me up" (p. 298). Joe then exits to fight—
and when he returns his hand is broken. This is the turning
point. Joe, "holding the hand out proudly," says:

Yes, it's broke. . . .(TOKIO *slowly reaches for a knife. He begins
  carefully to cut the glove*). Hallelujah! It's the beginning of
  the world! (MR. BONAPARTE, *his lips compressed, slowly turns
  his head away* . . . JOE *has become a fighter.* TOKIO *continues
  with his work.* JOE *begins to laugh loudly, victoriously, exul-
  tantly—with a deep thrill of satisfaction.*)

(p. 303)

Although the violin, which represents self-realization, is closed
to him now, Joe asserts that, "It's the beginning of the world!"
Is it? Or is it the end?
  In Act Three, Scene Two the crisis arrives. Joe has just killed
an opponent, Chocolate Drop, in the ring, and now he realizes
that he can never fight again. Nor can he return to music. Facing
his girl, Lorna, Joe appears to have a moment of insight:

JOE. . . . Lorna, I see what I did, I murdered myself, too! I've been running around in circles. Now I'm smashed! That's the truth. Yes, I was a real sparrow, and I wanted to be a fake eagle! But now I'm hung up by my finger tips—I'm not good—my feet are off the earth!

. . .

LORNA. You wanted to conquer the world—

JOE. Yes—

LORNA. But it's not the kings and dictators who do it—it's that kid in the park—

JOE. Yes, that boy who might have said, "I have myself; I am what I want to be!"

LORNA. And now, tonight, here, this minute—finding yourself again—that's what makes you a champ.

. . .

We have each other! Somewhere there must be happy boys and girls who can teach us the way of life! We'll find some city where poverty's no shame—where music is no crime—where there's no war in the streets—where a man is glad to be himself, to live and make his woman herself!

JOE. No more fighting, but where do we go?

LORNA. Tonight? Joe, we ride in your car. We speed through the night, across the park, over the Triboro Bridge—

Joe's reply indicates that his insight has not penerated very deep as yet, for he is still trying to solve his problems in a childish, irresponsible manner:

JOE (*taking* LORNA's *arms in his trembling hands*). Ride! That's it, we ride—clear my head. We'll drive through the night. When you mow down the night with headlights, nobody gets you! You're on top of the world then—nobody laughs! That's it—speed! We're off the earth—unconnected! We don't have to think! That's what speed's for, an easy way to live! Lorna darling, we'll burn up the night!

(pp. 315–316)

Thus, Joe has slipped back to where he was a moment before his insight ("My feet are off the earth!"); as a result, the outcome of the couple's search for happiness seems inevitable. The climax of the play arrives in the last scene. A telephone caller informs the Bonapartes that Joe and Lorna have been killed in an automobile accident. Whether it is an "accident" or a deliberate suicide is irrelevant; for Joe's death is merely the culmination in a series of self-destructive acts. The dramatic question posed in Act One, and developed throughout the action, has been answered: Joe changed his life—and ended in death. At the point of attack, when Joe betrayed his true self, his course toward doom was inevitably set. When Tokio, just before the turning point, instructed Joe to "Lay down," Odets—as he also did in *Awake and Sing!*—symbolized Joe's preparation for a "coffin." Now, at the conclusion of the play, Papa Bonaparte says: "Come, we bring-a him home . . . where he belong . . ." (p. 321). The moral of the play appears to be that man must live, not for his false self (the ring), but for his real self (the violin); and that "Two together"—Joe and Lorna—cannot be happy, not only because Joe has lost his real self, but because society is corrupted by false values: man must fight, like Frank Bonaparte, for a better world so that *all* can be happy. The bald statement of the dramatic problem dealt with in the play conveys, of course, none of the rich texture and density of the work itself.

In his characterization of Joe Bonaparte, which is deceptively simple on the surface, Odets attempts to fuse psychological and social motivation in *Golden Boy*. Joe is described as "cock-eyed." This personal disability, which accounts in part for the boy's feeling of shame and insignificance, also functions as a symbol within a social frame of reference. Immediately before Joe makes his first entrance Moody, the fight manager, tells Lorna: "I'd give me right eye for a good black boy" (p. 239). This suggests that Joe's strabismic eyes have something in common with Moody's willingness to sacrifice an eye for the sake of money.

One recalls Ralph saying: "It's a cock-eyed world," and Jacob replying: "Boys like you could fix it some day" (*Awake and Sing!*, p. 45). Joe's name—Bonaparte—is another example of personal and social complexity in the play:

MOODY. Didn't that name used to get you a little giggle in school? Tell the truth, Bonaparte. Didn't it?
JOE. Call me Joe.

(p. 242)

There is nothing more personal than a man's name. Joe's sensitivity about his name suggests that being an Italian in American society may involve exposure to snobbery and prejudice. More important, the name has an obvious symbolic significance. Like Napoleon, Joe wants "to conquer the world" (p. 315). Like Napoleon, Joe is a short man—he weighs one hundred and thirty-three pounds (p. 243)—and he suffers from an intense inferiority complex. Joe, like Napoleon, makes "war"—and ends in defeat. Although Napoleon was called "Son of the Revolution," he was, like Joe, the enemy of the revolution; like Napoleon, Joe is an individualist. In the thematic structure of the play Frank is the counterweight to the Napoleonic idea. Finally, as Napoleon's ambitions enlarged he tended increasingly to view men and armies as mere machines; in *Golden Boy*, Joe becomes similarly dehumanized. He tells Tokio: "When a bullet sings through the air it has no past—only a future—like me!" (p. 299). Lorna says: "You murdered that boy with the generous face—God knows where you hid the body!" (p. 308). And Joe asks Eddie Fuseli, the homosexual gangster who "owns a piece" of the fighter: "What the hell do you think I am? A machine?" (p. 309). Thus, it is not easy to separate personal and social causation in the play.

Given Joe's frustrations—personal and social—what solutions offer themselves? Frank is there, as noted previously, as one possible way of life; but Joe—unlike Ralph Berger in *Awake and Sing!*—is not attracted to such selfless social activity. Music is the strongest counterweight to the lure of "success." However, "when you leave your room . . . down in the street," says Joe, "it's war! Music can't help me there . . ." (p. 264). Hence, the Napoleonic mode of conduct presents itself as a "realistic" response. As Odets says in *Awake and Sing!*: "when one lives in the jungle one must look out for the wild life" (p. 37). In such a world the old adage, "Knowledge is power," seems false. Joe tells Lorna: "I read every page of the Encyclopaedia Britannica. My father's friend, Mr. Carp, has it. A shrimp with glasses had to do something" (p. 264). Note how skillfully Odets identifies Joe with Carp through the reference to size ("shrimp") and faulty eyesight ("glasses"). Of what value is music and abstract knowledge in a commercial society? As Lorna puts it: "Something's wrong somewhere" (p. 267). The only power that is respected in our society, Odets suggests, is economic power; and this power is generated by fists, bullets, and machines. An individual's frustration can easily find an outlet in socially approved power drives. "People have hurt my feelings for years. I never forget," Joe informs Lorna. "You can't get even with people by playing the fiddle. If music shot bullets I'd like it better . . ." (p. 264). Joe, according to the elder Bonaparte, thinks that fame will erase his feeling of insignificance (p. 256), but subsequent events disprove this hope:

EDDIE. A year ago Bonaparte was a rookie with a two-pants suit. Now he wears the best, eats the best, sleeps the best. He walks down the street respected—the golden boy! They howl their heads off when Bonaparate steps in the ring. . . .

JOE. There are other things.

(p. 309)

Joe is "respected"—but not by himself.

Love might save Joe from his terrible illusions—"you're real for me," he tells Lorna, "the way music was real" (p. 281)—but love in our time, as the play's climax suggests, demands both self-lessness in the lovers and stability in the environment. "Love is no solution of life!" says Frenchy in *Rocket to the Moon*. "You have to bring a whole balanced normal life to love if you want it to go!" (p. 404). Consequently, Joe is torn apart apart by inner conflict. Lorna tells him:

> You're a miserable creature. You want your arm in *gelt* up to the elbow. You'll take fame so people won't laugh or scorn your face. You'd give your soul for these things. But every time you turn your back your little soul kicks you in the teeth. It don't give in so easy.
>
> (p. 265)

Various characters help to illuminate different aspects of Joe's conflict. Frank remarks: "You're expecting opposition all the time" (p. 252). "I'll tell you a secret," Lorna says, "I don't like you. . . . You're too sufficient by yourself . . . too inside yourself" (p. 265). Tokio suggests, however, that Joe's cocky self-sufficiency is "seventy-five percent front" (p. 255). These, and other viewpoints on the central character, help to make Joe Bonaparte one of Odets' most complicated heroes. And it is, of course, Joe's inability to resolve his conflicts that eventually destroys him. "I gave [Chocolate Drop] the fury of a lifetime in that final punch!" Joe says in Act Three; but when the news comes that the other fighter is dead, Joe knows that he has murdered himself, too (p. 315). For Joe chose the wrong way to solve his problems, and his death in "Babylon" is clearly symbolic of his fate (p. 320).

Golden Boy, like *Awake and Sing!*, reveals complex patterns of imagery. In the earlier play, as noted, society is compared to a "jungle." In order to underline the vicious, predatory nature of modern society, Odets employs animal imagery throughout his dialogue and stage directions. For example, Papa Bonaparte says of Joe's ambition for fame and money: "He gotta wild wolf inside—eat him up!" (p. 295). Asked by Joe to explain her relationship to Moody, Lorna says: "He loved me in a world of enemies, of stags and bulls . . . and I loved him for that" (p. 283). However, Moody, according to Fuseli, is known as "the

Brown Fox" (p. 275). Fuseli describes Joe in these terms: "Like
a cat, never off his position" (p. 275). When Fuseli exits after
this remark, Odets says that the gangster "drifts out . . . on his
cat's feet" (p. 275). Moody refers to Fuseli as a "rat" (p. 276).
The punchy fighter Pepper, who is a mirror image of Joe should
the latter remain indefinitely in the ring, says of his mistress: "I
go for her like a bee and the flower" (p. 299). A further parallel
exists between Pepper's clandestine affair with his married lover,
and Joe's furtive meetings with Lorna. Furthermore Joe is becoming, like Pepper, increasingly dehumanized. When the golden
boy informs Moody that Lorna loves the younger man, for example, the manager retorts: "Crazy as a bat!" (p. 291). The
name "Carp," of course, looks in two directions; it not only
stresses the character's faultfinding and complaining—it is also
the name of a fish which inhabits sluggish ponds and streams.
Juxtaposed to the negative menagerie of images, however, is a
positive pattern of animal symbols. In his stage directions, for
instance, Odets describes Joe's house as follows: "Plaster busts
of Mozart and Beethoven are on the sideboard. A cage of love
birds at the other side of the room" (p. 244). Odets' linking of
music and love birds signals their positive function in the symbolic structure of the play. Lorna calls Joe's sister, Anna, and
the latter's husband, Siggie, "love birds" (p. 288). Roxy, who
also "owns a piece" of Joe, tells Fuseli that Papa Bonaparte "sits
on the kid's head like a bird's nest!" (p. 278); to which the
gangster—the most vicious animal in the Odetsian jungle—
replies: "When a bird sits on your head . . . you shoot him off"
(p. 279). At the crisis of the play, the reader will recall, Joe declares: "Yes, I was a real sparrow, and I wanted to be a fake
eagle!" (p. 315).

A second, and perhaps even more important, pattern of imagery in *Golden Boy* revolves around the theme of "prostitution."
By "prostitution," I intend the selling of one's self in our society
for money and fame; it is to use one's self and others as mere
objects. This is a course of action which ends, finally, in complete

dehumanization of the self. In the first Odetsian pattern of imagery man is largely reduced to an animal; in the second man becomes a thing. Thus Moody tells Lorna: "It's our last chance for a decent life, for getting married—we have to make [Joe] fight! He's *more* than a meal ticket—he's everything we want and need from life" (p. 261, italics in original). Joe resents Moody's attitude toward him: "He treats me like a possession! I'm just a little silver mine for him—he bangs me around with a shovel!" (p. 282). Moody expresses the terms of the relationship in a similar manner: "It's a business—Joe does his work, I do mine. Like this telephone—I pay the bill and I use it!" (p. 288). Lorna, who sleeps with Moody and who plans to marry him though she does not love him deeply, prostitutes herself out of gratitude and a desire for security. In Act One Lorna volunteers to use her charms in an effort to persuade Joe to fight (pp. 261–262). When Moody urges her in Act Two to keep Joe away from his family, however, Lorna resents the suggestion that she play the whore: "You expect me to sleep with that boy?" (p. 280).

Joe Bonaparte, as might be expected, is the chief prostitute in the play. When Moody attempts to get Joe to overcome his caution and to fight with complete abandon, Odets compares the manager's reasoning to a "siren song" (p. 259). In mythology the siren, who was often represented as one who carried off souls, was a minor god associated with death. Frequently the siren was depicted with the head, bust and arms of women, but otherwise with the form of birds. In the first pattern of imagery discussed above "birds" equal "love" and "self-realization." The most famous sirens in mythology were those who lured men to destruction. Disguised as a bird of love, Moody actually tempts Joe to pervert and destroy himself. Odets' prostitution motif is developed with elaborate care in Joe's characterization. "With music I'm never alone when I'm alone," Joe informs Lorna. *"Playing music . . . that's like saying, 'I am man'"* (p. 263, italics mine); "Who says I'm *married to music*?" Joe tells his brother;

"I take a vacation—the notes won't run away!" (p. 253, italics mine). It is interesting to note that *Time* quoted Odets in 1938 as saying he would not go to Hollywood to do the film version of *Golden Boy:* "They want to emasculate me," he said. When Joe Bonaparte abandons music for boxing, he emasculates himself; when he divorces himself from music, he marries prizefighting:

MOODY. . . . what's holding you back, Joe? You can tell me, Joe. We've set up housekeeping together, Joe, and I want you to tell me if you can't cook a steak—it don't matter. We're married anyway. . . .
JOE (*uneasily*). Who's being put to bed?
MOODY. What do you mean?
JOE. I don't like this seduction scene.

(p. 259)

After about a year of "wedded bliss" Joe is thoroughly corrupted: "Listen, Drake, I'm not the boy I used to be," Joe tells a newspaperman, "—the honeymoon's over. I don't blush and stammer these days. Bonaparte goes in and slugs with the best" (p. 305). If Moody is Joe's "mate," Eddie and Tokio are his new "parents." After Papa Bonaparte gives Joe the "word" to fight, the latter remarks: "Now I'm alone . . . you're my family now, Tokio—you and Eddie!" (p. 299). An aura of perverted sexuality hangs over Joe's new menage. Eddie Fuseli is called a "queer" (p. 292); and Tokio, though he is treated in a sympathetic manner, functions under a cloud of dubious masculinity. In one scene, for example, Tokio's "busy hands start up the back of [Joe's] legs," while the trainer whispers: "You're a real sweetheart. . . . You're getting good, honey . . ." (p. 298). Later, when Joe learns that Chocolate Drop is dying, "Tokio comes to [Joe], as tender as a mother" and offers encouragement (p. 313). Like Joe, Tokio has been seduced, corrupted and emasculated through compromise with the values of a commercial society. This interpretation receives added support when Eddie, just before the Chicolate Drop bout, says: "Tokio, I put fifty bucks on Bonaparte's nose for you. It's my appreciation to you . . ." (p. 297).

The theme of prostitution of one's self needs to be viewed in relation to the norm of "nature" in Odets' play. "There'sa olda remark," says Papa Bonaparte, "—never interfere in the laws of nature and you gonna be happy" (p. 248); "life'sa good," he adds shortly afterward. "Siggie and Anna fight—good! They love—good!" (p. 249). The elder Bonaparte insists to Carp: "What ever you got ina your nature to do isa not foolish!" (p. 250). When Carp asks Mr. Bonaparte if baseball is "foolish," the old man says: "No, if you like-a to do" (p. 250); but when Papa learns that Joe has been boxing, he declares: "Had a fight? That is foolish—not possible" (p. 251). It is "foolish" because Joe does not "like-a to do" boxing; it is not an expression of his "real nature." Odets' meaning is underlined in the following exchange:

LORNA. . . . Why don't you fight?
JOE. You have to be what you are—!
LORNA. Fight! see what happens—
JOE. Or end up in the bughouse!
LORNA. God's teeth! Who says you have to be one thing?
JOE. My nature isn't fighting!

(p. 264)

Nevertheless, Joe goes against his "nature"—and he destroys himself.

At the opposite pole from Joe is Frank, the "oldest son of the family, simple, intelligent, observant" (p. 250). Like Papa Bonaparte, Frank is a moral touchstone in the play. It is Frank's "nature" to fight for a better society:

FRANK. I'm not fooled by a lotta things Joe's fooled by. I don't get autos and custom-made suits. But I get what Joe don't.
. . .

EDDIE. What don't he get? . . .

FRANK (*modestly*). The pleasure of acting as you think! The satisfaction of staying where you belong, being what you are . . . at harmony with millions of others!

ROXY (*pricking up his ears*). Harmony? That's music! the family's starting up music again!

FRANK(*smiling*). That's right, that's music—

(p. 318)

Whereas Frank realizes his self, Joe foolishly destroys his self. Thus Odets skillfully juxtaposes the theme of music and the theme of prostitution in order to underscore Joe Bonaparte's ruinous flight from his real nature.

Odets develops the theme that a commercial society tempts man to violate the natural law and thus destroy himself through his emphasis in the play on man's attitude toward woman in such a world. Most of the male characters in *Golden Boy* can be arranged on a spectrum of responses to the female ranging from Papa Bonaparte at the near end to Eddie Fuseli at the far end. "My father likes everybody," Anna remarks. "But best of all he likes his horse, Dolly, who drives the fruit wagon" (p. 268). "My father never said one bad word to my mother in her whole lifetime," Anna adds later. "And she was a big nuisance right up till the day she died" (p. 269). Moody's underlying attitude toward Lorna is revealed when he calls her by the name of Papa Bonaparte's horse, "dolly-girl" (p. 286). In the same scene, Siggie arrives then and returns two hundred dollars to Joe from the old man. Siggie is "sore" because the money is "enough to choke a horse" (p. 287); and he adds: "I got a father-in-law nothing's nice to him but feeding his horse and giving a laugh and slicing philosophical salami . . ." (p. 287). Odets' meaning seems clear: Papa Bonaparte is a natural man who loves everybody and everything—including his horse, Dolly; Papa refuses to keep Joe's money because it has been earned in an unnatural way—and such earnings would "choke a horse." Moody, however, is completely corrupted and he expects to feed Lorna on such winnings. Joe reveals a similar depravity when, early in the play, he tells Lorna: "When you're lying in [Moody's] arms tonight tell him, for me, that the next World's Champ is feeding in his stable" (p. 266). In other words, Joe is the "horse," or "meal ticket," who will be "choked" by money. "I see a crowd of Eddie's all around me," Joe complains to the hoodlum, "suffocating me, burying me in good times and silk shirts!" (p. 308). The natural man, like Papa Bonaparte, loves; the unnatural man, like Joe, hates. "Joe," says Tokio, ". . . your heart ain't in fighting . . . your *hate* is. But a man with hate and nothing else . . . he's half a man . . . and half a man . . . is no man. Find something to love, or someone" (p. 306, italics in original).

Although Siggie has someone to love, he has been tainted by the "success" dream of our society. "Listen, pop," says Siggie, "I'm a natural man . . . Joe went in the boxing game 'cause he's ashamed to be poor. That's his way to enter a little enterprise. All other remarks are so much alfalfa!" And a moment later, Siggie adds: "My god is success . . . I'm prouda you, Joe . . . buy your sister's boy friend a new cab" (p. 270). In terms of the Odetsian polarities in *Golden Boy*, "natural man" and "success" are, of course, contradictory statements. It is all right, according to Siggie, for Joe to want money, and any argument against money is simply "alfalfa." The irony here is that money earned in an unnatural manner will "choke a horse," whereas adherence to the norm of nature amounts to the proper diet for a horse, namely, hay. Siggie has been confused by the "success" myth of our time, and by his inordinate desire for possession. Papa Bonaparte refuses to finance Siggie's dream of owning his own cab (the money that Papa has saved, significantly enough, has been spent on Joe's violin); and, consequently, Siggie complains: "Every time I talk money, [Papa] gives me that *horse laugh*" (p. 245, italics mine). That Siggie has been corrupted receives additional emphasis from the fact that once during a quarrel with Anna he strikes her:

MR. BONAPARTE. Hit your wife in private, not in public!
CARP. A man hits his wife and it is the first step to fascism!
SIGGIE (*to* CARP). What are you talking about, my little prince!
I love my wife. You don't stop talking how you hate yours.
(p. 247)

Here Siggie is at least partially identified with Carp, the man who reveres the German philosopher, Schopenhauer, who is noted not only for his pessimism, but also for his misogyny.

SIGGIE (*annoyed*). Women! Always buzzing around. . . .
CARP (*reflectively*). Women . . . the less we have to do with women the better. As Schopenhauer says, "Much ado about nothing . . . the comedy of reproduction." (*He wags his head bitterly.*) Women . . . !
(p. 246)

Siggie and Carp have something in common with Pepper. When Mr. Bonaparte says: "If [men] wasa fight for cause or for woman, woulda not be so bad," Pepper replies: "I fight for money and I like it" (p. 300). The values of an acquisitive society have, to one degree or another, corrupted the three men, and have turned them away from the natural life. And woman, of course, is an immemorial symbol of the natural world.

Lorna is the product of a marriage that was, however, far from natural. She tells Papa Bonaparte: ". . . my father's an old drunk son-of-a-bitch. . . . Twice a week he kicked my mother's face in. If I let myself go I'd be a drunkard in a year" (p. 269). Lorna's father, then, is in striking contrast with Mr. Bonaparte. Perhaps Lorna's relationship with Moody can be read, at least in part, as her search for a kind father image; if so, though, the affair would have to be viewed as still another perversion of the natural order. Similarly deranged in this sense is Roxy Gottlieb. For Roxy, Lorna has but one function in life: "a woman's place is in the hay" (p. 254), he says—and *hay is for horses*. Furthermore, there is a suggestion that Roxy is a homosexual:

Tokio. . . . If you want the goods delivered you have to treat [Joe] delicate, gentle—like a girl.

Roxy. Like a girl? Why didn't you say so before?

Moody. No, Roxy, not you—you just treat him like a human being.

(p. 255)

There is no doubt, though, about Eddie Fuseli's sexual inclinations (p. 292). What is merely a tendency in Carp's Schopenhauerian philosophy becomes a full-blown manifestation of pathology in Fuseli's person. "Don't ask me which is worst," remarks the homosexual gangster, "—women or spiders" (p. 290). There would seem to be no real love in a homosexual relationship, for such a situation is a violation of the natural order. Hence Eddie appears to dote on Joe, but at bottom he ruthlessly exploits the fighter for money. Even Joe becomes tainted through association with Eddie. For example, both men dress "almost identically" (p. 308) and Joe comes to feel that "Eddie's the only one here who understands me" (p. 297).

For one who, like Joe Bonaparte, has committed himself to such a world the drive for "success" can lead to only one end. Not surprising, then, the play is filled with references to death. In a short but stimulating discussion of *Golden Boy*, Kenneth Burke has called attention to some of this imagery, such as, Moody's remark to his wife: "Monica, if I had fifty bucks I'd buy myself a big juicy coffin" (p. 261) and Carp's reflection on the violin case: "It looks like a coffin for a baby" (p. 248). Actually, the death imagery in the play is more complex and pervasive than Burke suggests. Take, for instance, Act One, Scene Four; here are the stage directions which establish the scene:

Joe *and* Lorna *sit on a bench in the park. It is night. There is carousel music in the distance. Cars ride by in front of the boy and girl in the late spring night. Out of sight a traffic light changes from red to green and back again throughout the scene and casts its colors on the faces of the boy and girl.*

(p. 262)

Lorna is there in the park to entice Joe into boxing. The carousel music reminds the audience of Joe's old desire to play the violin, a proclivity that he now feels inwardly compelled to treat with contempt: "That's for kids," he snaps (p. 262). The traffic light symbolizes Joe's inner conflict, and the winking of the colored lights on the couple's faces is keyed to Lorna's opening dialogue: "Success and fame! [Green light: Go!] Or just a lousy living [Red light: Stop!]" (p. 262). Moreover, the employment of the traffic signals establishes a symbolic frame of reference for the subsequent automobile discussion in the scene, and for Joe's ultimate fate. In our society automobiles are powerful status symbols. When Lorna suggests that she would never leave Moody, Joe consoles himself by substituting an automobile for the woman:

JOE (*looking out ahead*). Those cars are poison in my blood. When you sit in a car and speed you're looking down at the world. Speed, speed, everything is speed—nobody gets me!
LORNA. You mean in the ring?
JOE. In or out, nobody gets me! Gee, I like to stroke that gas!
LORNA. You sound like Jack the Ripper.

(p. 266)

Joe wants to get to the top, and he wants to get there fast. Eddie Fuseli is linked to the "poison in [Joe's] blood" when Lorna later remarks of the gangster: "What exhaust pipe did he crawl out of?" (p. 275). The language of love ("stroke") is transformed into the language of murder ("Jack the Ripper"), as Joe, the unnatural man, becomes identified with a pervert who murdered women. Furthermore, the automobile—which was intended to carry Joe to the top of the world—becomes a coffin in which to bury him.

Finally, a word on credibility is in order. Critics have frequently objected that it is extremely unlikely for a boy with the sensitivity and hands of an artist to be proficient at boxing. Is this true? Two Nobel Prize winners in literature—Ernest Hemingway and Albert Camus—fought in the ring. Mickey Walker, one of the greatest prizefighters in ring history, turned to painting upon his retirement from the ring. Two heavyweight champions—Jim Corbett and Gene Tunney—confessed to having had poor hands for boxing. And the latter's interest in Shakespeare, as well as his friendship with George Bernard Shaw, is common knowledge. Such negative criticism of *Golden Boy*, then, proceeds from ignorance. Not uninformed, however, is W. C. Heinz's observation that there are two errors in the play. Fighters, as Heinz points out, do not train on the day of a fight; nor do they slip into their bathrobe before removing their headgear. (One might also speculate whether a fighter would eat cheesecake the day of a bout—although former heavyweight champion Floyd Patterson once admitted to having eaten chocolate candybars before an event.) In the "Appendix" to *Six Plays*, Clurman says that the "imperfections" of *Golden Boy* derive "from a certain lack of concreteness in details of plot and character . . . due to [Odets'] mere nodding acquaintance with most of the play's locale." As I have tried to suggest, however, Joe's two aptitudes—namely, his ability both to fiddle and to fight—are not necessarily incompatible, and the few errors of fact are so picayune that only a specialist, such as Heinz, might detect them. Moreover, if *Golden Boy* is an allegory, as Clurman, John Gassner and R. Baird Shuman maintain, then the "lack of concreteness" and the factual errors—which might, for some, seriously disfigure the piece—dwindle to insignificance. Similarly, the allegorical nature of Odets' play also makes the "either-or" situation depicted—either the fist or the fiddle—less unacceptable. (It is not a question of *aptitudes* here, but of realistic *alternatives*.) Nevertheless, one should not *over*emphasize the allegory. No recourse to an abstract conception behind the play's action, for instance, is really necessary in order to account for Joe's becoming a boxer. The history of the prize-ring in America reflects the unfortunate situation of minority groups in our society. Most of the early fighters were Irish; then came the Jews; after them the Italians; next the Negroes; and, finally, the Puerto Ricans. As each new group assimilated itself into society, finding easier, more conventional means

of employment, the attraction of the ring declined. Odets' protagonist becomes a boxer, at least in part, because he is an
underprivileged Italian-American in a world that puts a premium
on "success." So much for social motivation. That Joe was born
with a physical disability which compelled him to defend himself
with his fists against the cruel taunts of others in the neighbor-
hood jungle is further proof of realistic complexity in *Golden
Boy*.

For a long time Odets treated *Golden Boy*, which he had written for money, with contempt. This naïve view of creativity was
undermined years later, however, when the dramatist saw the
play again—"quite objectively," as he put it—at the Pasadena
Playhouse. "Gee," he remarked, "this is really quite a good play.
There's something written into it—a quality of American folk
legend—that I really had nothing to do with. It was a much
better play than I thought it was. So after that I made my peace
with that play" (*Harper's*, September 1966). True, the work has
a touch of Americana in it—but so have any number of *bad* plays.
(And speaking of bad plays, perhaps it should be noted here that
William Gibson presented a musical version of *Golden Boy*—
which was a box office hit—in 1964. A number of significant
changes in structure, character, language and theme were made
in the conversion of the original into a vehicle for Sammy Davis,
Jr. The less said about Gibson's musical adaptation of Odets'
play, however, the better.) *Golden Boy* endures because, as an
analytical study of the piece makes clear, it represents a triumph
of dramatic technique and artistry in the service of a theme
which continues to be relevant. If the play has "definite audience
impact in the theater" (Clurman), it is also true—and this is the
case with all important drama—that *Golden Boy* can survive a
rigorous study of its form and content *as literature*.

CHAPTER FOUR

Rocket to the Moon

> A man falls asleep in marriage. And after a time he wants
> to keep on sleeping, undisturbed. I'm surprised how little
> I've thought about it. Gee!—What I don't know would
> fill a book.
>
> —Ben Stark, Rocket to the Moon,
> p. 351

Rocket to the Moon: A Romance in Three Acts, which was
first presented by the Group Theater at the Belasco Theater on
November 24, 1938, is one of Clifford Odets' finest plays. As
the dramatist himself once remarked: "Rocket to the Moon
[reveals] a depth of perception, a web of sensory impressions
and a level of both personal and social experience not allotted
to the other [early] plays" ("Preface" to Six Plays, p. ix). When
the Theater Group at UCLA staged Rocket to the Moon a few
years ago, Odets told the journalist Cecil Smith that the play was
"about love and marriage in this country. They're playing it as
of 1939 but I should think its theme would be as relevant and
poignant today as it was then." Rocket to the Moon, as Odets
rightly pointed out, "is widely performed in Europe and by the
more advanced little theater organizations" (Los Angeles Times
Calendar, August 26, 1962, pp. 9–10). For some reason, however,
Rocket to the Moon has never been popular in America. Perhaps
the explanation lies in the curious but persistent critical myth

that the structure of the play is faulty. Another reason may be that in Act Three Odets is determined to treat his subject in an uncompromising fashion and refuses to give the audience—save for one unconvincing moment—a happy but spurious climax and conclusion.

The charge that *Rocket to the Moon* has a defective structure was made at the time the play was first produced; and, as is so often the case in criticism, that complaint has been perpetuated by one unthinking critic after the other down to the present moment. In the *Time* review of the 1939 production, for example, the writer claims that *Rocket to the Moon* "does not move in a straight line," and that Act Three "wobbles all over the place." Although the word "wobbles" suggests movement of some kind, Rosamond Gilder's review of the play in *Theater Arts* asserts that the last two acts are "static." Even the ordinarily perceptive Harold Clurman argues in *The Fervent Years* that Odets' play is badly constructed and thematically confused. I shall return to Clurman's specific criticism later. The subject again came up for discussion in 1962 when Cecil Smith interviewed Odets on the occasion of the UCLA production of *Rocket to the Moon*. Odets maintained that most people over the years simply "failed to understand the structure" of the play. A close analysis of the dramatic action in *Rocket to the Moon* should make clear that Odets' play is much more successfully integrated than critical opinion over the years has allowed.

Rocket to the Moon is a return to the tight, narrowly focused form of *Awake and Sing!*. Whereas *Golden Boy* extends over eighteen months, has twelve scenes, five sets and nineteen characters, *Rocket to the Moon* covers about two months, has four scenes, one set and eight characters. Which compares more closely with the twelve-month time-sequence, four scenes, one set and nine characters of *Awake and Sing!* than with the more expansive and fluid *Golden Boy*. Needless to add, of course, the *basic* form in all three plays is identical. The setting of *Rocket to the Moon* is a dentist's waiting room in a New York City office building; the time is summer and, as I hope to show in due course, the intense heat is made to function both structurally and thematically in the play.

About two-thirds of Act One is introductory in nature. The audience learns that Ben Stark, the dentist, and his wife, Belle, are unhappily married; that the couple are childless and struggling economically; that Ben is sorely frustrated in a number of ways—for example, he is a sensitive man who reads Shakespeare and often suspects that he is in the wrong profession; and, that Cleo Singer, the dentist's young and attractive secretary—who is likewise frustrated sexually and vocationally—represents a possible threat to the uncertain Stark marriage. The point of attack arrives when Belle's father, Mr. Prince, who has had everything in life except love, hurls a challenge to the similarly suffering Ben—which challenge constitutes the dramatic problem of the play:

PRINCE. Iceberg, listen . . . why don't you come up to see the world, the sea gulls and the ships to Europe? . . . When did you look at another woman last? The year they put the buffalo nickel on the market? Why don't you suddenly ride away, an airplane, a boat! Take a rocket to the moon! Explode! What holds you back? You don't want to hurt Belle's feelings? You'll die soon enough—

STARK. I'll just have to laugh at that!

PRINCE. Laugh. . . . But make a motto for yourself: "Out of the coffin by Labor Day!" Have an affair with—with—with this girl . . . this Miss Cleo. She'll make you a living man again.

(p. 350)

The major questions of the play, then, are clear: Will Ben have an affair with Cleo? If so, will he thereby solve the problems of his life and make a more satisfying existence for himself? Is love the answer to Ben's problems?

The protagonist's first response to Prince's challenge is frightened and peevish resistance. Throughout the play Ben Stark views his father-in-law as some kind of "devil." The name "Prince" is, of course, significant in this connection, as is the older man's "aristocratic air" (p. 339). After Prince's exit, Frenchy, a chiropodist from an office down the hall, enters:

STARK. I don't understand human nature, not the off-color things. Suddenly [Prince] tells me he wants to be an actor! I like normal people, like you.

FRENCHY. Hell, who's normal nowadays! Take that kid of yours, that Cleo—

STARK. Sometimes people embarrass me. The most ordinary people suddenly become sinister—

FRENCHY. Sinister? They're just sleepy.

STARK. What about Miss Singer? You were saying—

(p. 352)

Odets' writing here reveals a sensitive grasp of psychological processes, and in presentation it is skillfully indirect. For it is apparent that Ben Stark is unconsciously alarmed by the image of himself which he dimly perceives in Prince. Even the reference to his father-in-law's desire to be an actor reflects Ben's own submerged Shakespearean longings. Not only promiscuous love, but even artistic aspirations appear disconcertingly abnormal to this frustrated middle class dentist. (The thematic link between *Golden Boy* and *Rocket to the Moon* should be obvious here.) Frenchy's line—"Hell, who's normal nowadays!"—is picked up later in the play and expanded upon in terms of the theme. Similarly, Frenchy's remark that Ben is not "sinister" but merely "sleepy" looks back to the point of attack—"Out of the coffin by Labor Day!"—and forward to Act Three, when the chiropodist urges his friend to, "Leave the morals out" and to "be practical" (p. 405). The final line of the exchange between Ben and Frenchy focuses the attention of the audience on the all important Cleo Singer. And when the girl makes her next appearance, Odets says: "Because of [Ben's] previous scene with Prince [Cleo] now presents a challenge to him which he might never have come to alone" (p. 355). One should note here that in the previous scene between Ben and Prince reference was made to the Hotel Algiers, a place across from Ben's office which caters to lovers (p. 345), and the hotel becomes an important symbol in the play—as can be seen, for example, from the excellent conclusion to Act One:

STARK (*impatiently*). Mrs. Stark is not the terrible person many people think she is!

CLEO (*dismayed*). Oh, I didn't mean anything. . . .

STARK (*almost savagely*). She's one of the most loyal, sincere and helpful persons I've ever met!

CLEO (*in a small voice*). I'm sure she is, I'm sure of that. . . .

(CLEO *now disappears into the operating room. For a moment* STARK *stands there, wagging his head. His eye falls on the dental magazine. He picks it up, looks at the ad and then throws the magazine across the room. As he begins to fill his pipe his glance turns to the window, right. He moves over to the window and looks out at the Hotel Algiers.* CLEO's *voice from the operating room threshold turns him around with a guilty start. In a small contrite voice.*) Pardon me . . . did I tell you before? Your wife expects you home at seven.

STARK (*annoyed*). Yes, thanks—you told me—thanks!

CLEO (*meekly*). You're welcome, Dr. Stark.

(CLEO *disappears into the operating room again.* STARK *looks after her annoyed. For a moment he stands reflectively. Finally he strikes a match and begins to light his pipe.*)

(pp. 356–357)

In Act Two, Scene One, Ben and Cleo are drawn increasingly together and their obvious attraction for each other becomes a painful, and at times even a somewhat ludicrous, state of frustration. The point, I believe, needs to be emphasized. Throughout *Rocket to the Moon*, Odets—and this is one measure of his achievement—successfully walks a tightrope between the serious and the comic. Not many dramatists are capable of engaging the emotions of a sympathetic audience in the fate of a seemingly banal romance—what on the face of it could seem more unpromising than the affair of a middle-aged dentist and his young secretary?—and still have the tact to control the mood and tempo of the action with a light touch of irony and humor. Consider the conclusion of Scene One:

CLEO. Don't want to be lonely, never left alone! Why should I cry? I have a throat to sing with, a heart to love with! Why don't you love me, Dr. Stark? I was ten, then fifteen—I'm almost twenty now. Everything is in a hurry and you ought to love me.

STARK. Cleo please. . . .

CLEO. You're good, you're kind, you're like a father. Do you love your wife? I'm intuitive—I know you don't!

STARK. (*making a last effort to stop her*). Cleo!

CLEO. We're *both* alone, so alone. . . . But I won't have it that way. I'll change life.

STARK. You're wonderful. . . .

CLEO. You don't deserve me. Not you or any other man I ever met.

STARK (*in an agony of indecision*). Cleo, dear. . . .

CLEO (*shyly*). I'll call you Benny in a minute! (*After a throb of hesitation.*) Ben! Benny! . . . (*They are standing off from each other, poised on needles.*) Don't be afraid. . . .

STARK. . . . No? . . .

CLEO. Love me . . . Love me, Ben.

STARK. . . . Can't do that. . . .

CLEO. (*moving forward a step*). Put your arms up and around me.

STARK. Cleo. . . . (*Now they move in on each other. Everything else gone, they are together in a full, fierce embrace, together in a swelter of heat, misunderstanding, loneliness and simple sex.*)

(PP. 379–380)

There is a lyrical breathlessness here, a balance of romantic urgency and wry humor, and a strong dramatic line, that is far from common in the modern theater.

In Act Two, Scene Two, Ben and Belle have a serious confrontation, and the wife exits in a cold fury:

> [BEN] *wags his head angrily, strides around the room several times. Finally he looks out of the window, examining the Hotel Algiers. A sense of resolution grows into his appearance. Suddenly he puts his hand to his heart, not having noticed before how strongly it is beating.*
>
> (p. 395)

The turning point, as is usual in this type of structure, occurs at the conclusion to Act Two:

> STARK. . . . Tonight we'll be together, Cleo. . . . Alone, alone together. . . .
> CLEO. I don't trust you.
> STARK. You're more important to me than anything I know. Cleo, dear. . . .
> CLEO. What happened?
> STARK. Nothing. I only know I love you, Cleo.
> CLEO (*after a pause, suddenly*). Then hold me tight, Ben. Kiss me, love me—kiss me till I can't be kissed no more. Hold me. Don't let me be alone in the world, Ben. . . . Don't let me be alone. . . . (STARK *moves to her and they embrace passionately.*)
>
> (pp. 397–398)

Thus, Odets focuses the dramatic question first projected at the point of attack and developed throughout the action; moreover, the playwright foreshadows the crisis and climax, both of which become obligatory, since Ben *must* answer the question: Will he "let [Cleo] be alone in the world?" Will he stay on that rocket to the moon? Or will he return to Belle—and all that that return implies?

Conflict is maintained throughout the final act of the play. The entire resolution—crisis, climax and conclusion—explodes

within the restricted space of the last four pages of the published
text. Cleo asks: "What do you say, Ben? Don't stand there like a
dead man . . ." (p. 414). Which line looks back to the point of
attack, when Prince tells Ben: "Make a motto for yourself: 'Out
of the coffin by Labor Day!' " (p. 350). Cleo's question also prepares the audience for the following crisis:

CLEO (*almost crying*). Don't discuss [Prince], Ben. Tell me
what *our* plans are. What'll you do with me?
STARK: Cleo, I can't talk now. . . . This man standing here . . .
CLEO. No, you have to tell me now. Where do I stand? . . .
STARK (*evasively*). Stand? . . .
PRINCE (*harshly*). In short, will you leave your wife? (STARK *is
silent, unable to make an answer.* CLEO *looks at him appeal-
ingly.* PRINCE *stands in the background, unwilling to provoke*
CLEO's *wrath.*)

This is, of course, the point toward which the tension of the
play has been mounting—that moment in which the fate of Ben,
Belle and Cleo must be decided and the theme realized in full.
The climax flows immediately out of the crisis:

STARK (*lost*). Nothing. . . . I can't say. . . . Nothing. . . .
CLEO. You'll let me go away? (*She gets no reply from him. Half
stunned, she seats herself. Finally.*)
CLEO. I'd like to hold my breath and die.
PRINCE (*softly*). He'd let you do that, too.
STARK (*to* PRINCE). You're a dog, the lowest dog I ever met!
(*To* CLEO): Do you know what this man is trying to do?
CLEO (*crushed*). I don't care.
STARK (*gently*). Listen, Cleo . . . think. What can I give you?
All I can offer you is a second-hand life, dedicated to trifles and
troubles . . . and they go on forever. This isn't self-justification
. . . but facts are stubborn things, Cleo; I've wrestled with my-
self for weeks. This is how it must end. (*His voice trembling.*)
Try to understand . . . I can't say more. . . .

(p. 415)

Cleo then decides that none of the men in the play are worth her love. Nevertheless, she will go on searching for the right man. Prince advises her: "You'll never get what you're looking for! You want a life like Heifetz's music—up from the roots, perfect, clean, every note in place. But that, my girl, is music!" (p. 416). In the three plays discussed in this section—*Awake and Sing!*, *Golden Boy* and *Rocket to the Moon*—music is used as a symbol of the good life, perhaps of the "perfect" and hence the ultimately unattainable life. An increasing tension is discernible in Odets' work between what the dramatist wants to believe and the limits that reality establishes on romantic dreams. The tension, as I have suggested, was there from the beginning; for example, in *Awake and Sing!* Jacob's broken phonograph records are juxtaposed to Ralph's revolutionary gestures and the romantic flight of Hennie and Moe. In *Rocket to the Moon*, however, the urgency of young Cleo's search for love seems a bit wistful in the somber context of the play. Listening to Cleo's parting words one is reminded of the futile longings of Lorna Moon at the crisis in *Golden Boy*. Here, once again, is Lorna:

> Somewhere there must be happy boys and girls who can teach us the way of life! We'll find some city where poverty's no shame—where music is no crime!—where there's no war in the streets—where a man is glad to be himself, to live and make his woman herself!
>
> (p. 316)

This is Cleo:

> Don't you think there's a world of joyful men and women? Must all men live afraid to laugh and sing? Can't we sing at work and love our work? It's getting late to play at life; I want to *live* it. . . . You see? I don't ask for much. . . .
>
> (p. 416)

It may be, however, *too much*. In *Golden Boy* the lovers end

badly, but Frank Bonaparte is present to suggest better days in
the future. Similarly, Ralph's conversion in the last act of *Awake
and Sing!* foreshadows a world in which love can grow and
mature in dignity. At the conclusion of *Rocket to the Moon*
Odets does not wholly resist the temptation to add a positive
note before the curtain descends on an otherwise realistic play:

PRINCE (*at the door*). Go home, to my daughter. . . .
STARK (*slowly rises from his seat; calls* PRINCE *back*). Poppa,
    wait a minute. . . . For years I sat here, taking things for
    granted, my wife, everything. Then just for an hour my life
    was in a spotlight. . . . I saw myself clearly, realized who and
    what I was. Isn't that a beginning? Isn't it? . . .
PRINCE. Yes. . . .
STARK. And this is strange! . . . For the first time in years I don't
    feel guilty. . . . But I'll never take things for granted again.
    You see? Do you see, Poppa?
PRINCE. Go home, Benny. . . . (*He turns out the lamp.*)
STARK (*turning out the other lamp*). Yes, I, who sat here in this
    prison-office, closed off from the world . . . for the first time
    in years I looked out on the world and saw things as they
    really are. . . .
PRINCE (*wearily*). It's getting late. . . .
STARK (*almost laughing*). Sonofagun! . . . What I don't know
    would fill a book! (PRINCE *exits heavily.* STARK *turns out the
    last light, then exits, closing the door behind him. The room is
    dark, except for red neon lights of the Hotel Algiers and a
    spill of light from the hall.*)
                        Slow curtain

                                              (p. 418)

Although Odets avoids having Ben run away with Cleo in the
manner of Moe and Hennie in the earlier play, he spoils his
ending with this unconvincing final dialogue. I would not,
though, call this a serious defect in a structure otherwise noted
for its clear, plausible, rising line of action. As Otis Ferguson

says: "[*Rocket to the Moon*] is as tight a piece of dramatic joining as you will find, marvelous in the ingenuity with which the play moves forward by the use of three men, two women, two commentators, one dentist's office. It is not only that this ease in the the form means release from formalities as such. In this story of likely people trying to find their way out of the likeliest of difficulties (likely but not humdrum, it must be emphasized) the freedom from strain gives it the complete scope of honesty in dealing with the problems of people who have somehow to live and who dream of living happily." Consequently, it is difficult to understand the persistent claim that the structure of the play is faulty. *Rocket to the Moon* moves in a straight line of development; it is neither "static" nor "wobbly." Odets felt, as I have said, that most people "failed to understand the structure." Close analysis of the action seems to support the playwright's contention.

A word is in order on Odets' use of the hot summer weather in the action of the play. The torrid heat allows the playwright, as Rosamond Gilder has pointed out, to bring various characters on stage, for Ben Stark's office appears to be the only room with a water-cooler. More important, however, is that the oppressive summer intensifies the frustrations and passions of the characters. As might be expected, the stifling atmosphere mainly underscores the romantic and sexual emotions of Ben and Cleo. At one point, for example, Prince mops his brow and stares out thirstily at the Hotel Algiers, which place, as I have shown, becomes a symbol of Ben's desire for Cleo. Belle jealously objects to Cleo going about the office without stockings and wearing her hair in an upsweep (p. 336). In Act Two, while Ben is occupied on the telephone, Cleo hastily adjusts her undergarments. When Ben returns, Cleo says: "I never adjust my shoulder straps or girdle in public, as some women do. God knows, it's so warm I'm practically naked underneath"; to which—"with surprising asperity"—Ben replies: "You musn't say things like that!" (p. 366). Hence Odets, through repeated references to the heat

and to Cleo's body, contrives to keep the urgency of love and
sex constantly in the foreground of the action. But the blistering
summer weather also creates a slight aura of fantasy about the
events on stage, and at times lends a touch of "other worldliness"
to the characters' drab lives. Thus Cleo remarks: "People in the
city have a sweet kind of dizziness in the summer" (p. 375).
"They're frying eggs on the sidewalk," Cooper, another dentist,
says. "The public is staggering around" (p. 375). Clearly, then,
a good deal of that "web of sensory impressions" in *Rocket to
the Moon* which Odets spoke of in his "Preface" to the *Six Plays*
derives from the dramatist's careful manipulation of atmosphere.

The characters in *Rocket to the Moon* are among the most
realistic and complex that Odets has created. For example,
Prince tells Cleo that Ben "lost his enterprise, years ago. He's
no more resourceful. . . . My good daughter made him like that
—afraid to take a chance" (p. 368). Later Cleo repeats this
charge to Ben: "You don't go *out* to things any more. It's your
wife's fault" (p. 374). It would be an easy task for a dramatist
to push the entire responsibility onto the woman—the destructive bitch is a favorite character of American writers—and to
whitewash the hero. But Odets refuses the easy way. "I'm what I
am," says Ben, "it's not Belle's fault!" (p. 349). Perhaps Ben's
troubles, one might argue, extend back to his early days in an
orphan home (p. 348), for a child deprived of a mother's love
may grow up feeling strangely inadequate. This lack of certainty
about himself may account for Ben's need to have the approval
and love of others. "My husband lets people walk all over him—"
Belle informs Cooper. "Don't you think you're taking advantage
of his good nature?" (p. 338). Indeed, Ben's sensitive, brooding
nature probably impelled him away from the world long before
he had met Belle. Odets makes the point that Ben was interested
in botany as a young man (p. 330), and I have already commented on Ben's fondness for Shakespeare. Probably Ben became
a dentist because that line of work seemed more "practical," and
because he felt that Belle would not marry a man who wanted

to be a florist. (The thematic link between *Golden Boy* and *Rocket to the Moon* should, once more, be manifest.) Hence, both socio-economic and psychological forces help to account for Ben's plight. Reference to antecedent causal factors, of course, does not mean that Belle Stark has made no contribution to her husband's unhappiness. A different woman may have helped Ben to overcome the past, may have encouraged him to realize himself more fully. Unfortunately, however, Belle could not be that woman because she too has been twisted psychologically by circumstances in the past.

For Belle Stark is the product of an unhappy marriage. She informs Ben that her parents were "always quarreling" (pp. 330–331). Belle has an intense grudge against her father—"If you'd seen the life of hell he gave my mother," she tells Ben, "you'd understand" (p. 331)—and the suggestion is present that Belle has developed an unconscious enmity, or at least a resentment, toward men as a result of her early experience as a child. It is also suggested that Belle may be unsatisfactory as a sexual partner due to the Puritanical influence of her mother: "In the bargain," Prince complains to Ben, "[Belle's mother] had more respectability under the blankets than you have on Fifth Avenue!" (p. 347). An unfavorable background then has damaged Belle, too. "Ben, you have to love me all the time," she says. "I have to know my husband's there, loving me and needing me" (p. 335). Instead of making Belle timid and pliable, though, circumstances have molded Belle into a cold, harsh, aggressive person. In a way, Ben and Belle have exchanged "masculine" and "feminine" roles, inasmuch as Ben is rather passive and Belle is more active. One is reminded here of the same reversal of roles in *Awake and Sing!* and of the outrage against nature which accounted for the warped characters in *Golden Boy. Rocket to the Moon*, however, suggests a more complicated approach to character and environment than Odets demonstrated in his earlier plays.

Part of Belle's difficulty derives from the fact that she is unable to have children—there may be a combination of biological and psychological factors here—and hence she remains deeply frustrated in her "natural" role as a woman. Belle does not want her father to move in with the Starks because she believes that a husband and wife should live alone (p. 331). Yet—ironically—it is partly due to the fact that the couple *are* alone that they remain unhappy. Frustrated motherhood would seem to account for Belle's overprotective attitude toward Ben: "Any day now," she remarks to her husband, "I'm expecting to powder and diaper you" (p. 330). To complicate matters further, it is precisely the lack of children that renders Belle more insecure and jealous about Ben's possible waywardness. "You don't have children to hold you together," Prince tells Ben. "You're almost forty . . . a time for special adventures" (p. 349). Belle's general insecurity, the foundation of which was established in childhood but which has been perpetuated through the conditions of her marriage, manifests itself in other ways beside mere sexual jealousy. As Frenchy informs Ben: "every generous impulse on your part brings [Belle] closer to insecurity" (p. 353). Consequently, Belle has felt compelled to dislike Ben's Shakespeare teacher, Dr. Gladstone, evidently simply because Ben loved the man (p. 359). Such factors as these make Ben's announcement at the end of the play—"I insist this is a beginning"—seem rather hollow. "It's Labor Day on Monday," Prince reminds Ben; and one cannot help but feel that Ben, rather than making a "beginning," is returning to his "coffin" (p. 418).

Mr. Prince is another complex character. As is true of so many modern writers, Odets gives the audience options on how to interpret the man. Was Prince the cause of the unhappy marriage that produced Belle? Or was he the victim of a frigid and destructive woman? Perhaps the truth lies in a combination of factors? At any rate, Prince blames his wife and daughter for his misfortunes: "The two of them, my wife included—with their bills they ate holes in me like Swiss cheese . . ." (p. 341). In his directions Odets says that Prince is an "extremely self-confident man" (p. 339); but in the action of the play Prince manifests an intense desire to live with Ben and Belle. Why? To be sure, Prince is fond of his son-in-law; however, he dislikes Belle very much, and he is clearly aware of his daughter's rejection of him. Why then should he wish to move in with the couple? Apparently Prince is not as "self-confident" as Odets suggests; beneath the man's bluster there exists a loneliness, a dread of old age, and a hunger for love. "There are seven fundamental words in life," Prince tells Ben, "and one of these is love, and I didn't have it! And another one is love, and I didn't have it! *And the third of these is love, and I shall have it!*" (p. 409, italics in original). When Ben suggests that Prince was unfaithful to his wife, the older man stoutly defends himself: "Never! *But never!* Not once did I make a sexual deviation!" (p. 347, italics in original). No doubt, it was Belle who told Ben that her father was unfaithful to her mother. Should the audience believe Belle? Or is Prince correct in his claim of innocence? True, Prince has a yearning for Cleo; but his wife is dead now and his sexual longings in the present offer no proof of the man's past behavior. Similar ambiguity surrounds the question of Prince's artistic talent. "Without marriage," Prince asserts, "I would have been one of the greatest actors in the world!" (p. 347). Now it appears extremely unlikely that Prince might have been a *great* actor—but is there *any* truth to his claim? Ben seems dubious (p. 348). Odets, however, says: "There is about [Prince] the dignity and elegant portliness of a Jewish actor, a sort of aristocratic air" (p. 339). Prince declares that his wife "insulted [his] soul" (p. 347). Which remark echoes Jacob's belief expressed in *Awake and Sing!*: "Remember, a woman insults a man's soul like no other thing in the whole world!" (p. 48). In both instances, however, one feels that the man speaking has, in one way or another, contributed to his difficulties with woman. One is forced to conclude, then, that Prince, like the other characters in the play, is far from a simple creation.

The foregoing discussion of structure and character should make plain that love is the main subject matter of *Rocket to the Moon.* In *The Fervent Years,* Harold Clurman maintains that Odets' theme is confused. "As originally planned," says Clurman, "the play was about a meek little dentist ravaged through the love of a silly girl. . . . In the actual writing of the play the theme was transformed to that of the difficult quest for love in the modern world." But aren't there some suspiciously neat and oversubtle distinctions here? As my analysis of the play's action shows, there is nothing seriously defective about Odets' thematic structure. Why can't Ben *and* Cleo—*and* Prince, *and* Belle, *and* the others—all reveal the "difficult quest for love in the modern world"? In fact, that "quest" constitutes the "spine" of the play. Clurman also argues that Cleo steals the last act. This is not correct. Ben remains the protagonist from the point of attack, through the development and turning point, to the resolution. After the climax, it is true, Cleo tends to move toward the foreground—as did Hennie in *Awake and Sing!*—but this temporary advance is not evidence of gross structural defect. Furthermore, the conclusion of the play belongs to Ben. True, Odets injects a false note of optimism at the end when Ben says: "I insist this is a beginning," but Prince's statement that Monday is Labor Day—with its connotation of a "coffin"—and his weary attitude, tends to qualify the positive assertion. Further proof that there is no confusion between Ben's search for love and "the difficult quest for love in the modern world" lies in a consideration of Cleo, Cooper and Frenchy as agents in the "spine" of the play.

Some critics disparage Cleo Singer. Clurman, for example, calls her "rattle-brained," "silly" and "trivial"; John Gassner brands her "unimportant" and "commonplace"; Edmond M. Gagey regards her as "cheap" and "silly." Others feel that her awakening at the end of the play is unconvincing. In my opinion, Cleo Singer is Odets' most appealing female character, and one of the most attractive and forceful characters ever created by an American dramatist. Only some of Tennessee Williams's heroines have as much vitality on the stage as Cleo; but with the exception of Maggie in *Cat on a Hot Tin Roof*, all of Williams's memorable women are pathological cases. It must be a dour critic indeed who is not charmed and captivated by young Cleo, and compelled by her urgent desire to "live." Nor is her behavior at the end of the play so alarming; in fact, there is no real transformation. For Cleo has merely glimpsed the truth about Ben; her original desire to find love has not altered—indeed it has been intensified. Moreover, is it correct to say that Cleo's sentiments are too lofty for such a young girl? Aside from the fact that the average person expects a character in a play to be more articulate than such a one would be in life—what is so intellectually involved in Cleo's decision to go on searching for love? Every young person has felt the same desire. Nor would an acquaintance with, say, Plato's "Symposium" be a prerequisite for understanding such feelings. Throughout the play Cleo expresses a desire for love and a sense of personal dignity. "Mrs. Stark," Cleo complains to Prince, "she thinks I'm a dummy. Do this, do that!—I'm a person!" (p. 342). This is in Act One. In Act Three, Cleo informs another unacceptable male: "No man can take a bite out of me, like an apple and throw it away" (p. 411). Similarly, Cleo yearns for fulfillment in love throughout the play. "Nobody loves me!" she wails. "Millions of people moving around the city and nobody cares if you live or die" (p. 372). "Don't you think life is to live all you can and experience everything?" she asks Ben. "Isn't that the only way you can develop to be a real human being?" (p. 374). "I'm a girl, and I want to be a woman," she declares at the end, "and the man I love must help me be a woman!" (pp. 416–417). Cleo, I believe, remains in character throughout the action of the play. Of course she has altered somewhat—"I have more confidence than when I came here," she announces (p. 417)—but that change has been made credible. Luise Rainer, then Odets' wife, thought that Cleo should have married Prince. R. Baird Shuman says: "Such an ending would have been in character with Cleo . . . and would have been a more conclusive ending than the one which Odets

insisted upon." Given such a faulty interpretation of a central
character, one is not surprised when Shuman concludes that,
although *Rocket to the Moon* "does represent a broadening in
Odets' interests and social concerns, it does not mark an artistic
advance for him."

Phil Cooper is another Odetsian character in search of love.
In his case, however, economic problems are even more insistent
than they are in the lives of, say, Ben or Cleo: "Who's got time
to think about women! I'm trying to make a living! . . . Is there
a man in our generation with time to think about women? Show
me that man and I'll show you a loafer!" (p. 352). In Act Two
Cooper returns to this theme:

> If only they invented hydrants in the streets which give
> out milk and honey! . . . we'd be happier people. . . .
> Don't I try? Can anyone accuse me of indifference to my
> work? Why can't I make a living? I'm falling apart by
> inches. (*Suddenly sobbing.*) Where can I sail away? To
> where? I'm ashamed to live! An ostrich can hide his head.
> Diphtheria gets more respect than me! They coddle
> germs in laboratories—they feed the white mice twice a
> day. . . . Why don't somebody coddle *me*? (*Controlling
> himself now.*) What did I do to my fellow man? Why am
> I punished like this? (*Trembling again on the brink of
> sobs, but holding them back.*) Where is the God they told
> me about? Why should an innocent boy and an old lady
> suffer? I ask you to tell me, what is the Congress doing?
> Where are they in the hour of the needs of the people?
> . . . Where will it end if they can't use millions of Coopers?
>   (p. 376)

"O'Neill's and Steinbeck's proletarian heroes are often characterized by their lack of verbal coherence," says Robert Brustein,
"but Odets' heroes are singular for their extreme verbosity.
Rather than being speechless in the face of their dilemma, they
never stop talking about it." Alan S. Downer points out that

Odets has "an absolute ear for human speech," and that in this respect "he has been unequalled in the modern theater." It is important to add, however, that, as Gerald Weales says, "with Odets, colloquial speech is not simply reproduced; it takes an artistic form . . . [it is] a kind of literary prose." Phil Cooper is a "natural" lover frustrated by the circumstances of his life. "In my younger days I was inclined to poetry," he remarks. "In my older days I'm inclined to poverty" (p. 337). God might be, as the Church says, Love, but Mrs. Cooper is dead and "life is a war" (p. 376).

Perhaps Frenchy, the bachelor, is the chief raisonneur in the play. When Ben says: "A man would be a mad idealist to want a honeymoon all his life," Frenchy corrects him: "No, he'd be a woman. . . . The man who worries for the bucks is not the one to kiss his wife behind the ear" (p. 352). The conflict between the "love ethic" and the "business ethic," a prominent theme in modern literature, is on view here. Later in the play Frenchy is more articulate on the subject of love in our time:

FRENCHY (*with extreme seriousness*). . . . Love, for most people, is a curious sensation below the equator. Love—as they call it—is easy—even the rabbits do it! The girl I want . . . she'd have to be made in heaven. That's why I wait—

STARK. You're that good, you think?

FRENCHY (*correcting him*). That *bad*, Doc! *She'll* have to be the good one. This is why: Love is a beginning, a jumping-off place. It's like what heat is at the forge—makes the metal easy to handle and shape. *But love and the grace to use it!*—To develop, expand it, variate it!—Oh, dearie me, that's the problem, as the poet said!

STARK. Yes, I see your point. . . .

FRENCHY. Who can do that today? Who's got time and place for "love and the grace to use it?" Is it something apart, love? A good book you go to in a spare hour? An entertainment? Christ, no! It's a synthesis of good and bad, economics, work,

play, all contacts . . . it's not a Sunday suit for special occa-
sions. That's why Broadway songs are phony, Doc!—Love is
no solution of life! Au contraire, as the Frenchman says—the
opposite. You have to bring a whole balanced normal life
to love if you want it to go!

STARK. Yes, I see your point.

FRENCHY. In this day of stresses I don't see much normal life,
myself included. The woman's not a wife. She's the dependent
of a salesman who can't make sales and is ashamed to tell her
so, of a federal project worker . . . or a Cooper, a dentist . . .
the free exercise of love, I figure, gets harder every day.

(p. 404, italics in original)

This is the same viewpoint, the reader will recall, that Odets
expressed in *Awake and Sing!* and *Golden Boy,* namely, that
there can be no real love until the social environment is "healthy,"
until lovers can "bring a whole balanced normal life to love."
Need one be a Marxist in order to concur with this evaluation of
a serious contemporary situation?

The theme of love, as Odets remarked in 1962, remains relevant. Unless human nature changes, and the conditions of
modern life are drastically altered, the theme should continue
to be relevant. Surely it is silly to go on speaking of Odets in
terms of "proletarian drama." In making Odets a stereotype
figure of the thirties, the commonplace caricature of his career
neglects the fact that his plays written during the Great Depression transcend that specific era and, by projecting continuing
spiritual and emotional conflicts arising from our general social
situation in this broken century, assume universality. Although
Odets appeared to be waving a red flag in *Waiting for Lefty,* one
would have to be a member of a certain Congressional committee
to locate signs of ideological unAmericanism in, say, *Rocket to
the Moon.* Odets persisted in mouthing tough slogans as late as
1939 when, in the "Preface" to *Six Plays,* he said: "We are living
in a time when new art works should shoot bullets" (p. ix).

Odets' practice, however, was another matter. Gerald Rabkin and other critics overemphasize the importance of the Marxist metaphor in Odets' work in the thirties. There are, as I have attempted to show, many things other than economic going on in the early plays. By focusing too narrowly on the Marxist dimension of *Awake and Sing!*, *Golden Boy* and *Rocket to the Moon*, Rabkin—and, I repeat, he is certainly not alone here—undervalues not only the other elements in said plays but also all the pieces written after the thirties. This simply will not do. The approach is much too narrow. Even the writer in *Time* magazine was perceptive enough to note this fact in 1938:

> The reason Odets has gained and held a public that, by and large, does not share his Leftist ideas is obviously not the ideas themselves but his rich, compassionate, angry feeling for people, his tremendous dramatic punch, his dialogue, bracing as ozone. In every Odets play, regardless of its theme or its worth, at least once or twice during the evening every spectator feels that a fire hose has been turned on his body, that a fist has connected with his chin.

Yet even this concedes too much to Odets' "Leftist ideas" in respect to his better plays of the period. During the thirties Joseph Wood Krutch never tired of reminding his readers that Odets' plays did not depend for their appeal on Marx. Radicalism is apparent in *Awake and Sing!*—which survives in spite of its agit-prop ending—but Marxism disappears almost from view in *Golden Boy* and *Rocket to the Moon*. *Golden Boy*, as Krutch points out, "may be very readily though not inevitably interpreted in the Marxian terms which Mr. Odets would no doubt insist upon," but the play owes its "excellence to a warmth of imagination rather than to an intellectual creed." Elsewhere Krutch says of *Golden Boy*—but his remarks could as well be applied to *Rocket to the Moon*—that "Odets keeps his political theories in the background where they belong and writes a play which does not depend for its appeal upon a concern with his economic opinions. The agonies of his characters are real and affecting, whatever one may think of the reasons for their existence." These are wise words, and many a contemporary critic would profit from a consideration of them prior to taking another look at Odets' early work. Finally, almost every approach to Odets in the past has been prone to overemphasize theme in his plays, and to neglect the means through which the dramatist expresses his view of life. In the first part of this study I have sought to illuminate Odets' dramaturgy—his complex construction, his rich characterizations, his unforgettable dialogue—and in the analytical chapters that follow I shall continue to stress both the "what" and the "how" of the plays. For Odets is a dramatist—not a philosopher—and as such he is one of the finest writers we have produced in the American theater. And this judgment rests, I believe, not only on three plays of the thirties, but also on three pieces written *after* the thirties.

CLIFFORD ODETS: AFTER THE THIRTIES

CHAPTER FIVE

After the Thirties

What did I want? To be a great man? Get my picture on a postage stamp?

—Ben Gordon, *Paradise Lost*,
p. 203

One thing we need and badly is heroes.

—Clifford Odets, *New York Herald Tribune*,
August 7, 1958

In his diary for 1940 Clifford Odets wrote: "Hugo . . . inspired me, made me aspire; I wanted to be a good and noble man, longed to do heroic deeds with my bare hands, thirsted to be kind to people, particularly the weak and humble and oppressed. . . ." It is easy to sneer at such sentiments, to put them down to immaturity or posturing or mere neuroticism. And without doubt there was often a discrepancy between Odets' aspirations and his actions. The same might be said, however, about all of us. In my first chapter I argued that Odets' plays are unusual in that, unlike "proletarian literature," love is present in them to a remarkably high degree. And not a few people have attested to the fact that Odets was a genuine lover of humanity. This is too rare a quality in any age, least of all our own, to be despised. Viewing Odets' situation at the start of the forties

97

Harold Clurman said: "As a man and artist he would grow no more unless he found people, a cause, an idea, or an ideal to which he could now make a gift of his love (that is, his talent) to replace his old enthusiasms, loyalties, fervor. Such men as he could not live and mature alone. Such as he must be forever attached to a body of people and a body of belief greater than themselves. They alone could offer nurture to his spirit, serve as the recipient of his passion, the counterweight of his ego." The stock summary of Odets' career is that he was not equal to the challenge of changing times—that he lost his revolutionary zeal, sold out to the movies, and ended a "failure." Thus Malcolm Goldstein cooly and confidently declares: "After the first six plays, handsomely brought together in an omnibus volume in 1939, Odets' work dwindled in relevance to the age, until finally, after 1954, he could give the stage nothing at all." In the chapters that follow I shall discuss the plays that Odets wrote after 1939 —*Night Music* (1940), *Clash by Night* (1941), *The Big Knife* (1948), *The Country Girl* (1950) and *The Flowering Peach* (1954)—in an effort to discover whether all these plays are quite so shoddy as the reports would have it. Odets' "relevance to the age," as Goldstein puts it, seems far from being wholly understood by those who would dispatch him summarily as a mere relic of the thirties.

If Odets' early plays reflect the mood of the Great Depression (and nobody denies that they do), his later plays express the tensions of the forties and fifties. I am aware, of course, that my statement runs counter to the accepted piety about Odets— namely, that his post-Depression writing bears witness to a failure of nerve, and that he is another illustration of the inherent inferiority of the Found Generation. The postwar years have been given a number of titles, such as, "The Age of Anxiety," "The Years of Neurosis," "The Silent Generation," "The Dismal Decades," "The Age of Hesitation," "The Age of Survival," and so forth. None of the names suggest an attractive period. Chester E. Eisinger has made an extensive study of the fiction of the forties and has arrived at the conclusion that *all* the writers of the period—whether they "emerged" in the twenties, or the thirties, or the forties—reveal the same lack of intellectual surety. "The cultural life which the writer found everywhere about him in the forties," says Eisinger, "was marked by incoherence and uncertainty. . . . Rebellion and reform were unacceptable tactics, and many writers saw no alternative but to withdraw from the political scene, that is, as artists to turn their attention elsewhere. . . . With all forces thus conspiring to destroy the self, fiction set about recording the survival of the self." What Eisinger says of fiction applies as well to American drama. We all know this; it is another of our stereotypes. Yet when we come to evaluate specific writers—writers like Odets—we fail to apply what we know. But is it fair to make a single writer, or a group of writers who came of age in the thirties, a scapegoat for the problems of a later age?

Eric Goldman has dubbed the period 1945–1955 the "crucial decade." During that decade the American people, as Goldman sees it, learned to live with a complex world situation that was not amenable to the quick total solution. Odets—who believed in quick total solutions when he had his characters shout "Strike!" at the end of *Waiting for Lefty*—was slowly forced to adjust himself to this altered state of affairs. Like most mortals, Odets continued in part to function in terms of the past; however, he also sought to come to grips with changing historical circumstances. True, Odets did not make a "great Beginning"—but then a "great Beginning" is generally suspect. It is in his serious creative work, not in his public utterances, that Odets' growth and maturity are most in evidence. In his press interviews, it is true, Odets often sounds like the caricature of himself that hostile observers all too happily present to us. As W. J. Weatherby (who is not unsympathetic) says in the *Washington Post* on April 2, 1961: "Sometimes [Odets'] anger seems archaic, as if he is still hitting at targets that no longer exist or have at least changed their position, almost as if he is trying to work himself up into the conditions in which he did his best work. Many of the other writers of the thirties are the same; writers trying to recapture their creative anger of yesterday in the cooling atmosphere of the cold war." Reading over the newspaper interviews that Odets granted in the years after 1940, one *does* get the impression quite often that the playwright was more of an activist, and an optimist, than decorum in the Age of the Absurd would permit. To leave it at that, though, would be much too simple. Some of the expectations of the thirties have proved to be illusory—but does that mean that *all* the values espoused by the men of that time remain foolish and antiquated? To think so is to drift with the times, to substitute a kind of cultural determinism for hard value judgments.

Yet, as I have insisted, Odets was very much caught up in the problems of the "crucial decade," too. In one of the important works of our period, *The End of Ideology*, Daniel Bell says:

> One can have causes and passions only when one knows against whom to fight. The writers of the twenties . . . scorned bourgeois mores. The radicals of the thirties fought "capitalism," and later, fascism, and for some, Stalinism. Today, intellectually, emotionally, who is the enemy that one can fight? . . .
>
> The ideologist—Communist, existentialist, religionist— wants to live at some extreme, and criticizes the ordinary man for failing to live at the level of grandeur. One can try to do so if there is the genuine possibility that the next moment could be, actually, a "transforming moment" when salvation or revolution or genuine passion could be achieved. But such chiliastic moments are illusions. And what is left is the unheroic, day-to-day routine of living.

Two years after these lines appeared Odets told Pete Hamill of the *New York Post* (September 16, 1962):

In one of [my future] plays, I plan to have an old-

fashioned man give his views, which are essentially my
views. Am I an old-fashioned man? One begins to feel
that. This is no longer a country of individualism. The
concept of morality has changed. There is a sort of new
Calvinism, a new piety. There is no longer the sense of
being against something. The idea of "the enemy" has
gone out of American life, and I don't think that's a good
thing.

Odets repeated these reflections two months later when he
told a *Time* reporter (December 14, 1962): "We don't know
who the enemy is with a capital E. This is a frightening thing.
Who gives a goddam about moon shots when you see zombies
walking around with lost souls?"

In the forties and fifties it was easy to believe that the "enemy
. . . with a capital E" was a myth; Daniel Bell seemed correct in
his assertion that even the enemy with a small "e" had disappeared from American life. Odets' last produced play, *The Flowering Peach*, expresses a tension in the development of Noah between the longing for "chiliastic moments" and the "unheroic,
day-to-day routine of living" that characterized the mood of the
times. Although Odets often sounded as though he was still
waiting for Lefty in the fifties, his creative work told a different,
more complex, story. As the dramatist informed Arthur Wagner:

> I find that those things often come out best when I don't
> know what's going to happen, and in fact, most of the
> time I don't know what I know or what I think until I
> say it. Ask me what I think about the world, about the
> kind of morality in this country, oh, I can give you some
> intellectual talk about it, but it's not till I write a play
> that I know what I really think, that I know where I
> really am in the whole mess and can really make a state-
> ment that I didn't know was in me to make.

However, Odets' lingering belief during the "crucial decade," in the possibility of mankind's spiritual renewal made him appear "an old-fashioned man." "Idealism," he told Henry Hewes in 1955, "seems to me at a new low in our world; the grab for success is frightening." On August 7, 1958, Joe Hyams in the *New York Herald Tribune* quoted Odets as follows:

> No young people are speaking out. It is difficult these times for American men or women to find their identity, to find out who they are. In order to know yourself and be a whole person, you must know what you are for, as well as what you are against. But it is unpopular today to be against anything. One thing we need and badly is heroes. As Emerson said, a hero must be a minority of one. He must be an ethical model who breaks the mold of conformity, but this is an age of conformity.

Today Odets' militant belief in individualism seems less archiac than it did in the forties and fifties. The mood of the times has changed again. A number of social movements in the sixties, whatever one's attitude toward some of them might be, suggests that youth is at last breaking "the mold of conformity," that it is returning to a more rebellious stance; in short, the idea of the "enemy"—sometimes with a capital E, sometimes without—has come back into fashion again. Odets' belief in man during "The Dismal Decades" now appears to be vindicated.

What compromised Odets' position as a spokesman for humanistic values, however, was his own *unheroic* submission to the House Un-American Activities Committee in 1952 and his own "grab for success" represented by the plush life he enjoyed for years in Hollywood.

Odets' trip to Washington does not make for inspirational reading. Throughout the ignominious proceedings Odets stressed the Communist Party's negative evaluation of his plays during the thirties; the committee, however, insisted on recalling the more favorable reviews. Odets wished to focus on the artistic side of his life, to give some sense of how he felt about his work; the committee had not the slightest interest in his artistic worth or integrity. Odets had been brought to the capital to prove his loyalty, to suffer through the ritual of self-abasement, and to name names. It was not important, really, that all but one of the persons named had been previously denounced before the committee; the political rite required that Odets prove himself a "good citizen." (There is also some question whether *The Country Girl* would have been made into a motion picture had Odets not complied with the committee.) Nor was it a matter of interest to the committee that Communism in 1934 and 1935 was a different matter from Communism in 1952, that the main movement of American political life in the thirties was left of center. Odets told the committee:

> At that time one believed that perhaps all of our problems could be worked out by some kind of socialism, and I believed that then. . . . I must point out that in those days not only myself but no one had a sense, or very few people had a sense, of the Soviet Union as a country opposed to our interests anyway. I think it was during that time that we began to recognize the Soviet Union, began to move into a kind of amnesty with that country, in terms of trade, for instance.

Odets might have added that a hopeful and sentimental view of Stalinism prevailed—on both the left and the right—not only during the Second World War but at least as late as 1948. In 1944 Communist Party membership in the United States was at an all time high of 80,000; in 1948 Henry Wallace, running on the Communist-backed Progressive ticket, pulled more than a million votes. The committeee was not concerned with hard questions, fine distinctions, and the ambiguity and tragedy of human experience—they wanted clarity, cooperation, simplicity. Odets found it difficult, though, to explain certain matters. "My relationship with the Communist Party over the years," Odets insisted, "was a very distant one." The committee presented evidence of over twenty-five instances in which, up to 1950, Odets had lent his name to questionable groups. The playwright was vague, however, on how or to whom he had given permission to use his name. What is the explanation for the playwright's behavior? "Since [Odets'] commitment was never primarily intellectual," argues Gerald Rabkin, "he never formally rejected it in the manner of the intellectuals who, having made themselves political men, one day awake with horror to a sense of betrayal and find it necessary to destroy their radical roots." If this is true it does not speak kindly, of course, for Odets' intellectual maturity or sophistication. Odets, however, offered another explanation:

MR. ODETS. If I may say so, the foolish position of a man like myself is that he has no party to belong to. And I think that I share this foolish, empty position with thousands of sincere and earnest-thinking liberals in the United States. We have no party to join because we cannot give our allegiance to the Communist Party.

MR. WALTER. You feel that the Democratic Party is too reactionary for you?

MR. ODETS. I don't think I said that, sir.

MR. WALTER. There is a very clear inference.

MR. ODETS. We know that there are all sorts of people within the Democratic Party.

MR. WALTER. Yes. For which I apologize every two years.

It was not a good day for Odets, who wearily concluded his testimony by avowing that if he had it to do over again he would "pick very carefully and would be careful" where he put his signature. He said a liberal these days has to pick his "way very carefully . . . or . . . remain silent. Of the two, I must tell you frankly I would try to pick the first way, because the little I have to contribute to the betterment or welfare of the American people could not permit me to remain silent." Four years later another famous American playwright, Arthur Miller, appeared before the same committee; but Miller, who refused to name names, came out of the hearings as something of a hero. Obviously, the same cannot be said of Odets. The diarist who had "wanted to be a good and noble man, longed to do heroic deeds," appeared to be very far removed from his ego-ideal in Washington.

The press—both the Right and the Left—assaulted Odets. The conservatives sneered at him for his radicalism. *Newsweek*, for example, referred to Odets' testimony as a "switcheroo": "Odets, who also wrote *Awake and Sing!*[,] . . . warbled like a canary" (June 2, 1952). The Left hated him for his cooperation with the witch-hunters. Thus, *The Daily Worker* reminded Odets that he had defended the Communists involved in the Foley Square case in 1949 ("Millions of all colors and creeds believe, with those Communists," Odets said at that time, "that the two leading parties of the country, no matter what their avowed intentions, are against the square break, shake, deal or whatever you choose to call it!") and that he had once written a monologue called *I Can't Sleep* (1936) about a man who had betrayed his class ("The blood of the mother and brother is breaking upon my head. I hear them cry, 'You forgot, you forgot!' They don't let me sleep," Odets had written. "Hungry men I hear. All night the broken-hearted children. Look at me—no place to hide, no place to run away. Look in my face. Look at me, look, look, look!!!"). *The Daily Compass*, a Leftish New York newspaper, reprinted an article Odets had written on December 9, 1951, or three days after J. Edward Bromberg—who had refused to name names for the committee—had died. Odets had known Bromberg from Group Theater days. In the obituary Odets said: "Men are growing smaller. . . . Am I wrong in saying that, now that citizens of our world are hounded out of home, honor, livelihood and painfully-accreted career by the tricks and twists of shameless shabby politicians banded into yapping packs? And, too, is it not a commonplace of the day that most of us in the face of these evident truths do little more than purse our lips, shrug and perhaps privately sigh?" Later another friend from

Group Theater days, the motion picture star John Garfield, (formerly Jules Garfield), went before the investigating committee in Washington. Unlike Odets, Garfield insisted that he had never been a member of the Communist Party; nevertheless, the Hollywood studios were afraid to use the actor in future films, and Garfield died shortly afterward in New York City. Odets betrayed evidence of guilt feelings over having survived the witch-hunt. At Garfield's grave, for example, the playwright sobbed brokenly and unashamedly with his face in his hands; later he wrote to the newspapers: "Julie, dear friend, I will always love you." Whatever else might be affirmed of Odets he remained, in the words of W. J. Weatherby, "a too sensitive man still without armor."

The other part of Odets' life that mocked his demand for heroes was, as I have said, his long and financially rewarding occupation as a scenarist, and sometimes a director, in Hollywood. In 1949 Odets informed Seymour Peck:

> What do they mean, sellout? If people think I'm a millionaire, this is a misapprehension. People don't know that when I went to Hollywood in 1942 I had to wire John Garfield for two thousand bucks to get me and my wife out there. I went to Hollywood because I had to earn a living and digest a great deal of experience and settle into marriage and raise a family. There's nothing mysterious about it. And I did not stop writing. I laid out four or five plays in Hollywood.

(Odets appears to have made an error in his remarks to Peck, for the playwright divorced Luise Rainer in 1941 and did not marry Bette Grayson until 1943). In an interview with Bob Thomas of the Associated Press on October 26, 1959, Odets stressed his continuing idealism throughout the Hollywood years:

> After I finished *None But the Lonely Heart* [1943], MGM signed me to a fantastic deal to write and direct. For

over a year I did nothing. I sat in the basement of my big house and did little water colors, which were costing MGM about $500 a painting.

Finally I told my agent to cancel the deal, which would still have paid me $250,000 or $300,000. He told me I was crazy, and I had to threaten him before he would do it. Then I went back East to write some more plays.

According to Harold Clurman, Hollywood had always represented "Sin" to Odets. When Odets first went out to the motion picture capital he attempted to play the messiah and tried to convert the other studio workers to his own muddled political philosophy. Such behavior puzzled Clurman: "[Odets] had to believe more in himself and in his ideas rather than try to hammer the virtue of both into people's heads. . . . It was a profoundly human pattern of adjustment through coercion. It is often followed by adjustment through self-abasement." Perhaps one might say that Odets, frightened by his willingness to compromise with his ideals, sought to escape the guilt and complications of his false position by an attempt to remake the film colony in his own cherished ego image, ending an internal threat by external gestures. Odets, wishing to escape the confinement of an "either-or" situation, wanted to be both an artist and a "success," wanted to be both respected and wealthy. When he went to Washington in 1952, Odets informed the investigating committee that he had quit the Party in 1935 because the little commissars tired to tell him what to write. "I could only write out of my own experience, out of my own incentive," Odets explained. "I couldn't be given a theme and handle it. . . . It meant to me, if I may say it this way, a loss of integrity." These are noble words; yet Odets permitted the Hollywood bosses to dictate to him for over twenty years. In 1961 Odets told Arthur Wagner: "The creative writer always starts with a state of being. He doesn't start with something outside himself. He starts with something inside himself. . . . The form, then, is always dictated

by the material . . ."; but he exposed the plight of the artist in
Hollywood when, in 1963, he informed Michael J. Mendelsohn:
"You do not sit down in Hollywood if you are a writer, even if
you are a director, to express a state of being. . . . The returns
that must come in are against that. . . . I have tried it; I have not
been successful." Of course, there was an important difference
between the ideology that the Communist press sought to impose
on Odets' serious stage plays and the claptrap he was compelled
to write for the motion picture studios. William Faulkner, who
also wrote film scripts, always maintained that hack writing in
no way interfered with his creation of major fiction. Odets,
however, seems to have felt that motion picture writing was a
betrayal of his own standards, and that, in committing himself to
such writing, he had suffered "a loss of integrity."

Nevertheless, Odets could not always admit this painful truth
to himself; he could not always be candid about his false position. Frequently Odets argued, for example, that cinema work
was a practical and realistic compromise which permitted him to
give his best efforts to the Broadway stage. At other times, perhaps with some justification, Odets claimed that film writing—
considered purely from the technical side—had sharpened his
dramaturgy. Occasionally he offered still other motives for his
remaining on the movie payroll: "California is all right for bring-
ing up children," he remarked to Pete Hamill, "but I never really
thought of living there all my life." This was in 1962—twenty-
five years after his first trip to Hollywood! That same year Odets
told a *Time* reporter:

> There is the mistaken idea that if you stay on Broadway
> and do plays—no matter how bad—this makes you a moral,
> right-living man. Come to Hollywood, and this makes
> you a wrong-living man. All the really great artists are pro-
> fessional craftsmen who write everything. But there is
> this idea in the United States that there's something nasty,
> unsavory or immoral about doing professional craftsman-
> ship.

This is an important point, for Odets liked to insist on the distinction between "art" and "professional craftsmanship." Hence, he told Mendelsohn:

> I suppose that by now I've written . . . fifteen or eighteen, close to twenty films. One need not be ashamed of them. I have not expressed anywhere any loss of standards. I haven't dehumanized people in them. . . . It's professional work; I'm a professional writer. And I am never ashamed of the professional competence which is in these scripts. I have never down-graded human beings or a certain kind of morality. I'm not ashamed of any of them. . . .

Odets, one feels, protests too much.

"Something happens to our good writers at a certain age," Ernest Hemingway wrote in *The Green Hills of Africa* in 1935. "We destroy them in many ways. First economically. They make money. . . . Then our writers when they have made some money increase their standard of living and they are caught." Odets seemed to echo Hemingway when Bob Thomas interviewed the dramatist in 1959:

> The rewards for a writer in this country and this time are fantastically great. It is difficult for a writer not to be changed by success. He writes one way when he is struggling for recognition and another way when his belly is full. . . . Most American writers have a writing span of only ten or twelve years. It was true of Melville and Whitman. It may have taken Whitman several years to write *Leaves of Grass*, but once it was published he had little else to give. Hemingway is another whose span of effective writing was brief. I don't know why it is. Except that maybe when these authors have had success, some chemical change takes place. They become curators of their own museum.

This is a complex problem. In a well-known essay on F. Scott Fitzgerald, William Troy says: "One wonders whether a certain coyness toward the things of the mind is not one reason for the lack of development in most American writers." But this would seem to place *all* the blame upon the writer, and ignore the question of society's share in the problem. Not that the writer is exempt from the consequences of making individual, and agonizing, choices. By refusing to exist solely for his serious work, and by compromising his integrity for a lucrative income in Hollywood, Odets failed (to employ existentialist jargon) to live an "authentic" existence. Ironically Odets, who was forever demanding that men be individualists, failed the first test of individualism—namely, of choosing to be his highest and best self despite the consequences.

The result was a severe guilty conscience which finally completely undermined Odets' artistic confidence. After 1954 Odets began many plays, but he brought none of them to completion. The last nine years of Odets' life, then, represent a real loss to the American drama. When Odets died, Brooks Atkinson, writing in *The New York Times* (September 3, 1963), recalled having seen the playwright on television in a 1962 panel discussion involving the recent death of Marilyn Monroe: "Using the vocabulary of astronomy, [Odets] said that she was like one of the stars that are bound to a dark companion. The dark companion of her private miseries finally extinguished the star that the public knew." Atkinson, however, seems to have drawn the wrong conclusion from Odets' explanation. "He, too, had a dark companion," says Atkinson. "It consisted in the waywardness with which he indulged himself in hobbies. Having a vivid private life, he did not need continual reassurance from the public. Although he was always full of ideas for plays and blandly convinced of his own genius, he was unable to accept the harsh disciplines of writing and staging plays on Broadway." It takes as much "discipline" to write an insincere movie as to write a truthful play. Furthermore, Odets had eleven plays produced on Broadway, which would seem to testify to a certain amount of "discipline" in the writer. It seems more likely that Odets' "dark companion" was his "private misery," or as the dramatist himself put it to Mendelsohn, his "neurotic illness"—that psychological conflict (whatever its origin) which had never been really resolved in the thirties and which, presumably, had left the playwright weakened in his struggle with false values. I shall return to this subject later.

"I don't have much of a sense of accomplishment," Odets declared to Joe Hyams in 1958. "My best four or five plays are ahead," he told Sidney Skolsky. "I feel it . . . sense it, . . ." (*New York Post*, October 23, 1959). But the plays, unfortunately, never materialized. Odets' last completed film was *Wild in the Country* (1961), featuring Elvis Presley. That same year Odets received a cash prize of a thousand dollars and an Award of Merit for the Drama by the American Academy of Arts and Letters. Previous citations had been given to Sidney Kingsley, John van Druten and Enid Bagnold. The Award of Merit, then, was a dubious distinction. The year he died Odets was working on a television series for NBC. "We want to be optimistic, truthful and happy." Odets told a magazine writer about the forthcoming series. "Those are the key words. Robert Frost once said something about using potatoes in one of his poems and mentioned that he didn't mind using potatoes in poems as long as they were well scrubbed. That's how we feel. We will want our potatoes well scrubbed." According to the terms of the television contract, Odets was to write some plays himself and select the rest from among the offerings of other writers. After the playwright's death the show, which was widely publicized, collapsed after the initial thirteen weeks. The two plays by the author of *Wild in the Country* were not well-received. Evidently Odets' "potatoes" had been *too* "well scrubbed" and had lost their savor.

Over the years Odets' bitterness about the turn his life had taken after Group Theater days frequently, and painfully, erupted in interviews. "Grin and bear it," he snapped in 1948 on one of his periodic returns from California to New York. "I took my filthy salary every week and rolled an inner eye around an inner landscape." When Mendelsohn asked Odets: "Suppose there were no film industry today. Where would you be?", Odets replied:

> Well, in some ways it would be much better for me, because I might have been more productive in the serious aspects of my work instead of the mere craft aspects. . . . I would have scrounged around this way and that way, gotten out from under this big tent and pitched smaller tents in many a wild and strange terrain. And good would have come out of it, more good than has come out of my present way of life. . . . You see, the European concept of a "decent poverty," in which framework you continue to grow and exist creatively, is unknown to America. We're so much here for success and its din and its awards and rewards, that we do not understand this concept of a decent poverty. . . . [M]ake a small success, the movies snap you up, and then [you're] well on [your] way to being lost. Because talent—what's talent? In our country there's no profound training, such as, let's say the training of a German musician. . . . But in this country, where there's not that cultural heritage to pass on, if a fellow has a little talent, what happens? It's as evanescent as smoke. He's not well grounded in the past of drama, really. He doesn't write out of any cultural stream or continuity. So that the talent just disappears—like smoke. Before you know it, he has become a hack. He laments it, he has no respect for the work—or for himself.

While Jerry Tallmer was writing an obituary piece on Odets for the *New York Post*, he received a phone call from Pete Hamill, who had interviewed the playwright for the same paper the previous year. "You're working on Odets," Tallmer reports Hamill as saying. "My God, I wish I had the letter to show you. . . . I'd sent him the interview. . . . And he wrote me this letter. It was like, you know, thanks, a nice article—and then what he said, if I could only read it to you, was: 'You're twenty-eight years old, kid. Don't do what I did. Don't screw it up.' "

On July 23, 1963, less than a year after the above words were written, Odets—the man who felt that he had "screwed it up"—entered Cedars of Lebanon Hospital in Los Angeles for a gastric disturbance. Perhaps Odets was reminded then of Hank Teagle's words to Charlie Castle, the wealthy movie star, in *The Big Knife*: "You've *sold* out! . . . Stop torturing yourself . . . don't resist! Your wild, native idealism is a fatal flaw in the context of your life out here. Half-idealism is the peritonitis of the soul—America is full of it!" (p. 58, italics in original). Odets' pains in the stomach were diagnosed as cancer, however, and the doctors abandoned hope of saving the patient. The playwright died on Wednesday night, August 14th. Funeral services were conducted in the Little Church of the Flowers at Forest Lawn Memorial Park in Glendale; afterward Odets' body was cremated. He was survived by two children, two sisters, and his father. Odets also left behind eleven plays.

The death of Clifford Odets served, as might be expected, as an occasion for critical estimates of the man who had once been the most famous playwright in America. The reaction of the general reader, Bryllion Fagin pointed out in the *Baltimore Sun* (September 1, 1963), "reflected either complete ignorance of him or surprise that he was fifty-seven." Two years later Margaret Brenman Gibson, writing in *The New York Times* (June 13, 1965), took a backward glance at Odets' death notices and said: "The newspapers and magazines with few exceptions printed obituaries which were strangely personal, some faintly accusatory, others supercilious; almost all were offhand." Mrs. Gibson, a true Odetsian, was angry—and she had reason to be. *Newsweek*, for example, dispatched the dramatist whose career covered twenty years in the American theater in a narrow—in more ways than one—twenty-two line column (August 26, 1963). Three days earlier *Time*, which had devoted its cover story to Odets in December 1938, had similarly discharged its duty in a summary fashion. Indeed, the *Time* obituary was so disgraceful that Dorothy Parker (who twenty-three years earlier was said to have gone to F. Scott Fitzgerald's wake in California, found it distressingly unattended, and repeated Owl-Eyes's remark at Gatsby's funeral: "The poor son-of-a-bitch"), John Houseman, Gore Vidal, Christopher Isherwood and others felt called upon to protest the magazine's fifty-five word piece on Odets (August 30, 1963). In all the announcements of Odets' passing one complaint—whether openly expressed or not—appeared to be present: the playwright, after getting off to a brilliant start, had died a "failure."

Even in the academic world, where one would expect the intelligence, balance and patient inquiry lacking in journalism and popular magazines, Odets' "failure" seemed to be taken pretty much for granted. In 1965, for example, Malcolm Goldstein said: "Although [Odets'] well-wishers were hopeful that the [NBC] series would belie the strictures of the obituaries, the program was too dismal to last. . . ." I find the critic's reasoning here rather curious. Because the television plays that Odets wrote are bad, does that prove that *The Flowering Peach*, say, is also bad? Goldstein—and he is only one of a chorus here—blandly assumes that everyone will agree that *all* of Odets' late work is without merit. Evidence for this assumption, I might add, is not available in the assessment of Odets; all the reader gets is Goldstein's conclusions, or generalizations. What is missing, unfortunately, is the analytical process by which the critic arrived at his judgment. The result is caricature, and the perpetuation of a stereotype. Gerald Rabkin's thesis-dominated study, *Drama and Commitment*, suffers, as I have previously suggested, from a similar rigidity in its approach.

In 1963 Catharine Hughes, a playwright, sought to persuade the readers of *Commonweal* that Odets' "periodic disavowals that he had sold out were more true than anyone realized. It may be that they reflected merely an unconscious—and accurate—

evaluation of his own talent. . . ." After reducing Odets' stature
to that of a merely "capable and occasionally exciting" dramatist, however, Miss Hughes suddenly betrayed signs of confusion and decided uneasiness over her generalizations. Perhaps
Odets was a better dramatist than she had allowed? Miss Hughes
rose valiantly to the occasion. "The 'tragedy,' if such it be," she
added hastily, "lies in the fact that one can never be *sure*." Ah,
sweet mystery of life!

Clifford Odets, in spite of whatever else might be said for and
against him, wrote six plays that are among the best works in
the American drama. Unless there are no longer any objective
standards by which to evaluate plays there should be no doubt—
or mystery—about Odets' achievement. Although the Hollywood
years eventually took their toll and prevented Odets from writing for the stage after 1954, it is wrongheaded to assume that
the playwright's inner struggle between idealism and materialism did not result in his creating any important works between
Night Music and *The Flowering Peach*. Recently Pauline Kael,
ridiculing Michelangelo Antonioni's grossly overrated film *Blow-
Up*, remarked: ". . . Odets, even in late [film] work like his
dialogue for *Sweet Smell of Success* . . . managed to convey both
hate and infatuation [with a corrupt milieu]. Love-hate is what
makes drama not only exciting but possible, and it certainly isn't
necessary for Antonioni to resolve his conflicting feelings." Un-
resolved ambivalence is at the core of much modern American
writing. "Love-hate" makes Theodore Dreiser's autobiographical
piece, "My Brother, Paul," one of the most moving things the
novelist ever wrote. Faulkner's love for and hatred of the flesh
account, in part, for the structural and thematic polarities of
Light in August. Fitzgerald's ambivalent feelings toward the rich
provided, on at least one level, the driving force for his work.
O'Neill's love-hate conflict centering on his family informs every
line of his greatest play, *Long Day's Journey Into Night*. Similar
tensions distinguish the work of Arthur Miller and Tennessee

Williams. Clifford Odets, no less than the other writers mentioned, fashioned powerful and meaningful drama out of the conflicts that tormented him.

Throughout his life it was characteristic of Odets to oscillate between emotional extremes: He sought protection from his father, or father surrogates, but at the same time he rebelled against his feeling of dependence; he shaved his hair off and grew a beard in order to keep the world at bay (even in middle age, according to William Gibson, Odets was "always suspicious of what the world wanted from him"), but he also longed to merge himself with others in an effort to escape his agonizing sense of loneliness; he scorned the dollar—and he pursued it avidly; he loved the theater—and he spent most of his time in Hollywood; he was a sensitive, introspective man—and he played the tough, extrovert rebel. The contradictions could be multiplied. Behind these polarities was a still deeper neurotic conflict, but one that awaits, as I have said, more precise biographical information and the insights of psychoanalysis in order to be understood. The dark subterranean forces which drove the young Odets toward suicide were never, presumably, wholly recognized or completely routed. A psychoanalyst, perhaps, might argue that at least part of Odets' persistent political naïveté was traceable to unconscious causation, or to those hidden conflicts which had impelled the dramatist to embrace "Marxism," or the "total solution," in the first place. Although inner conflict was painful to Odets the man, Odets the playwright was more often than not able to transform his suffering into highly unified dramatic art. "Anger," Odets told Joe Hyams, "is one of my best integrations, psychologically speaking. I don't think I will ever lose it." This was in 1958—four years after *The Flowering Peach*. If Odets never lost his anger (he was still sounding off the year that he died), he did lose the "integration" of art; something, quite obviously, had gone wrong with Odets' delicate creative apparatus. In view of the fact that *The Flowering Peach* is such a remarkable play—"mature" in both form and content—it is difficult to say with real certainty why Odets failed to be seriously productive after 1954. Perhaps the playwright was simply written out. As yet, in spite of our increasing sophistication in the field of psychology, we know relatively little about creativity. All that one can repeat here is that the "dark companion" of Odets' "private miseries finally extinguished" the artist "that the public knew." Apparently, the same "dark companion," as I have said, tempted Odets to "scrub" too many commercial "potatoes," with the result that the effective exercise of art—through some intricate form of emotional and moral retribution—at last became impossible for him.

Shortly after Odets' death, *The New York Times* carried the following tribute to the playwright by Harold Clurman:

> The bulk of Odets' work was self-portrayal. He was an impassioned romantic, what he himself called a "moral idealist." His central theme was the difficulty of attaining maturity in a world where money as a token of success and status plays so dominant a role. This has very little to do with being a "reformer." His very flesh experienced the lure of those false gods. He struggled against their temptations all his life. He could neither wholly succumb nor yet entirely defeat them. . . . Most of Odets' work was a confession. He told us of his anguish at sharing those values in our civilization that he despised. He begged for protection from the contaminations against which he always raged and which he realized infected him. Stronger than the sound of torment that rose from his clash by night was the urgency of hope, a belief in ultimate salvation, a desperately noble affirmation of what was purest in himself and the exalted ideals of his race and his country. Here we find the source of Odets' importance. His work reflected not only his own faltering but the time and place with which he struggled.

These are eloquent words, moving in their compassion, justice and truth. Yet—it seems necessary to add—the same language might be employed in the name of a poor dramatist, too. What makes for Odets' "importance" is not alone that his best work projects a deep inner conflict that is also *our* conflict—although this is a significant feature of his plays—but that he works his spell as an accomplished playwright, as an artist in a medium he has mastered. Which is to insist that in his best work Odets controls his "state of being" through an integrated structure, or "form"; that he projects characters who, while they represent warring aspects of his own "being," exist independently of him and attain the status of unforgettable creations; that his language—perhaps the finest ever written by an American dramatist—is as alive today as ever it was on an opening night because Odets was a true poet of the theater; and, finally, that his plays are rich because, though he had a "central theme," he had other things to "say" too—all of which impart to his best writing that density and diversity one expects of literature, especially the literature of our time. And, I hasten to repeat, what has just been said applies not only to Odets' work of the thirties, but also to three plays—*The Big Knife, The Country Girl,* and *The Flowering Peach*—written *after* the thirties.

Can it seriously be maintained, then, that Clifford Odets was a "failure?"

CHAPTER SIX

Night Music

There are two ways to look, Mr. Takis—to the past or the future. We know a famous case in history where a woman kept looking back on a mean narrow past, the same thing can happen to you.

—A. L. Rosenberger, *Night Music*,
p. 189

Night Music: A Comedy in Twelve Scenes, though admittedly defective in dramatic art, is an important play in the later work of Clifford Odets. When the play appeared—which was first presented by the Group at the Broadhurst Theater on February 22, 1940—reviewers maintained that Odets betrayed the influence of William Saroyan. Such claims, however, remain difficult to prove. Perhaps another line of approach might be more fruitful. One still finds studies in which it is asserted that Odets' plays are structured in the Chekhovian mode; but as I pointed out earlier, and as I tried to show in my analysis of *Awake and Sing!*, *Golden Boy* and *Rocket to the Moon*, the basic dramatic action of these early works is Ibsenite, with the Chekhovian influence— stronger in *Awake and Sing!* than in the other two plays—providing specific surface techniques such as counterpoint and cross-purpose dialogue. If *Night Music* is a failure the reason is partly traceable to Odets' inability to integrate Ibsenite and Chekhovian structure as he had previously done, or to find a satisfactory alternative structure. "Content presents the task," Friedrich Hebbel wrote in his *Journal*, "form, the solution." Behind Odets' structural difficulty, as I shall argue later, lies a conceptual confusion. Which is to say that in 1940 Odets had reached a turning point in his career. *Night Music* is worth more than a casual glance because it reveals Odets spread-eagled between the old and the new, and searching for a way to express his altered perception of life.

The twelve scenes of *Night Music* are divided into three acts. There are eight sets and twenty-eight speaking lines in the play, which might suggest the episodic nature of the work. Although the action moves from a Saturday evening in October to the following Monday morning, the concentrated time-sequence, as R. Baird Shuman points out, does not result in "a heightened intensity." Deep-lying problems of content cannot be overcome by the employment of superficial structural mechanisms. Resorting to the transitional technique of *Golden Boy*—which also dealt with a large cast and many scenes—Odets uses cinematic fades to move the action. Once again, however, the playwright exposes himself to the charge that he is merely tinkering with the external side of the formal problem, for the filmic devices fail to create the desired illusion of movement or fluidity. Harold Clurman, who directed the play, was well aware that *Night Music* "lacked definite theme, logical plot progression, coherent passion"; he "agreed that the play was too long, but [he] refused to cut any of its scenes. The structure of the play, such as it was, needed every scene, though the play's excesses were obvious." In his "Introduction" to the published play (I have been quoting from *The Fervent Years*), Clurman argues "that among [Odets'] longer plays it is the most integrated in its feeling and the most completely conceived." Although Clurman is a perceptive and sensitive critic, and though he makes some trenchant observations on *Night Music*, it is nevertheless impossible to concur with his view that the play is unified. For *Night Music* is too uncertain

in its conception, and too divided in its motivation to be a satis-
factorily executed play.

Although the points of decisive change are neither clear nor
compelling, *Night Music* betrays traces of an Ibsenite structure.
In Scene One the audience learns that Fay Tucker, a struggling
actress, has innocently jeopardized Steve Takis' job. While Steve
was standing on a Manhattan corner with two monkeys, about to
return with them to his Hollywood studio, one of the animals
frightened Fay, resulting in the young man's arrest. Having lost
his wallet in the confusion, and having to endure the possibility
of not finding another job very easily, Steve is at odds with Fay.
By Scene Two some vague dramatic questions appear to be
present, such as, Will Steve Takis—the aggressively surly but
fundamentally decent hero of the piece—fall in love with Fay
Tucker? The dramatic problem (which uncomfortably suggests
so many trite Hollywood boy-meets-girl affairs) adumbrates
movement from initial antagonism, through increasing com-
plication, to final happy ending. Other questions dimly raised
are, Will the positive influence of Fay and the guardian angel
detective, Abraham Lincoln Rosenberger, soften Steve's harsh
and pugnacious attitude toward the world? Will Steve discover
his real self and find a constructive aim in life? Act One, which
like the following act is divided into five scenes, ends with Fay
in love with Steve. During Act Two, Steve resists returning Fay's
love, but the play tends to circle statically until Scene Five, which
concludes with the hero holding Fay "silently, with pride and
dignity." Says Steve: "You're my girl, Fay" (p. 200). And if
Night Music can be said to have a turning point, this is it, for the
questions are focused: Will Steve marry Fay now, and if so,
will Steve alter his outlook on life? The resolution appears in the
final scene of the play. When Steve loses his Hollywood job, he
is "ready to resign from the human race" (p. 233), but Fay and
Rosenberger persuade the young man to go on fighting for love
and happiness. Odets concludes the action with the three char-

acters—Steve, Fay and Rosenberger—making an exit "as one" (p. 237).

In his review of *Night Music*, Joseph Wood Krutch described the structure of the play as "centripetal." With more accuracy, perhaps, the form of the play (to the extent that the piece *has* a form) could be called "centrifugal." For Steve Takis is at the center of the structure, and all the action of the play proceeds outward from the center. The "spine" of the play, as more than one critic has observed, is "to find a home." If one visualizes the structure of the piece in graphic terms, one might see the form as a wheel with Steve Takis as the hub and the various characters he encounters over the weekend as so many spokes revolving around him. It is the movement of the wheel which conveys the theme of "homelessness." Thus Fay, Rosenberger, the actress who has lost her job, the sailor who cannot find a room in the Hotel Algiers, Mr. George whose wife is dead, Roy Brown who has never had a wife, Al and The Little Man, both of whom have wives but still remain "homeless," Fay's parents, Eddie Bellows—all these characters, and others, reflect the situation of Steve and participate in his loneliness and alienation. I shall regard some of these characters more closely later; here I should like to point out that it is this form, which I have called "centrifugal," that distinguishes Chekhov's plays.

According to Winifred L. Dusenbury; "The [Chekhovian] technique [in *Night Music*] appropriately reinforces the theme of loneliness by emphasizing the separateness of each character from the others." Actually, however, there is little or no cross-purpose dialogue in *Night Music* to support Dusenbury's interpretation. Where is the scene in the later play which compares, say, with that one in *Awake and Sing!* where Moe agonizes over Hennie, concealing his pain behind the line: "What the hell kind of house is this it ain't got an orange!!"—while Myron dazedly recalls Nora Bayes singing "When It's Apple Blossom Time in Normandy" (p. 58)? As Odets' choice of a title suggests, music—not logic—is the informing principle of the the-

matic structure of *Night Music*. ("It is not a thesis," says Clurman—further confusing the issue by making an Ibsenite, or
logical, structure, identical with a "message" play—"it is the
'melody' that permeates the play.") And music, of course, again
suggests Chekhov, who was fond of complicating his centrifugal
structure by recourse to counterpoint. "Only a master," John
Gassner correctly observes, "can sustain counterpoint interestingly for any length of time in drama, as in music." Although
Odets used contrapuntal structure in a masterful way in *Awake
and Sing!*, he failed to build such effects into *Night Music*. Once
again, there is no scene in the later play which resembles the one
in *Awake and Sing!* where Jacob embraces Ralph, both men
crying with frustration and humiliation, while in the adjacent
room a tango blares mockingly and Morty roars with laughter.
Consequently, the centrifugal structure of *Night Music* is imper-
fectly developed and the play remains loose and baggy because
Odets is unable to "sustain counterpoint interestingly for any
length of time."

The fundamental problem in *Night Music* lies, as I have
suggested, in Odets' confused approach to his subject. "Odets,"
Mordecai Gorelik says, "has never been able to strike a balance
between his amazing intuitive grasp of the American scene
and the oversimplified pattern into which he forces his materials."
Whatever one may think of this criticism as applied to the body
of Odets' work, there seems little doubt that Gorelik's observation is apt in regard to *Night Music*. Gerald Rabkin arrives at
a similar interpretation. "Steve's predicament," says Rabkin, "is
given an economic base, since his aggression is motivated by the
fact of his deprivation. . . . But a sense of man's inability to con-
front reality and change the world vitiates the social implication
of *Night Music*. . . . The theme [is] not the determination of the
economically deprived to gain their deserved rights, but rather
a despairing acknowledgment of the futility of gestures of protest." Rabkin argues that for Odets, social "dislocation . . . now
informs *all* strata of society." So far there is not much to quarrel

with here. But then the critic, like the playwright he is dissecting, goes on to confuse the whole point of the thematic problem. After declaring that Odets' "answer"—namely, "a blind faith in man's possibilities"—is a "false solution," Rabkin concludes that "despite [Odets'] attempt at wistfulness, his world is a real one, and demands real solutions." But suppose there are no "solutions"? For behind the Have and Have Not dichotomy of the play lies a spiritual problem. George R. Kernodle is certainly correct when he perceives this fact; he errs, however, when he asserts that Odets now "sees man's problem as purely a problem of the inner spirit." The truth of the matter, as previously noted, is that Odets is profoundly disoriented, and he writes, as George Jean Nathan unsympathetically expressed it, like "a man volubly and indignantly waiting for an ideational street-car that never shows up." The angry gestures that Odets trots out are unconvincing not only because the fire has fled the radical cause, or because the "dislocation . . . now informs *all* strata of society" (Rabkin exaggerates for the sake of his thesis, by the way, since *all* classes are not represented in *Night Music*), but because the basic problem is, or seems to be, largely metaphysical and hence not amenable to an activist "solution." Perhaps a fuller discussion of character and theme in *Night Music* will make my point clearer.

Viewed from one perspective, Steve Takis appears to be the unhappy victim of social injustice. Employed at the age of twenty-three (p. 85) in the capacity of an "eighteen-fifty-a-week errand boy" in a Hollywood studio (p. 208), Steve is treated as of less importance than the monkeys he tends. This point is underlined at the start of the play when Fay defends Steve against a policeman: "Lieutenant, you have no right to talk that way to another human being!" (p. 8). Throughout *Night Music* Steve's "homelessness" is given a socio-economic interpretation, and the Odetsian "solution" is presented in strident activist terms. For example, Rosenberger tells Steve: "You are feeling mad. Why shouldn't you feel mad? In your whole life you never had a pretzel. You think you have to tell me it's a classified world?" (p. 189). Even Fay strikes a belligerent stance on the subject: "It's war to make a living, to keep respect, to be in love! . . . Don't you see you're at war, right now, yesterday, last year—*and right here*?!" (p. 234, italics in original). One of the rapid ideological exchanges between Rosenberger and Steve echoes a similar dialogue in *Awake and Sing!*:

ROSENBERGER. A certain late Cardinal, an old friend of mine, he spoke like you.
STEVE. He spoke? *Spoke?* Why didn't he *do?*
ROSENBERGER. Maybe he died too soon. But you won't die so soon. Fix it, make it, change it.
STEVE. I'm not that good.
ROSENBERGER. You can learn. You are the younger generation. The whole country is looking to you.

(pp. 180–181, italics in original)

Here is a passage from the earlier play:

JACOB. There's an expression—"strong as iron you must be."
RALPH. It's a cock-eyed world.
JACOB. Boys like you could fix it some day . . .
RALPH. I don't get all that.
JACOB. For years, I watched you grow up. Wait! You'll graduate from my university.

(p. 45)

When he wrote *Awake and Sing!*, Odets believed that Marxism was the answer to Ralph's problems, and though the structure of that play is not completely satisfactory, the work as a whole achieves a high degree of unity. In *Night Music*, however, Odets' faith in the efficacy of any form of activism is obviously faint; consequently, the disillusioned dramatist feels compelled to increase the volume of his protest in order to conceal the emptiness of his hopes. *Golden Boy* and *Rocket to the Moon* were largely free of such defects. Perhaps Odets, when he wrote these plays, still believed in Marxism (he was always to believe, with varying degrees of intensity, in some form of activism) but he was able to keep his ideological commitments from disfiguring his art. Unhappily, *Night Music* represents a loss of artistic control. Thus Odets is constrained to drag in statements by George Washington ("The preservation of the sacred fire of liberty . . . is in the hands of the people") and to pose marriage as an answer to the unhappiness of Steve and Fay ("Who told you not to make a new political party?" Rosenberger counsels the lovers. "Make it and call it 'Party-to-Marry-My-Girl!'" [p. 235]) in a pathetic effort to offer some "solution" to the difficulties posed by the play. Equally distressing are Rosenberger's—and presumably Odets'—aims for good activists: "No old man can rest if you don't use your health to fight, to conquer disease and poverty, dirt and ignorance. . . . Go, go with love and health—your wonderful country never needed you more . . ." (p. 236). What makes such sentiments especially clumsy and embarrassing to read is that the remedy proposed bears absolutely no relationship to the deeper issues posed by Odets in the play.

In *Awake and Sing!* Odets was able to integrate personal and social causation. Analysis of *Night Music* reveals, however, a split in motivation. Take, for example, Steve's constant references to his late mother. In a scene on a park bench, Steve tells Fay:

> Gee, I'm pooped. . . . Didn't sleep much on the plane. (*After yawning*) There's like a smell of geraniums an' I hear my mother say, "Go to bed, Stevie, tomorrow's another day." . . . Every window in our house had geraniums —two rooms equal house. Since my mother died I can't stand Brochton. I don't want no one to mention her—I can't stand it.
>
> (pp. 89–90)

Undoubtedly, Odets wished the audience to grasp some related significance in "two rooms equal house," the death of Mrs. Takis, and Steve's homelessness. Whatever Odets' intention, though, the playwright fails to establish any concrete causal connection between the Takis' economic situation and the protagonist's sense of loss over his mother's death. In the park scene referred to above, Fay puts "a protecting arm around [Steve]; his head falls on her shoulder; she gathers him tighter to herself" (p. 107), which suggests that Fay has come to fill the space in Steve's life vacated by his mother. In short, much of the hero's anguish and aggression derives from a level of experience which bears little or no relation to economic or social circumstances. Mrs. Takis' death from cancer would not seem socially significant unless one felt that research scientists were malingering in regard to the cancer problem in a perserve effort to eliminate the economically impoverished. The idea is, of course, absurd. Yet Odets repeatedly presents Steve Takis in such a way as to suggest that society has somehow victimized the young man by depriving him of his mother. Hence, when Fay slaps Steve for using vulgar language, the hero says: "When I'm hit that way it's like my mother died. . . . I'm off my top!" (p. 176). Indeed, Steve's love for his mother is so intense that one begins to suspect the presence of an oedipal attachment.

"What a sweet girl she was!" Steve says of his mother. "My father musta loved her like a sonofabitch" (p. 119). Mrs. Takis is also associated with the hero's love of music, for the clarinet he plays was given to him by his mother (p. 37). Referring to himself as a "harmony boy who mighta been," Steve accuses America of "keepin' me there on a low A when I'm good enough for a high C!" (p. 180). Baffled by his intense feelings, Steve can only express himself through his music:

Now he begins to play on the clarinet. . . . His music is soft and gentle, lonely, filled with yearning. Whatever his pride and fear

of repudiation prevented him from saying to the girl he is now
able to express in his music. In the next room FAY *lifts her*
head and then sits upright on the bed. . . . She understands
STEVE's *music. . . .*

(p. 198)

Fay "understands Steve's music," it seems clear, in the same
way that the late Mrs. Takis used to understand her son's "yearning." Whereas the scent of geraniums in the park reminds Steve
of his mother and thus prepares the way for Fay's adoption of
the role of a surrogate mother, the sound of music here once
again evokes the ghost of Steve's mother and once more casts Fay
in the image of the departed Mrs. Takis. In many ways, then,
Steve is a mama's boy. ("Yum yum" is one of the hero's favorite
expressions of mockery; but this character tag, like the clarinet,
merely underscores Steve's oral orientation to life.) Viewed in
this light, Steve's exaggerated aggression is a defence against his
passivity and dependence. "You're like some sort of wild animal,
Mr. Takis," Fay complains at one point. "Don't you think you
overdo it a little?" (pp. 78–79). Throughout the play, Fay, not
Steve, is the aggressor. "A girl isn't supposed to pick," Steve informs Fay; "—A girl is passive, don't you know that yet?" (p.
181). And when Fay persists in assuming the lead in the romance,
Steve cries: "Hell, a nice girl don't talk that way. A girl's supposed to be passive . . ." (p. 195). There is no help for it: what
emerges most patently from a close analysis of Steve Takis is the
fact that his basic problem is psychological—he is still searching
for a lost mother. Too wide a gulf separates this individual character problem from the social theme of homelessness, with the
result that the play collapses for want of unity.

If Steve Takis' fundamental problem seems hardly susceptible
to some form of group action, Odets' depiction of Fay Tucker,
Abe Rosenberger, and several other characters makes even plainer
the painful discrepancy between the basic issue in the play and
the spurious interpretation of it given by the dramatist. Odets'

characterization of Fay looks back to a theme developed earlier in *Rocket to the Moon*. In the previous play, Mr. Prince describes Ben Stark's existence as follows:

> A life where every day is Monday. There used to be a week-end, but now it's always Monday. Awnings up, awnings down, coat on, coat off. Sweat in summer, freeze in winter—a movie, a bridge game, an auto ride to Peeks-kill. Gas is twenty cents a gallon, worry about the bills, write a budget—the maid is too expensive—you bought a pair of shoes *last* month. You're old, you're getting old —she's old. Yesterday you didn't look in my face. Tomorrow you forgot I'm here. Two aspirin pills are good for headaches. The world is getting . . . so dull, let me sleep, let me sleep! You sneeze, you have a cold. No, that was last month. No, it's now. Which is now and which is then?
>
> (p. 349, italics in original)

Here is Fay Tucker expressing her disgust with life in *Night Music*:

> Nothing, nothing, I tell you nothing happens! Shampoo your hair. Wash out a pair of stockings before you go to bed. Cousin Gert's very sick. Mr. Jones is expected to die. Did my nails last night. Went to bed early. Cleaned up around the house. Fixed my drawer or handkerchief box. Bought some cold cream and writing paper, but who will I write to? Wished I was dead. It's Lent. Lent is over. Quarreled, but didn't want to hurt the family's feelings. Went to high school reunion. Stayed home—did the dishes. Father has a cold, mother has a chill. Business very poor. Ate a water ice.
>
> (p. 99)

Fay's boredom would seem to bear little relation to economic conditions; indeed, the sense of emptiness she expresses has much in common with the spiritual sterility that is so marked a feature

of modern life and literature. One finds references to boredom
in the Existentialists and in the Theater of the Absurd, but also
in writers as far removed from one another ideologically as, say,
Georges Bernanos and Alberto Moravia. On the very first page
of *The Diary of a Country Priest*, Bernanos writes:

> My parish is bored stiff; no other word for it. Like so
> many others! We can see them being eaten up by boredom,
> and we can't do anything about it. Some day perhaps we
> shall catch it ourselves—become aware of the cancerous
> growth within us. You can keep going a long time with
> that in you.

In *The Empty Canvas*, Moravia writes:

> However far back into the years I probe in memory, I
> recall having suffered always from boredom. But it is im-
> portant to understand what I mean by this word. For
> many people boredom is the opposite of amusement; and
> amusement means distraction, forgetfulness. For me,
> boredom is not the opposite of amusement; I might even
> go so far as to say that in certain of its aspects it actually
> resembles amusement inasmuch as it gives rise to distrac-
> tion and forgetfulness, even if of a very special type. Bore-
> dom to me consists in a kind of insufficiency, or inade-
> quacy, or lack of reality.

For Bernanos, "we can't do anything about" the "cancerous
growth" of boredom; for Moravia, "love" is the answer—but a
love which is very difficult to attain. Without necessarily mini-
mizing the importance of love in the scheme of things, it seems
reasonable to suggest that a certain amount of tragedy is inevitable in life—with or without love; that some degree of pain,
disillusionment and boredom is inescapable. Evidently Odets
found it hard to accept this fact. Recoiling violently from the
thematic realism of *Rocket to the Moon*, the playwright is led
into asserting the easy "solution" of romantic love, supported by

group action, in an effort to overcome what Moravia calls a "lack
of reality." Hence, Odets has Steve Takis offer the following as
an answer to Fay's speech on boredom:

> Don't stand an' take people's guff. You're a nice girl—
> don't stand and take it like a dumb Swede or a hunky.
> . . .
> Give it back with two fists if someone yells or gives you
> hell. Be an American!
>
> (p. 121)

Later in the play Eddie Bellows, Fay's fiancé, defends the
young lady's reluctance to settle for a life resembling the one her
parents endure:

> She wants more than she has and she *should* want more!
> (*To* FAY) You'd be a traitor to your country's flag if you
> didn't. A dozen pair of finest silken hose, not two. A
> house with eight rooms, not four. A car in the twelve
> hundred class, such as I've got outside—*eight* cylinders,
> not six!
> . . .
> I find Fay's ideals quite normal. Those are the ideals that
> put this country on top of the heap!
>
> (p. 151, italics in original)

After this speech Rosenberger informs Eddie that "not one
human thought came out of your mouth" (p. 155). But has
Eddie misunderstood the significance of Fay's discontent any
more grievously than has Odets himself?

A similar confusion reigns in Odets' treatment of the other
characters. The playwright suggests that the source of Rosenberger's loneliness is his unmarried state: "I always liked a clean,
wholesome home. I wasn't lucky. . . . For every man, they say,
there is a woman somewhere in the world. Maybe mine was hiding in an Eskimo Igloo" (p. 167). But Al—Abe's brother-in-law
—is married, and he is "bored to death!" (p. 140). "I don't

know where my youth went," Al laments. "I had it, and then I
didn't have it. Marrying Mr. Rosenberger's sister didn't help me"
(pp. 123–124). 'Why do I live?" Al adds. "What for?" (p. 125,
italics in original). "Some marriages can be very beautiful," says
Mr. George, the callous night clerk at the Hotel Algiers. "I was
married very happy till Mrs. George died three years ago" (pp.
125–126). It would be unusual for the George marriage to be
"beautiful," however, in view of the fact that none of the other
marriages in Night Music seem to be happy ones. Take, for example, The Little Man, who says:

> I'd like to tell my wife what I think of her. You don't
> know me, do you? That's no way to talk about your wife.
> . . . I'm the man nobody knows. I'm very bold, but some
> nights I'm gripped by unbearable shame and shyness.
>
> (p. 97)

Like Jacob in Awake and Sing!, The Little Man has a dog for
a companion. (At the conclusion of Rocket to the Moon, the
reader will recall, Prince remarks: "My mind is blank. Next week
I'll buy myself a dog" [p. 418].) The Little Man says:

> My wife claims babies would spoil her figger. Can you tie
> that? And she drinks a case of beer a day and she claims
> a child would spoil her figger. I used to have a motto for
> myself, "Fifty and Nifty!," but it don't work no more.
> . . . I'm sixty now.
>
> . . .
>
> Had my tonsils out. On top of that, neuritis is stabbin'
> every nerve. The saddest part is when you go to the doctor
> and he says, "It's your imagination, five dollars, please."
> . . . [To STEVE and FAY] You're both young and that's
> very nice—it is very nice when you're young. Youth,
> youth. . . . But I don't look my age. Here's one for the
> lesson book, boys and girls: if you got money, you got
> nerve. . . . If you ain't got money, you ain't got nerve.
>
> (pp. 95–97)

It seems impossible to believe that money would really cure the "cancerous growth" that is destroying The Little Man; yet Odets concludes the speech by suggesting that a change in this character's financial situation would alter the essential passivity he shares with Steve Takis or the pervasive boredom he has in common with Fay and Al.

In my analysis of *Awake and Sing!* and *Golden Boy*, I had occasion to discuss the various patterns of imagery in those plays and I tried to show how skillfully Odets used the resources of language in support of his theme. It is still another measure of Odets' basic confusion in *Night Music* that his imagery is indecisive and jumbled. As in *Golden Boy*, animal imagery is conspicuous in the later play. When Steve visits Fay's room for the first time, for example, he remarks: "All that's missin' is the horses!" (p. 74). The hero then proceeds to sing the following song:

> Move over, Mr. Horse. Gimme room in your stall. How are the oats, Brother Horse? Gimme room in your stall. Didn't you ever wish you were dead? Brother Horse, giddiap, Brother Horse! I got those nobody-nothing blues! I'm feelin' like the King of the Jews! Oh, you Brother Horse, eating oats by the peck. Brother Horse, Brother Horse, send a dish over to me. How's your father? How's your mother, Brother Horse? Got no mother, got no father, anywhere! Some fun, Brother Horse!
>
> (p. 75)

When Al informs Steve about Rosenberger's cancer, he says: "Tomorrow, after thirty-two honorable years on the police force, they are retiring him like an old horse. So you can afford to treat him with respect!" (p. 187). Odets' point, it would seem, is that Fay, Steve and Rosenberger have been reduced to the level of animals, and that such a condition violates human dignity.

In the opening scene of the play, Steve Takis is called a "parrot" and a "snipe," and is warned by a policeman: "In a minute you won't have a feather in your tail!" (p. 6). Later another character, Mrs. Scott, tells the hero that Broadway plays "fall like sparrows" (p. 26). And Rosenberger, glancing around at the Hotel Algiers, remarks: "It's a nest of fine-plumed birds here" (p. 61). The bird imagery, like the horse imagery, is intended to place man in the Odetsian world. Hence the bird becomes a metaphor for man's aspirations to soar above his squalid circumstances. Fay refers to Steve as the "Sweet Swan of Brochton" (p. 223); but the young man objects to the title:

STEVE. An' this *swan* stuff don't go. Or anyway, the swan's a goose.

FAY (*with a seeming increase of stature*). I want you to know you're a swan to *me*. Look at me, Steve. Look at me—!

STEVE (*avoiding her look*). Don't horse me around, Fay.

(p. 226, italics in original)

Note the reference to "horse" in the above exchange. Once again, Odets reveals a thematic tension between, on the one hand, "horses" and "flightless birds," and on the other, "swans" or "birds that fly." At the conclusion of the play, Fay tells Steve: "Now you're a swan" (p. 236).

The imagery in *Night Music* is confusing, however, because the title of the play derives from the following dialogue:

FAY (*listening*). Do you hear what I hear?

ROSENBERGER. What?

FAY. The last cricket, the very last. . . . Crickets are my favorite animals in all the world. They're never down in the mouth. All night they make their music. . . .

ROSENBERGER (*shrugging*). Say, what kind of problems can a cricket have . . . ?

FAY. Night music. . . . If they can sing, I can sing. I'm more than them. *We're* more than them. . . . We can sing through any night!

ROSENBERGER (*judicially*). A very human thought, Miss Tucker.

(pp. 160–161, italics in original)

Later in the same scene, however, Steve explodes: "They say

there's jobs? That's cricket water!" (p. 178). "What kinda life where you gotta compare yourself to crickets? *They're bugs!*" (p. 179, italics in original). Nobody in the play answers Steve's question in a satisfactory way. If Fay's belief is, unlike Eddie Bellows' philosophy, a "very human" one, and if Odets uses that belief for the title of his play—why then does he permit his protagonist to undercut the symbolism of the cricket and its "night music"? If the symbolism of the cricket is valid, however, why then does Odets insist on comparing Steve to a "swan"?

No matter which element of *Night Music* we isolate for analysis —structure, character, imagery or theme—we encounter evidence of confusion, failure and uncertainty in Odets. Psychological motivation opposed to social motivation and activism offered as a remedy for an immedicable boredom—Odets really has diverse themes in *Night Music*, but he treats them as one, unable to see that they are distinct and unable to discover a way to dramatize them effectively and to make them cohere. The various themes exist side by side in *Night Music*, compete with one another, remain contradictory, and finally destroy the integrity of the piece.

CHAPTER SEVEN

Clash by Night

You're like me, [Mae]. . . . You were born an' now you'd
like to get unborn! That's why I drink this varnish, lady
—to get unborn! Perpetual motion—born, everybody's
getting born! Two strangers hit the hay one June night
and suddenly there you are! Well, why not get unborn
the same way?

Earl Pfeiffer, *Clash by Night,*
pp. 103–104

While *Night Music* was still in rehearsal, Clifford Odets began
keeping a daily journal. In "Genesis of a Play"—an article Odets
later wrote which appeared in *The New York Times* on February 1, 1942—the dramatist described "how certain remote
thoughts and feelings collect themselves around a theatrical
spine and become a play." The play in question, dubbed *The
Trio Play* in the journal, later became *Clash by Night.* Here,
according to Odets, is his first note for the new play:

May 19: Every time you refuse to live a relationship with another person to its most potential depth you are committing
a sin against yourself and the other involved. . . . It is one of
the rock bottom vices which infest American life from top to
bottom. . . . Much better to refuse a relationship wholly, never
starting it, than to deal half heartedly or less with it. Rather

live alone than keep yourself shut to the man or woman with whom you spend time. . . . Eschew once and for all relationships which are not humanly productive, but first make an effort to make them so; for they are the sleeping pills of modern life, and in this life there are enough other things which make one want to sleep!

. . .

August 8: . . . The theme is taking shape in my mind, intensely personal but generally significant feeling behind it. The theme . . . has to do with the need of a new morality, with a return to voluntarily assumed forms in a world of democracy where there are no forms but plenty of appetite and irresponsibility.

. . .

October 21: Part of the theme of this play is about how men irresponsibly wait for the voice and strong arm of Authority to bring them to life. . . . Nothing stands for Authority and we wait for its voice! . . . The children are looking for the father to arrange their lives for them!

These notes were entered in Odets' journal after *Night Music* had closed with a brief run of two weeks. (And speaking of *Night Music*, it is worth observing that Abe Rosenberger functions in that play as a father figure, or "magic helper," to Steve and Fay.) While writing *Clash by Night*, Odets watched the Group Theater pass into history; in addition, Luise Rainer divorced the playwright. Odets' basic feeling of homelessness, then, was greatly intensified at this time. *Clash by Night*, which opened twenty days after Pearl Harbor, was even blacker in mood than *Night Music*. Indeed, one is tempted to speak of these two works as representing Odets' "dark night of the soul." The theme of *Clash by Night*, which Odets called "intensely personal but generally significant," has not been adequately explained by critics. "[Odets'] protests are significant," according to Harold Clurman in *Lies Like Truth*, "because one feels love in him, and whatever it is that wounds this love must be wrong. When his love turns black, as it did in *Clash by Night,* one is not as offended as one becomes with the literary pessimism of those who, one feels, are only fragmentarily connected with ordinary life." But why should one be "offended" when a playwright's "love turns black"? At any rate, Odets' capacity for love is not wholly absent from *Clash by Night.* Nor had the grim events of 1940 and 1941 completely crushed the dramatist who had written *Awake and Sing!* On February 9, 1947, J. B. Newmann, interviewed by a feature writer for *PM,* recalled having gone to Staten Island in 1941 with Odets and Boris Aronson to look for the sets of *Clash by Night.* "I could see then that he had feeling and enthusiasm for what the eye sees," the art dealer reflected. "It was 'Stop! Stop!,' and 'Look! Look at this building!' He saw small things. Everything meant something to him." Newmann emphasized that Odets was "full of love. Love is his driving force. That is a holy quality." No doubt, W. David Sievers is correct in underlining the influence of Erich Fromm's *Escape from Freedom* on Odets' construction in *Clash by Night.* According-ing to Sievers, Odets reported to a questionnaire that, though "he had read a large number of books by the Freudians, . . . his most mature evaluation of Freud reached him through the William Alanson White Institute of Psychiatry and the work of Erich Fromm and Harry Stack Sullivan." One can readily understand how Odets, the ex-Marxist, would favor the theories of Fromm to those of Freud. Nevertheless, Odets' deepest inspiration in the writing of *Clash by Night* is suggested by the title of the piece, which was taken, of course, from the famous last stanza of Matthew Arnold's *Dover Beach,* and which Odets reproduced on the flyleaf of the published text of the play. I shall explore this theme later in the chapter. First, however, I should like to analyze the logical structure of *Clash by Night* and to discuss each of the principal characters.

Odets' notations in his daily journal are of prime importance in a consideration of structure in *Clash by Night*:

July 27: The heat is unbearable, except that one bears it. Too, speaking of atmosphere, the climate of the trio play will be exactly that of the weather here. Muggy, forboding, the never-bursting-open sky. Why? I feel it must be that way. It is weather in which anything can happen. All courses of conduct are possible, men and women may suddenly weep, reverse their entire lives under this leaden sky; relaxed amiabilities, hatreds, exquisite tenderness, love, sudden murderous wrath, all may happen in this climate. Out of a long chain of seeming dull trivia is born a shattering explosion, that is the line of the new play.

. . .

August 1: . . . I am working in what is a new way for me. The first draft is irregular, sketchy, a sort of charcoal sketch of where the main scenes are to be on a well-defined simple line of plot movement. I am not filling in the characters, hoping in this way later to make characters and plot line coextensive from start to finish.

The play does have "a well-defined simple line of plot movement." The triangle situation at the core of the action involves Mae Wilenski, thrity-four, the bored wife of a sporadically employed carpenter, Jerry, who possesses scant intelligence or emotional maturity. Earl Pfeiffer, a friend of Jerry's, comes to live with the couple—and the inevitable occurs.

Clash by Night is structured into two long acts. Although the tempo of Scene One is slow—the entire scene is introductory in nature and covers forty-two pages of text—there is a compensatory gain in mood and characterization. "The first half of the play offers by far the richest material for actors and audience alike," says Rosamond Gilder. "It is warm with life and with the irrelevant and mysterious action of human beings living on this 'darkling plain'. . . ." Gilder is a bit too indulgent toward the first half of the play, I think, yet there is no question but that the opening scene in which Mae Wilenski's discontent is delineated and her future relations with Earl Pfeiffer left in doubt is skillfully managed. The point of attack, which is unusually delayed, arrives near the end of Scene Two, or roughly one-third of the way through the play. The "trio," in addition to some other characters, are at a public pavilion on a hot July night. Suddenly Mae and Earl find themselves alone, and the woman, stimulated by a few drinks, reveals her dissatisfaction with Jerry:

EARL. I interpret you to say you don't love your husband. . . . Now suppose I slipped right through those remarks . . . and carried the ball down to the goal posts . . . ? Could you go for me? . . . Could you?

MAE. You're crude, Earl.

EARL. I never claimed a polish.

MAE. You impress me as one of those who needs a new suit or a love affair, but he don't know which.

EARL (*stung, but hiding it by gulping down a drink*). You can't make me any smaller . . . I happen to be preshrunk. (*Hiding his chagrin*) Want another drink? (*And grinning.*)

MAE. No.

EARL (*Taking his displeasure out in a jibe*). Can't you be pleased?

MAE. That Joe Doyle [a friend, who is at the pavilion with his girl, Peggy] is more of a man than you'll ever be, you and Jerry together! (*Quietly*) Now let's drop the whole topic.

EARL (*unable to resist a final taunt*). Well, maybe I can fix it up with Doyle—

(MAE *drops her waving fan to the table and smartly slaps Earl across the face. For a moment he seems stunned. Then slowly a sickly grin comes to his face.*) Let there be peace on earth, cookie.

(pp. 79–81)

Although the sexual attraction between Mae and Earl is at last out in the open, it is not yet clear what course the two characters will take. Past experience with mates has left both individuals with ambivalent feelings toward the opposite sex, and this situation promises both inner and outer conflict. "It is weather," Odets says in his journal, "in which anything can happen." Whatever happens, though, it is quite plain that there can never be "peace on earth" between Mae and Earl, for their natures are such as to preclude any permanently tranquil relationship. Thus, Odets seeks "to make character and plot line coextensive from start to finish."

Throughout Scene Three the desperately lonely Earl pursues Mae with a passion intensified by the torrifying summer sun. Mae, though increasingly displeased with Jerry, continues to resist. At the conclusion of the scene Mae and Earl quarrel bitterly, and the latter exits, slamming his bedroom door behind him:

MAE *stands in her place at the table, the swelling tango music from the radio seemingly emblematic of her inner feelings. Slowly she turns and moves to* EARL's *door. After an intense moment of hesitation, she calls softly, "Earl . . ." He quietly opens his door; they look at each other in silence. She enters the room and the door closes behind them. In the empty kitchen the tango music pours out of the radio.*

(p. 114)

Jerry learns the truth about Mae and Earl in the following scene, but he manages to master his rage. Act One ends, then, in a state of things where a crucial alteration one way or another is imminent.

The play's turning point is reached in Act Two, Scene One when Jerry informs his wife that he is willing to forget the past and start over again:

JERRY. You won't be sorry, Mae. It's my intention to bury the past deep in the ground. You'll see, Mae, I'll work my fingers to the bone. Lots of jobs comin' up now, don't worry. . . .

MAE (*abruptly standing*). Jerry, please—! (*Holding back tears*) Don't go on talking that way . . . it won't help.

JERRY (*uncomprehendingly*). Won't help?

MAE. You musn't have false hopes. . . . I'd give an arm to take back the grief I caused you. . . . But now I can't make this any different. . . . We're moving tomorrow. . . .

JERRY (*finally*). With him . . . ?

MAE. Yes . . .

. . .

JERRY. Mae, pray for me . . . I don't know what I'll do. . . .

EARL. You need some cash. . . . Take this.

JERRY. What you think—! You are—! . . . (*Then in one swoop* JERRY *picks up the hammer off the step and poises it for a throw . . .*)

MAE. Jerry, don't throw that! (*But* JERRY *hurls the hammer at* EARL. *It whizzes past his head and smashes one of the windows. . . .*)

JERRY. You are . . . think? . . . (JERRY *sways like a drunkard and then keels over in a dead faint.*)

(pp. 187–190)

Mae's decision to abandon her husband—to reach out for what she conceives to be happiness—drives Jerry to act, which in turn forces the resolution. Hence, Jerry's violent reaction here foreshadows the climax of the play.

The crisis occurs in the next scene. Vincent Kress, Jerry's uncle, prods his nephew into taking revenge on Mae and Earl:

KRESS. You're twice his size. I'm only half his size an' I wouldn't have it! With my hands—like that—he'd struggle in my hands . . . no mercy!—no, no! . . .

(p. 206)

Kress continues to torment and to goad the confused Jerry:

KRESS. Shoved the vinegar sponge in your mouth! Laughin' at *you*!

JERRY. Laughin' at *me*! . . .

KRESS. Him, at this very table here, sippin' the coffee outa your own coffee pot! . . .

JERRY. At me, at me! (*His face darkening even more.*)

KRESS. Yes, at you!

JERRY (*jumping to his feet*). Oh, I can't stand it! . . . I'll lose my mind!

KRESS (*quivering with hatred*). Batter his brains out!

(pp. 208–209, italics in original)

The climax occurs in the next, and last, scene of the play. Jerry goes to the movie theater where Earl is employed, climbs into the projection booth, and confronts his rival. Frightened, Earl seizes a heavy wrench:

EARL. You tried to murder me once tonight.

JERRY (*still advancing*). Still my real friend when it comes down to it. . . . (EARL, *cornered, tightens his grip on the handle of the wrench and hits* JERRY *on the head with it.* JERRY, *blinded by the shock, staggers backwards; slowly puzzled amazement and pain of the heart dawn into his face. Crying out like a child*) Oh, Earl, how you have hurt me!

EARL (*in a low intense voice*). You want it again . . . ? (*Bitter anger welling up in him*) I love Mae, she loves me—that's made in heaven! You can't change it—no laws can change it! Now get outa here! . . .

(*The two men stare at each other,* EARL *keeping his firm grip on the wrench.* JERRY's *murderous feelings are ebbing back to him. He slowly stands, his heavy face pale, a thin trickle of blood running to his mouth; he shoots the bolt off the door.*)

JERRY (*in a whisper*). But you can't have her . . . you'll never get her . . . (*Now* JERRY *slowly moves forward, one arm lifted to ward off the blows of the wrench.* EARL *moves backward to match the other's step. This ballet of hunter and hunted is done in deadly silence, excepting the buzzing of the machinery and the music off the sound track. Now* JERRY *gets the wrench again, on the right shoulder this time; but now he is insensitive to pain. Suddenly* JERRY *has* EARL *in his hands.* EARL *flails out with the wrench several times but is in too close for a good swing.*)

JERRY (*whispering*). You can't . . . hurt me no more. . . .

EARL (*whispering*). I love her . . . always love her . . . (*Suddenly the end begins—*JERRY *has* EARL *by the throat.* EARL *struggles, flails his arms around, but he is caught for good. He rips* JERRY's *shirt to shreds but is unable to loose himself from the terrible grip*) No, Jerry, no!! (*And another shake*) Let up . . . up!! . . . stoppp!! . . . (*The aimless swings of* EARL's *arms begin to lose their vigor: he is being strangled to death.*)

(pp. 235–238, italics in original)

The conclusion follows immediately upon the climax. Mae, Peggy and Joe Doyle arrive and listen with horror as Jerry prays inside the projection booth over the body of Earl Pfeiffer:

JOE (*coming to* MAE). The door's locked . . . I'll go for help. . . .

MAE. No! . . . wait a minute . . . no help! That boat has sailed, I know it. . . . Love's a superstition. . . . Did you mean that talk you said, Doyle? Then go and live it. . . . Don't let this throw you, Peg. You're young and strong, you got a future. Go on, the fist of God is in your back! Now get out of here. . . . Gee, I wonder how the poor live. . . . (MAE *controls her trembling lips, tightens her body and with quiet intentness moves to the foot of the ladder; holding onto a rung for support she slowly raps at the door.*) (*With a thousand years of awful patience*) Jerry . . . it's Mae . . . it's Mae, Jerry. (JERRY, *within, is buried in incoherent prayer.*)

(pp. 241–242)

It is easy to see that *Clash by Night* is constructed "on a well-defined simple line of plot movement." Unhappily, however, the plot involves a banal triangle which is exceedingly protracted in treatment. My focusing on the crucial points in the structure

of the action fails to suggest the elaboration Odets allows himself in each of the play's early scenes. The first scene, as noted, is
extremely long for an introduction, but since it artfully establishes atmosphere and motivation it largely escapes censure. It
is difficult, though, to justify some of the other scenes which
seem definitely overlong for what the dramatist is trying to say.
Why did Odets fashion *Clash by Night* in two acts? Probably he
wished to emphasize the contrast between the "dull trivia" of
the first half and the "shattering explosion" of the second. Most
reviewers, however, found fault with Act Two. For example,
Joseph Wood Krutch remarked: "The catastrophe . . . seems
weak or at least less imaginative than the opening passages lead
one to hope." At first sight this criticism appears perverse: How
can Odets' catastrophe be described as "weak"? If anything, one
feels, Earl's violent death at the hands of the crazed Jerry Wilenski is too strong, *too* "imaginative." In short, the resolution of
Clash by Night smacks of melodrama. And perhaps melodrama
is what Krutch intends by "weak." But melodrama seems like the
wrong word. For Jerry's destruction of Earl Pfeiffer does not sacrifice truth to life for the sake of theatrical show. What makes
the ending *appear* melodramatic, perhaps, is the too stark contrast between the halves of the play. The structure of *Othello*,
which also deals with a jealous husband who commits murder,
is very much like *Clash by Night* in its overall development. In
Shakespeare's masterpiece there is the leisurely paced first half
juxtaposed with the rapid tempo of the second half, in which
Iago goads Othello into killing Desdemona. Yet *Othello*, in spite
of its status as a classic, has not infrequently been attacked on the
score of its structure. (See, for example, A. C. Bradley's discussion of the play.) What saves Shakespeare's tragedy is, among
other virtues, its poetry and the fact that the great dramatist
was working within a non-representational convention. Odets—
certainly no Shakespeare—was committed to the realistic convention of the modern drama, and as a result he failed to lift his
catastrophe to the level of tragedy. In a serious prose drama

(and, it might be argued, even in poetic drama) violence is generally best perpetrated off-stage. Odets' problem with structure and tempo in *Clash by Night*, as was true of *Night Music*, merely indicates the presence of deeper difficulties in respect to character and theme.

Consider Mae Wilenski. When Odets introduces his heroine she is singing an old popular song: " 'I'm the Sheik of Araby, this land belongs to me. At night when you're asleep, into your tent I'll creep . . .' " (p. 4). From the beginning, then, we are made aware that Mae is discontented with her husband and that she would welcome, whether she consciously realizes it or not, a new lover. Seven weeks prior to the opening of the play, we learn through exposition, Mae gave birth to a baby girl (p. 7). This fact is made important:

EARL. I wasn't made for the quiet life. Or was I? They say your taste changes every seven years. You believe in that?
MAE. Every seven years? . . . it's possible.

(p. 25)

Later we learn that Mae and Jerry have been married for seven years (p. 33). The number seven, then, is associated with Jerry —with everything that relates to Jerry, including the baby—and with Mae's growing hunger for a new life. Odets is at pains to establish sympathy for Mae. Thus, Peggy says: "When mother was sick you couldn't get [Mae] out of our house. She's a wonderful nurse . . ." (p. 65). And Mae informs Peggy: "Young or old, you'll love the man who gives you confidence. And you'll sleep on floors and like it, if you love him" (p. 110). Which seems intended to suggest that had Mae married the right man perhaps she would not strike the audience as being such an unattractive character. The fault, Odets seeks to persuade us, lies not in Mae herself but in the circumstances of her life.

"My shoulders aren't strong enough for crosses," the heroine tells Earl. "Maybe I belong to a weak generation. My father always said I did—the great Johnny Cavanaugh—with the smoke pearl studs!" (p. 75). Nothing more is said about "the great Johnny Cavanaugh," however, and Odets' attempt to cast light into Mae's parental background is merely distracting. Has Mae —like Georgie in the later *The Country Girl*—a father complex that would account, at least in part, for her dissatisfaction in marriage? The "only man" that Mae "ever loved," she informs Earl, "was a Pennsylvania politician—weighed over two hundred" (p. 76). And what distinguished this individual in Mae's opinion? What, according to Mae, makes a man? She gives Earl the formula:

> Confidence! He gives you confidence, and he never breaks it down! He fights the blizzards and the floods for you. He gives you consideration. . . . He makes her more of a woman instead of less. . . . I guess I'm a hold-over from another century! Didn't there used to be big, comfortable men? Or was it a dream? Today they're little and nervous, sparrows! But I dream of eagles. . . .

(pp. 77–78)

Is Mae's search for "big, comfortable men" a search for a father surrogate? ("The children," Odets wrote in his daily journal, "are looking for the father to arrange their lives for them!") If so, it seems doubtful whether Mae would be content with *any* man. A good play may, of course, raise a number of provocative questions and in its total effect may seem to overlap the empirical world, rendering an illusion of that density which constitutes real life. But is that how one should interpret *Clash by Night*? Or is Odets merely projecting a mishmash? Why didn't the Pennsylvania politician, who was a "real man," marry Mae during the three years that she lived with him? Too much is left uncomfortably vague and unexplained in Mae's character. Not that Odets fails entirely to portray a complex, as opposed to a confusing, character in Mae. "I don't like [Earl] calling you Jeremiah that way," Mae tells Jerry in Scene One. "It's a way of walking over you—patronizing—I don't like it. He's not that good" (p. 45). This is a subtle touch, for Mae's complaint against Earl, toward whom she is drawn, mirrors her own contempt for Jerry. When Jerry, upon discovering the nature of Mae's relationship with Earl, says: "You're bad, both bad . . . ," Mae replies: "That's too simple." And immediately she confesses to Earl: "I'm tired . . . I've been tired for years. I'm bad and I'm tired . . ." (p. 162). Such moments of quiet, economical illumination of character are, however, rare in the play.

Mae Wilenski, according to Rosamond Gilder, "is the incarnation of the type that exists everywhere . . . of the desperate and the discontented, seeking always for something unachieved; seeking security and finding it demanding; seeking peace and finding it dull; seeking love and finding it dangerous." True enough. But Odets, in spite of his efforts, fails to render Mae a very sympathetic character. E. V. R. Wyatt, another female reviewer, was less charitable than Miss Gilder toward Odets' heroine: "Mae is . . . restless, bored, shrewd but with a potential devotion to her baby that a good beating from her husband might have consolidated. . . . [Mae] fails to make clear why her husband considered her a good wife. Her relationship with Pfeiffer never rises above lustfulness." *Clash by Night* has often been compared with *Rocket to the Moon*. All the two plays have in common, though, is a torrid atmosphere and a triangle situation. Ben Stark and Cleo Singer are much more attractive than Mae and Earl; Belle Stark is far more complex than Jerry Wilenski. The characters in the later play are almost hopelessly drab. Alternation of mood, a rhythmic Chekhovian quality which distinguishes the lyrical and passionate *Rocket to the Moon*, is largely absent from *Clash by Night*. And, though Odets succeeds at times in rasing the sexual relationship of Mae and Earl above the merely carnal, the predominant impression one derives from the action is that the affair is gross and selfish.

Perhaps Odets never saw Mae with the clarity required to make her a satisfactory creation. Consider, once more, his notes for the play: "Every time you refuse to live a relationship with another person to its most potential depth you are committing a sin against yourself and the other involved. . . . Much better to refuse a relationship wholly, never starting it, than to deal half-heartedly or less with it. . . . Eschew once and for all relationships which are not humanly productive, but first make an effort to make them so. . . ." Throughout the play Odets stresses Mae's complaints against her husband, and even at the end speaks of her "thousand years of awful patience" (p. 242). Actually, though, Mae has not been patient at all. Why did Mae marry Jerry in the first place? We are never persuaded that Mae had to marry Jerry, nor are we convinced that she has tried to live a relationship in "depth" with him. Indeed, Odets stacks the cards from the start, for Jerry, who is both infantile and stupid, could not have returned a mature and patient love even had Mae been disposed to offer one. Odets' view of Mae, then, seems unsteady. He had the same difficulty with Hennie Berger in *Awake and Sing!*. Like Mae, Hennie marries a weak man whom she does not, and presumably cannot or will not, love; and in the end she runs off with another man, deserting not only her husband but her child as well. The problems involved in *Awake and Sing!* were fully discussed in my second chapter. Suffice it here to add that Hennie, like Mae, remains one of Odets' least attractive female creations. For it is almost impossible to make a mother who is willing to abandon her child, or who is even willing to contemplate such an action, a sympathetic figure.

Jerry Wilenski is thirty-seven years old, but he remains "child-hearted" (p. 3). As John O'Hara points out, however, Jerry is closer to an "idiot" than a child. Odets wavers between presenting Jerry as a kind of gentle Dostoevskian "innocent" and a stupid, unperceptive, neurotically regressed brute. "Oh,` you don't know what people feel," Mae complains to her husband. "You think they're like your carpenter work—hammer a nail in them and they stand up straight!" (p. 15). Jerry is so dull that he insists that Earl move in with the Wilenski family; he arranges for Earl to escort Mae home from the summer pavilion; and he even urges Earl to take Mae to an amusement park. "You come around with your friend, a man I've never seen before! You jump up and down, like a kid with a new toy—practically push me into his bed!" Mae shouts at Jerry in the revelation scene. " 'Call her Mae, call him Earl!'—I didn't know the man ten minutes before you had his arms around my neck!" (pp. 152–153). This situation prompts W. David Sievers to speak of Jerry's "latent homosexuality often associated with passive dependency. . . . The homosexual theme now is clear: man kills the thing he loves. In this case, Jerry kills Earl, not Mae, for he felt betrayed by the man whom unconsciously he had loved and revered as a 'magic helper.' " Perhaps. What *is* "clear," however, is Jerry's love for Mae and his intense mother fixation.

In the disclosure scene, for instance, Mae and Earl bring home a teddy bear for the baby. Grinning at Jerry, Earl remarks: "Mae says this looks just like you" (p. 143). Shortly afterward, stunned by what he has just learned about his wife and his best friend, Jerry says: "I can go sleep in poppa's room, if you don't wanna talk to me, momma—I mean, Mae" (p. 157). At the conclusion of this scene, Earl "picks up the teddy bear from the table, several times bending it at the waist—a doleful 'Momma, Momma' answers him" (p. 164). In Act Two Jerry tells Mae:

> You want it to be like my mother died? To say she went on a journey? She'll be back?—it's just a journey? My wife an' child is on a journey, but they'll be back? You want the sun all covered with tear drops again?
>
> (p. 202)

Odets suggests that Jerry's infantilism can be explained in terms of socio-economic pressures. Repeated references to the unemployment problem are used to underscore, not only Jerry's helplessness, but the plight of all the emasculated men in the play.

Jerry's father, for example, plays an old Polish song on his concertina "about the little old house, where you wanna go

back, but you can't find out where it is no more, the house . . ."
(pp. 10–11). "Poor poppa worked hard all his life," Jerry continues sadly. "Now he plays in bars for drinks. It's the day of rest
in his life, an old man . . . he's ashamed" (p. 30). Later Jerry
expands on this subject:

> . . . You are just in the world on a rain check, as I see it.
> Nobody knows what'll happen next. . . . Everything boils
> down to worry . . . nobody don't sleep a whole night's
> sleep no more. You could wake up some day an' find
> you're an old man with a tool kit under your arm an' they
> don't want you—not even your wife. Like my father—
> my mother didn't speak to him for three years before she
> died.
>
> (p. 127)

Like father, like son. Jerry buys Mae a watch and a refrigerator
on the installment plan, and then is unable to keep up the pay-
ments (pp. 93–94). He is forced to ask Mae—in a "squirming"
manner—for his lunch and carfare money (p. 95). The exact
relationship between Jerry's infantilism and the structure of society is, however, far from obvious. As I pointed out above, Odets
presents the same difficulty in his characterization of Mae. Are
Mae and Jerry both suffering from a parent fixation? Much of the
evidence of the play suggests that this is indeed the case. But if so,
why then does Mae speak of a difference in the "generations"?
Why does Odets shift the blame to social factors? Odets fuses
personal and social causation, or at least suggests a clear link
between the two, in *Awake and Sing!*, *Golden Boy* and *Rocket
to the Moon*. It is doubtful, though, whether he succeeds in the
difficult task of reconciling the subjective and the objective in
Clash by Night. The same criticism, the reader will recall, was
directed at *Night Music*.

Earl Pfeiffer is another example of Odets' split vision in *Clash
by Night*. Earl informs Mae: "My mother passed away the year
I was born" (p. 70). Afterward the following dialogue ensues:

MAE. [Jerry] thinks I'm a Red Cross nurse—you have to watch him every minute! He doesn't know there's a battle of the bread and butter. He expects his wife to fight those battles! He says money isn't everything. Maybe not, but it's ninety nine point nine of everything! I guess the truth is he's a momma's boy....

EARL. Who isn't?

MAE. Are you?

(p. 74)

Earl evades Mae's question. Later, though, he tells Mae: "I'm always outside looking in! . . . The blues for home . . . but where is home? . . . Help me, Mae, help me!" (p. 105). Speaking of his ex-wife, Earl says: "It took me six months to be poisoned by that woman, an' six years to get over it! We began with a toast and ended with a funeral oration!" (p. 36). Earl's basic complaint against his ex-wife is that she "didn't make a home" (p. 105). This remark fails to resolve the conflict, however, between social and psychological motivation in the play. Much of Earl's language suggests that he is searching unconsciously for a lost maternal nipple. His favorite word, for instance, is "delicious": "A delicious night for beer" (p. 19); "A delicious situation!" (p. 39); ". . . wouldn't that be delicious?" (p. 104); and so forth. The loss of Earl's mother—and the same was true in the case of Steve Takis in *Night Music*—has no manifest connection with social causation. Earl's marriage failed because his wife refused to provide a home—but how was the Great Depression responsible for that refusal? One can see how an unfavorable socio-economic condition might intensify an already existing psychological difficulty. Odets suggests, however, a more direct causal relationship —yet he fails to supply evidence in support of his claim.

Vincent Kress represents the Fascist mentality which springs from the soil of economic and social misery. Kress is a repulsive character, a voyeur (p. 64), who spends his time cadging drinks and preaching a Hitlerite philosophy. When Earl asks Kress if he is working, the latter replies: "Would be if my name was Berko-witz. . . . What's happenin' in this country!" (p. 54). Later Kress says of Earl: "In the new order of things we'd string his kind up on trees! A great man said it, social justice for all" (pp. 176–177). Apparently Kress has been reading *Mein Kampf*, for he exposes his ideal of "justice" when he asserts: "Don't the world belong to the strong? . . . We spoil women here. All that schoolin' an' free speech—I don't see what it gets 'em. . . . Jerry, that's so much liverwurst, that love business! I tell you, give 'er the whip!" (p. 205).

Abe Horowitz, "a fatherly and good-hearted Jew" (p. 226), is presumably the repository of "Marxist" values in the play. Abe is about fifty years old, happily married, and the father of three children. "Tomorrow's another day," Abe philosophizes. "Make a plan. Have respect—do your work with respect" (p. 230). In view of the fact that Abe Horowitz works in the projection booth with Earl, it remains difficult to see how he can perform his "work with respect," for Odets makes plain that the films present an untrue picture of reality.

The chief counterweight to the affair between Mae and Earl, however, is lodged in the romance involving Joe and Peggy. Harold Clurman regards the young couple as representing "a kind of ideologic afterthought." Evidently Odets had difficulty believing in Joe and Peggy himself, for neither of the two charac-ters ever really spring into life; hence the subplot fails to offset the dreary atmosphere of the central situation. Furthermore, Odets does not meaningfully relate Joe and Peggy to the other motifs in the play. At the start, for example, Mae disparages Joe for not marrying Peggy immediately (pp. 13–14); thus Joe is made to seem a weakling for keeping Peggy engaged for two years. This would place Joe, then, in the category of a "momma's boy." Later, though, Mae switches her tactics: "That Joe Doyle," she snaps to Earl, "is more of a man than you'll ever be, you and Jerry together!" (p. 80). If Joe *is* a "man," how did he arrive at his enviable state of development? Odets offers no evidence to suggest why Joe, or Abe Horowitz, should be immune to the socio-economic forces that have maimed the other male characters in the play. This situation is not in itself necessarily blameworthy. In everyday experience we recognize the existence of both freedom and determinism, and we learn somehow to live with the contradiction. It is certainly valid for a playwright to include both orders of experience within a single play. Nevertheless, one feels that in *Clash by Night* Odets—far from being scrupulously attentive to the density of life—is merely confused. Much of the play, as I have tried to show, reveals "sick hurry" and "divided aims" (to borrow a couple more phrases from Matthew Arnold). In an attempt to underline the message of the piece, Odets has Joe Doyle deliver a long speech to Peggy:

> We're *all* afraid! Earl, Jerry, Mae, millions like them, clinging to a goofy dream—expecting life to be a picnic. . . . Who taught them that? Radio, songs, the movies— you're the greatest people going. Paradise is just around the corner. . . . Don't cultivate your plot of ground—tomorrow you might win a thousand acre farm! What farm? The dream farm! . . . Am I blue? . . . Sure, sometimes. Because I see what happens when we wait for Paradise. Tricky Otto comes along, with a forelock and a mustache. Then he tells them why they're blue. "You been wronged," he says. "They done you dirt. Now come along with me. Take orders, park your brains, don't think, don't worry; poppa tucks you in at night!" . . . And where does that end? In violence, destruction, cripples by the carload! . . . But is that the end for us? No, sweetheart, not while a brain burns in my head. And not because we're better than them. But because we know the facts—the anti-picnic facts. Because we know that Paradise begins in responsibility. And because we have the will to see, the honest will to learn. Yes, Peg, it's a time to learn, a time to begin—it's time to love and face the future—!
>
> (pp. 217–218, italics in original)

This crudely didactic passage raises a serious thematic problem. Is Mae guilty for not loving Jerry sufficiently—or is she to be applauded for seeking happiness with Earl? In his daily journal, and in the speech above, Odets suggests that Mae has not faced reality in a mature fashion. Yet throughout the play Odets attempts to present Mae in a decidedly sympathetic light. Gerald Rabkin says: "Nowhere in the play is it implied that the dilemma of the principle characters is motivated by the false ideals which they have learned from society. Nowhere is the corrosive influence of radio, songs, and the movies manifest." Although Odets *does* try to suggest a relationship between the infidelity of Mae and social pressures (Mae's singing of "The Shiek of Araby" in Scene One, Mae and Earl dancing to popular music in Scene Two, the tango music that blares loudly from the radio when Earl seduces Mae in Scene Three, the movie dialogue that counterpoints Jerry's killing of Earl—are all obvious examples) his attempt fails largely because, like the subplot, it seems another "ideologic after-thought." In sum: personal and social motivation in *Clash by Night* bear little or no integral relationship to each other.

What makes the thematic confusion of *Clash by Night* especially distressing is one's realization that Odets started with the promise of writing a really important play. For one of the central themes of modern literature, as I reminded the reader in my discussion of *Night Music*, is the "death of God." The title of Odets' play leads one to expect a treatment of this theme in terms of contemporary anxiety, despair, loneliness, the "dull trivia" of everyday experience, and the search for a substitute faith. True, the atmosphere of the play and certain details of character and language reveal the presence of this theme. Unfortunately, however, Odets was confused at this point in his career —part of him was looking back at earlier themes, part of him was exploring new areas of thought and feeling—with the result that the "spiritual" theme of *Clash by Night* is almost lost from view.

In the opening scene of his play, Odets deliberately seeks to duplicate the situation described in *Dover Beach*. Thus, the night is "calm," the "moon lies fair" on the "sea," and the characters talk about faith and love. Says Jerry:

> I was thinkin' of the stars an' how far away they are, an' that you feel pretty small in the world by comparison. Even when you're dead, the stars go on—
>
> (p. 4)

Suddenly Jerry realizes that his last words must have reminded Peggy of something unpleasant. But the girl says: "Just because my mother died nine weeks ago doesn't mean we can't talk about those things. . . . I feel confident my mother's in a better place" (p. 5). Peggy's belief, however, seems ironical in the thematic context of Arnold's poem. Later she remarks:

> It's a nervous world, a shocking world. I don't understand it, I just don't understand. . . . Thank God there are summers to relax in. . . . Was it a dream? I had some sort of dream when I was a child. . . . I remember words like "nobility, generosity, courage" . . . (*Suddenly*) I want to admire something, someone—!
>
> (pp. 122–123)

Further irony resides in Peggy's thanking God for "summers to relax in"—for it is the heat of the summer which encourages the affair that ends in Earl's death.

Jerry Wilenski also "had some sort of dream" as a child. He tells his father:

> We had those Christmas cards when I was a boy—a little warm house in the snow, yellow lights in the windows . . . remember? It was wonnerful . . . a place where they told you what to do, like in school. . . . You didn't have to have no brains—he told you what to do. . . . I wished it was like on the Christmas cards again, so nice an' warm, a wonnerful home. . . . I wished I never grew up now!
>
> (p. 223)

This speech might relate to Arnold's lost "Sea of Faith," but part of it also echoes Joe Doyle's long monologue which clearly imposes a sociological interpretation on the situation. This is not to say that the various elements—religious, psychological and socio-economic—might not be united; it is merely to note that in *Clash by Night* Odets fails to unite them. True, he makes an effort to do so. For example, Vincent Kress has been trained for the priesthood (p. 54), but in an age without God lost absolutist beliefs are redirected toward authoritarian dictators. When Jerry goes after Earl at the end of the play his hatred is complicated by "a wave of religious feeling . . . giving him a curious tenderness which he will carry into the booth" (p. 233). Jerry's insane religious calm is shattered the moment Earl strikes him—then the murderous aggression is triggered. The play ends, as noted, with Jerry praying over the body of Earl. Confusion in Odets, though, serves to lessen the impact of this feature of the play.

In Arnold's poem love between a man and woman is offered as an alternative to the loss of meaning in life. This theme was always present in Odets' work, and in the case of *Awake and Sing!* was a cause of difficulty in critical interpretation. Hennie and Moe seek "paradise" in each other's arms, but it is hard to explain why Odets has the revolutionary Ralph favor this "irresponsible" decision. In *Golden Boy*, Joe and Lorna die in an automobile crash, which suggests that love cannot exist in a society committed to false values. *Clash by Night* reveals a continuing tension in Odets' imagination. Not only is the dramatist's grasp of Mae Wilenski unsteady, but his hold on Joe and Peggy is equally shaky. How, in a world without God, can Mae's speech to the Roman Catholic lovers at the conclusion of the piece possess any conviction? For everything in the play makes it clear that men now are "on a darkling plain," and that human love is not up to the challenge of "the world." Even if Peggy and Joe were not Christians, Mae's exhortation to them would still appear to be meaningless within the specific situation depicted in the play.

Finally, the *Dover Beach* motif colors much of the imagery

of Odets' play. In Act One, Scene Two, Potter, who owns the summer pavilion, informs Jerry: "Yesterday a little girl drowned right off here" (p. 57). Unconsciously, Jerry identifies the "little girl" with his own child, and the loss of the one suggests the loss of the other. Thus, the "sea" becomes a metaphor for life's "melancholy, long, withdrawing roar." Says Jerry: "Yesterday some poor little girl drowned right here. . . . No one knows what's gonna happen next. Lucky we got our religion . . ." (p. 62); and "Only July an' they're drownin' like flies. Two weeks ago a little girl drowned at Potter's Pavilion . . . now here's another one [in the newspapers]. This picture shows the father by the body . . ." (p. 92). "People drownin' like flies . . ." (p. 124). "An' a little girl drowned. It sticks in my mind. . . . They wanna take my child!" (pp. 213–214). At one point in the action, Joe Doyle tells Peggy: "Marriage is not a convent. It's not a harbor—it's the open world, Peg. It's being out at sea in a boat" (p. 121). And later Mae describes Jerry's attitude toward her as follows: "Mae, Mae!—wash my face, comb my hair, be my wife, cook, account-ant, nurse, bed-mate and bottle washer! And for that I give you bed and board, a seat at my right, and dry up the ocean of your life!" (p. 161). Other examples of such imagery could be cited. Enough has been said above, however, to suggest why this net-work of symbols is rendered largely ineffective within the con-fused thematic organization of the play.

One is compelled, in final judgment, to say that *Clash by Night*, like *Night Music*, fails as a play. Consciously and/or unconsciously, though, Odets seems to have learned from his experience with the two plays. In *The Big Knife* the dramatist resolves the personal and social conflicts that rend *Night Music* and *Clash by Night* by limiting his approach largely to social causation; *The Country Girl* reveals an Odets who focuses almost entirely on psychological motivation. If some of the complexity of the earlier plays is lost in this relatively one-sided approach, at least the confusions of *Night Music* and *Clash by Night* are avoided. This, however, is to put the subject in too negative a light. It might be argued that Odets' strategy in *The Big Knife* and *The Country Girl* is a dramaturgical illustration of the architectural precept: "Less is more." *The Country Girl*, for example, discloses an unusual gift in the former "social" dramatist for psychological observation—for in this play, as I shall attempt to show, Odets plunges deeper into individual motivation than he was willing, or able, to do previously. Finally, in *The Flowering Peach* Odets returns to the "spiritual" theme treated confusedly in *Night Music* and *Clash by Night*; and though he does not return to the subject in precisely the same terms, he constructs a "religious" play that is as good as anything else in the body of his work.

CHAPTER EIGHT

The Big Knife

*Look at me! Can you face it? Look at this dripping fat of
the land? Could you ever know that all my life I yearned
for a world and people to call out the best in me? How
can life be so empty? But it can't be! It can't! It's proven
—statistics and graphs prove it—we are the world's hap-
piest, earth's best.*

—Charlie Castle, *The Big Knife*,
p. 72

Four days before *The Big Knife* opened at the National Theater in New York on February 24, 1949, Seymour Peck of *The
New York Times* interviewed Odets in Boston. The dramatist—
who was now forty-two and who had not had a play on Broadway in eight years—said:

The big knife is that force in modern life which is against
people and their aspirations, which seeks to cut people
off in their best flower. The play may be about the struggle
of a gifted actor to retain his integrity against the combination of inner and outer corruptions which assail him,
but this struggle can be found in the lives of countless
people who are not on the wealthy level of a movie star.
I have nothing against Hollywood per se. I do have something against a large set-up which destroys people and eats

them up. I chose Hollywood for the setting for *The Big Knife* because I know it. I don't know any other company town. But this is an objective play about thousands of people, I don't care what industry they're in.

Although the New York reviewers were not kind to *The Big Knife*, the play was still running at the National when Russell Rhodes interviewed Odets for the *New York Herald Tribune* on May 1, 1949. On this occasion, Odets said:

I wanted to write a play about the moral values of success. The protagonist of the play could have been a governor of a state or anybody in high position. But who better than a movie star? He's a glamorous, corrupt beach-comber, trapped in a big-money world; a familiar Holly-wood type, ruined by fabulous success, blown up out of all proportion to his talents. The point the play illustrates is the continual split between how people should live and how they really live. . . . The moral dilemma is purposely exaggerated to the nth degree. I admit I helped myself by choosing the melodramatic form, and to make the play's issues immediate and clear, I deliberately caused the crises and crucial relationships of the characters. . . . No critic has hit the chief fault of this play: Where is the actor going if he quits Hollywood? He has nothing to go to, no alternative choice. In *Golden Boy* is was simple— the fist or the fiddle—a man of moral devotion swerved between opposing demands. That crack about how could you feel sorry for a poor guy sold into slavery for six thou-sand bucks a week for fourteen years is quite out of con-text, an attempt to be funny. Is that all there is to this play? What about the other dilemmas destroying the actor?

What I can't understand is why they acted as if this play weren't pure melodrama. I wrote it objectively as such. The material seemed to dictate the melodramatic

form. . . . I don't say I'm Shakespeare, but nobody criti-
cizes *Macbeth* for inconsistencies or because it's melodrama. Chekhov was the ideal playwright—all character
and nothing happens. But people crave excitement and
movement.

I have quoted Odets at considerable length because, of all his
plays, none have been so misunderstood and maligned as *The
Big Knife*.

The structure of the piece is divided into three acts, with two
scenes in the final act. "The action takes place in the playroom
of Charlie Castle's Beverly Hills house, in the present day" (p.
4). Unity of place contributes to the increasing tension generated
by the conflicts in the play. The time-sequence covers about a
week and a half. When the play opens Charlie Castle has reached
a turning point in his life. Marcus Hoff, the actor's employer,
wants Charlie to sign a contract, but the protagonist is reluctant
to do so because part of him loathes film work, and also because
his wife, Marion, who is separated from him, threatens divorce
if Charlie commits himself to Hoff. If Charlie does not sign,
however, Hoff will reveal that the star, in the company of a
woman, was responsible for an automobile accident in which a
child was killed, and that the drunken actor had permitted his
friend and publicity man, Buddy Bliss, to go to jail for him. Even
if it were not for Hoff's blackmail threat Charlie would face a
problem of unemployment—or at least of very uncertain employment—as a stage actor if he failed to sign the contract. The central issue of the play, then, is Charlie Castle's conflict between
integrity and corruption, or between idealism and materialism.
A depraved environment—represented by Marcus Hoff, Hollywood and the whole society which the film capital symbolizes—
exerts strong pressue on Charlie to surrender, fully and irrevo-
cably, to his worst self, or "dark companion."

The point of attack occurs about midway in Act One:

MARION (*earnestly*). . . . Charlie, I don't want you to sign that contract—you've given the studio their pound of flesh. . . . We arrived here in a pumpkin coach and we can damn well leave the same way!

. . .

CHARLIE (*impatiently*). Just what do you expect me to do? Pick up, without a backward glance—and what? Go back and act in shows?

MARION. What's wrong with shows? You started in the theater. We'd go back to New York, yes—the theater still can give you a reasonable living. And away from this atmosphere of flattery and deceit we might make our marriage work.

CHARLIE. The theater's a stunted bleeding stump. Even stars have to wait years for one decent play. . . . I have to face one horny fact: I'm Hoff's prisoner now, and signing the contract is the ransom fee! . . . I didn't have the nerve that night, in this room . . . I made the wrong decision. . . .

. . .

MARION. . . . It was a difficult choice that night. We failed together, but now we have a second chance. It's a gamble—I know what Hoff can do if you refuse to sign. . . . But if you sign, you sink in even deeper than before. Refuse to sign, Charlie. . . .

CHARLIE. All right, I'll try. I haven't agreed to sign. I've been stalling for months. . . .

(pp. 14–16)

In spite of Charlie's determination to resist Hoff, however, the protagonist—intimidated by the Hollywood tycoon's blackmail threat—finally signs the contract. Afterward Charlie's self-loathing is intensified.

The turning point in the action arrives, not at the end of Act Two where it normally occurs, but at the conclusion of Act Three, Scene One. The girl who was with Charlie the night of the accident—her name is Dixie Evans but in the Rhodes interview Odets calls her "Banquo's ghost"—returns and threatens to reveal the truth about the accident. In order to silence her the studio plans to murder the girl. Smiley Coy—Hoff's "perfect tool and factotum" (p. 21)—informs Charlie of the plot. Appalled, Charlie decides to phone his agent, Nat Danziger, and Hoff for a showdown:

> Coy. Now don't fuss me, Charlie. There's no time to lose. Just keep in mind that the day you first scheme . . . you marry the scheme and the scheme's children. Right this minute . . . everything you are depends on a few drinks in a trollop's guts.
>
> CHARLIE (*flaring*). But what the hell do you think she is? A moth? A bug? . . . Murder is indivisible, Smiley. I'm finding that out. Like chastity, there's no such thing as a small amount of it. I'm finding that out. . . .
>
> Coy . . . . You mishandle your friends, Ella. . . .
>
> CHARLIE. . . . You're not my friend. That pathetic little girl is my friend. . . .
>
> (pp. 61–63)

This is the turning point because it forces Charlie to make a decision which is literally a matter of life and death.

In the last scene of the play Charlie and Hoff argue bitterly about Dixie Evans, and Charlie—revealing a renewed strength of character in the face of his difficulties—ends by striking Hoff. Although the producer exits affirming that Charlie's "acting days are over," and though Coy adds that "The studio has no further interest in that girl," Nat Danziger knows better: "There are things beyond money to [Hoff]," the agent declares, "—but *this* much money not" (p. 69, italics in original). In other words, Dixie's life remains in danger. Earlier in the scene Charlie says: "Today I see what Marcus Shriner Hoff and his horny partners would do for me: they'd murder! Now . . . I realize what I am!" (pp. 66–67). After Hoff and Coy exit, Charlie repeats this insight: "Now . . . I realize what I am" (p. 69). The crisis of the play follows shortly afterward: "Isn't it true?" Charlie remarks

to Marion. "Aren't the times beyond us, cold and lonely? Far
away as the stars." (Which reminds one of the *Dover Beach*
mood of Odets' previous play.) Charlie continues: "Nat's alternative is for me to sit tight and let Hoff protect his property. . . .
And me . . . I can pick up the telephone . . . and call the police.
. . . Marion, help me, help me! . . . I can't give myself up!" (p. 72).
The phone rings then; it is Buddy Bliss, whose wife seduced the
drunken Charlie at the end of Act One:

CHARLIE (*hanging up and turning to* MARION. *His voice low and
bitter, flat*). Connie came home tight. . . . They had a fight. . . .
She's leaving Buddy. She brought my name in. . . . (*Here*
MARION *understands* CHARLIE'S *meaning and turns away,
momentarily sickened.* CHARLIE *is talking with bitter self-
revulsion*) You see, you do it! . . . (*Stopping*) I'll go up and
bathe and change my clothes . . . Marion . . . Everything that
embitters you . . . I pledge you a better future. It begins
tonight.

(pp. 72–73)

Charlie brings about the climax by going upstairs, slashing his
wrists, and drowning himself in his bathtub. Unknown to
Charlie, Smiley Coy has bribed two policemen to kill the drunken
Dixie Evans. When the actor's death is discovered, Hank Teagle,
a writer, says: "He . . . killed himself . . . because that was the
only way he could live. You don't recognize a final act of faith . . .
when you see one . . ." (p. 76). As the curtain descends, Marion
screams: "Help! . . . Help! . . . Help!!!" And Odets adds the directions: "HANK *has his arms around her, but the word does not
stop and it will never stop in this life*" (p. 77).

Although the structure of *The Big Knife* is tight, it has not
escaped being censured by a number of critics. Kappo Phelan, for
example, believes that the attack is ill-chosen: "Certainly the play
which presents its catastrophe [*sic*]—that Christmas Eve when
the enormous pressure put upon the hero proved too much for
his integrity—only in talk and never in *action* cannot be said to

be worth much as document or drama." But Odets' technique here is perfectly conventional—that is to say, Ibsenite—and there is no reason why he is obliged to go back to the beginning of things for his point of attack. Perhaps the playwright makes too much of Charlie's conflict over signing the contract in the opening act. One might get the mistaken impression that this problem is inextricably wedded to the major dramatic question involving Charlie's basic integrity. I would not be inclined, however, to view this problem as a serious defect of structure. Yet Gerald Rabkin says:

> The real issue involved is simple: should the artist, luxuriating in material splendor at the expense of his artistic integrity, chuck it all to return to a meaningful existence? Stated in these terms, the issue seems hardly one to induce suicide. But Odets obviously felt the problem was not dramatically sufficient, and therefore felt constrained to project the dilemma in terms of a plot which deals with intrigue and suggested murder. The difficulty with this scheme from a dramatic viewpoint is that the real issue— the acceptance or rejection of Hollywood values—is in no way related to the machinery of the plot. If Charlie Castle is blackmailed into signing his contract, what happens to the element of choice which is crucial to the larger, more serious, dramatic issue?

Rabkin appears to go astray in his analysis of the structure. Since Charlie signs the contract in Act One, the major dramatic question must logically focus elsewhere. Aside from the fact that blackmail does not necessarily prevent Charlie from choosing jail as an alternative, the protagonist proves his intergity when he decides to sacrifice his life rather than witness the death of Dixie Evans. I shall return to this problem later. Furthermore, my analysis of the stuctrure refutes the charge that there is a split between "the real issue" and "the machinery of the plot" in the play. Odets drives Charlie Castle into a situation which fully reveals what the actor's willingness to "scheme" entails in terms of human values. All good plays deal with men trapped in extreme situations.

Which raises the question of melodrama in the structure of *The Big Knife*. There is little inner development on the part of Charlie Castle (he moves from intense self-loathing in Act One to self-destruction as "a final act of faith" at the climax) and as a result, Odets, as noted above, felt constrained to "deliberately" heighten "the crises and crucial relationships of the characters." Some readers may feel that Charlie is only too painfully aware of the truth about himself all through the play; consequently, his supposed self-discovery—"Now . . . I realize what I am" (three times in the last scene)—is somewhat contrived in order to round out the play with the protagonist's suicide. Yet one might also argue that there is an element of realism here. Every man has a breaking point. A man may "know" the truth about himself for years, but he may avoid acting resolutely in that knowledge until enough pressure has accumulated to propel him into action. The line between tragedy and melodrama, as Odets suggested when he discussed *Macbeth* in relation to *The Big Knife*, is far from clearly defined. Most attempts to clarify the distinctions between the two forms fail to be very informative. Malcolm Goldstein tries to solve the problem by calling *The Big Knife* a "melodramatic tragedy." It is difficult, however, to see how such a classification clarifies anything generically about Odets' play; indeed, Goldstein's definition seems to me to be semantically meaningless. Most critics apparently believe that whenever the integrity of a character is violated for the sake of action and/or theme the work in question can be called a melodrama. If this description is a valid one then it cannot be affirmed that Odets has written a melodrama, for at no time in the action does the playwright falsify Charlie Castle's character. Similar problems of interpretation along these lines might also be cited. Each reader will have to decide for himself about the respective merits of "tragedy" and "melodrama," and to what extent "truth" can be attained in either form. In his introduction to a recent edition of William Archer's *Playmaking*, John Gassner says: "A play is good or bad not because of its observance of this or that theatrical convention, but because it commends itself to us by the quality of its sympathies and antipathies, by its wit or its passion, and by its illuminations." If so, Odets' *The Big Knife* would seem to have much about it that "commends itself to us."

In *Clash by Night*, the reader will remember, Odets failed to fuse the marital infidelity with his attack on the movies. *The Big Knife* is another matter, however, for here Hollywood moves to the forefront of the action. At one point, Charlie Castle says:

> Why am I surprised by them? Isn't every human being a mechanism to them? Don't they slowly, inch by inch, murder everyone they use? Don't they murder the highest dreams and hopes of a whole great people with the movies they make? This whole movie thing is a murder of the people. Only we hit them on the heads, under the hair— nobody sees the marks.
>
> (p. 70)

Art means nothing to the Hollywood bosses. Says Charlie: "The studio paid [Hank Teagle] one thousand dollars a week for the last four years, and [they] can't remember his name or what he wrote" (pp. 59–60). Making movies is a business; money, not the love of beauty and truth, is the prime mover at the executive level. "I have nothing against you personally, understand?" Hoff informs Charlie during their negotiations. "But I am beholden to our stockholders. They control our every action—they are our invisible but ever-present monitors" (p. 68). This situation, by the way, does not necessarily reflect Odets' belief in "class warfare" (as Goldstein has it), but merely illustrates the primacy of commercial values in our society—the same values which have made the television of today, like the Hollywood of the past, a "cultural wasteland." It only confuses matters to view *The Big Knife* in the perspective of the thirties.

Actually, Odets is at great pains to show that things have changed since *Golden Boy*. Thus, Charlie tells Hank:

> When I came home from Germany . . . I saw most of the war dead were here. . . . And Roosevelt was dead . . . and we plunged ourselves, all of us, into the noble work of making the buck reproduce itself! . . . What, pray tell, does [a man] do? (*Bitterly*) Become a union organizer?

To which Hank replies: "I can't invent last-act curtains for a world that doesn't have one" (p. 58). This is not to say, though, that *Golden Boy* and *The Big Knife* have nothing in common. In both plays, for example, money and success are seen to be corrupting influences:

CHARLIE. What do I have to justify? Do I have to be in politics to hold my head up? What, making money? Is that the sin?
MARION. Your sin is living against your own nature. You're denatured—that's your sin!

(p. 34)

With the movie columnist, Patty Benedict, Charlie "is all gayness and glitter . . . a mask assumed and played lightly and guyingly, except when her back is turned" (p. 7). When Charlie, seeking to persuade Marion to acquiesce in his false position, says: "Come on now, be yourself," his wife replies: "That's another good local remark: 'Be yourself,' which means, 'Be just like me, *don't* be yourself!' " (p. 35, italics in original). At one point, Charlie compares himself to Macbeth (Shakespeare's play was apparently very much on Odets' mind in writing *The Big Knife*) as he says: ". . . Macbeth is an allegory, too: one by one, he kills his better selves" (p. 70). Odets also employs a suggestion of "homosexuality," as he did in *Golden Boy*, as a symbol for man's perversion of natural relations. Charlie Castle is, of course, the chief focus of this symbolism. Early in the play Charlie, echoing Joe Bonaparte, refers to himself as "half a man" (p. 13). He calls his colored servant, "Boy friend" (p. 16). To his agent,

Charlie declares: "Someone has to get tough with me before I float away. Sounds girlish, doesn't it?" (p. 17). The agent, in turn, addresses Charlie as "Lovey" (p. 18) and "Darling" (p. 19). Smiley Coy calls Charlie, "Ella" (p. 27). Other characters also partake of this "girlish" symbolism. When Charlie urges certain demands on Hoff, for instance, the latter says: "I'm like a girl in a summer-time canoe—I can't say no!" (p. 26). Obviously, Odets is not interested in homosexuality in a psychological, or clinical, sense. The dramatist is availing himself of a poetic metaphor—the point of which is underlined when Charlie tells his agent:

> Don't get me wrong, Nat. I live out here like a rajah and I love it! But what about the work? The place is hell on married life! I can't make peace with this place—I don't wanna live under the same blanket with Marcus Hoff and his feudal friends. The color of their money is getting pale white, with blood-shot eyes and I don't want it!
>
> (p. 20)

Behind the sweet talk of the characters, then, lies mutual hatred and distrust: "The free giving of hearts out here," Charlie remarks, "begins to freeze my blood. Boy, if I didn't love people so much . . . how I'd hate 'em!" (p. 27).

Does Charlie Castle really "love people"? Is "this dripping fat of the land" worth our consideration? Some critics were inclined to answer in the negative. John Mason Brown, for example, called Charlie "callow, egocentric, and verminous," a man who "never once seems to think about the child he has slain or to do anything for its parents." Is this true? In Act One, Marion tells Charlie: "I know you, deeply, darling. . . . I know the sleepless nights you've had since Christmas Eve" (p. 15). Odets, in his directions, notes that Charlie "is apt to mask his best qualities behind a cynical, guying manner and certain jazzy small-talk" (p. 6). If Charlie were not a man who still possessed a touch of idealism, he would not be in moral conflict throughout the play. For the truly corrupt are beyond—or beneath—such agonies of the spirit. (In this respect *The Big Knife* resembles Hemingway's autobiographical short story, "The Snows of Kilimanjaro.") Nat Danziger tells Charlie: "Business and idealism don't mix—it's oil and water. Darling, you expect too much from yourself. A movie isn't a movie to you—it's a gospel" (p. 20). Smiley Coy counsels the protagonist as follows: "Ideals, kid? Nowadays? A lost crusade. . . . Don't study life—get used to it" (p. 43). Bitterness frequently corrodes Charlie's outlook on life; he asks the writer, Hank: "Do you say in your book it isn't easy to go to hell today? That there's nothing left to sin against? . . . Correction! There's health left to sin against! Health—the last, nervous conviction of the time! We're sick at heart, but we'll increase the life span! What for? Nobody knows!" (p. 58). Hank, however, attempts to dissect Charlie's rationalizations, to probe the soul of his friend and to expose the deepest source of the actor's suffering:

> You've *sold* out! You'll be here for another fourteen years! Stop torturing yourself, Charlie—don't resist! Your wild, native idealism is a fatal flaw in the context of your life out here. Half-idealism is the peritonitis of the soul —America is full of it! Give up and really march to Hoff's bugle call! Forget what you used to be! That's the only way you'll find a reasonable happiness and pass it on to your wife! No half man ever made a woman happy!
>
> (p. 58, italics in original)

The "woman"—Marion—has her own complaints to register:

> Aren't you the one who says he wants to live a certain way and do a certain kind of work? . . . And then pushes a pie in the face of everything he says? Men like Hoff and Coy have their own integrity—they're what they are! The beetle and the fervid Christian can't be equally corrupted! You can laugh—you can snort! But the critic who called you the van Gogh of the American theater saw, as I did, that you had a Christian fervor! . . . And now you're noth-

ing, common trash—coarsened down to something I don't
even recognize! . . . Don't think I ever condoned what you
did to Buddy. Or my part in what you did! . . . But you're
helpless, you're sick and unhappy . . . and I go on, trying
to help a little, defenseless because you're sick. You feel
guilty and it makes you vicious! You've taken the cheap
way out—your passion of the heart has become a passion
of the appetites! Despite your best intentions, you're a
horror . . . and every day you make me less a woman and
more the rug under your feet!

(pp. 34–35)

This seems to me to be one of the most impressive speeches
in the body of Odets' work, and therefore proof that the dramatist, as distinct from the screenwriter, still had his famous "sting"
at least as late as 1949.

Some critics argue that we never see the protagonist when he
was supposed to have been the better man just described by
Marion. But is it really necessary for Odets to show us Charlie
Castle in, say, his altar boy suit in order for us to believe in his
former, more noble, self? For one thing, Charlie's better self, as
I have already pointed out, is discernible throughout the play.
Charlie's struggle between idealism and materialism is "there"
for us to see, and in that conflict of values both sides of the protagonist's nature are revealed. For another thing, exposition
makes clear what kind of a man Charlie was in the past. At the
beginning of the play, for instance, Charlie recalls his boyhood:

My uncle's books . . . I'll bet he had a thousand! He had
a nose for the rebels—London, Upton Sinclair—all the
way back to Ibsen and Hugo. Hugo's the one who helped
me nibble my way through billions of polly seeds. Sounds
grandiose, but Hugo said to me: "Be a good boy, Charlie.
Love people, do good, help the lost and fallen, make the
world happy, if you can!"

(p. 8)

Now Charlie conceals his guilty conscience behind cynicism. Thus Buddy Bliss informs Patty Benedict: "Charlie's slogan—if you got a message send for Western Union" (p. 8). Often Charlie succumbs to bitter self-justification as a defense against his tormented conscience: "I say the hell with bargaining, down with public opinion! Down with not being what we are!" (p. 49). To see only the surface of Charlie Castle, who is perhaps the most tormented character Odets ever created, is to miss the whole significance of *The Big Knife*. This movie star, sickened by compromise and driven to self-destruction in an effort to expiate his sins, is an unforgettable character. And for this to be so, by the way, it is not absolutely necessary that everyone *like* Charlie Castle (who *likes* Macbeth?), a point which did not seem to be very clear to reviewers and critics of the play.

Most critical approaches to *The Big Knife*, in fact, end up hopelessly and irrelevantly entangled in biographical parallels. True, the play suggests strong correspondences between Odets and Castle. For example, Charlie, like the dramatist, comes from Philadelphia; and when the actor says: "We're homesick all our lives, but adults don't talk about it, do they?" (p. 8), one is reminded of Odets' remark to Mendelsohn: "I've always *felt* homeless. I have never felt that I had a home." And when Charlie tells Marion: "You go on grieving for the past. . . . What the hell was Charlie Cass? A hot-head with clenched fists and a big, yammering mouth!" (p. 34), it is difficult not to believe that the older Odets is passing judgment on the Odets of the thirties. But so what? The important thing is what precisely the artist does with his personal experience, how he transmutes it into dramatic terms. Yet this side of the problem, since it allows less scope for interesting copy and windy pontificating, is generally neglected in what passes for criticism in American drama. Near the end of the play Charlie Castle informs his wife that "everyone needs a cause to touch greatness" (p. 71), and to a man the critics leap to their feet and declare that *The Big Knife* "fails" because Odets, like his protagonist, is no longer able to believe in causes. This is a strange conclusion. In the thirties, critics who did not share Odets' Marxist mystique rightly deplored his radical outbursts, for the playwright's propensity for causes might very easily have wrecked him as a serious artist. Why then should the absence of such tendencies be lamented in the forties and after? Criticism of *The Big Knife* is, one regrets to say, almost uniformly shoddy.

According to Harold Clurman, for example, Odets shifts the guilt to society and—worst of all—assumes a defeatist attitude. "One cannot be a progressive," Clurman solemnly intones, "and believe that the evils of our society must necessarily prostrate us." Charlie's line: "Don't get me wrong, Nat. I live out here like a rajah and I love it!" would seem to underline the protagonist's complicty with society in his corruption, and would therefore appear to be proof that Odets projects a complex view of the problem. Why is the word "progressive," clearly an honorific one for the critic, trotted out as some kind of aesthetic value? Why must a playwright be a "progressive" in order to have a large claim on our attention? And even if it were completely accurate to describe *The Big Knife* as "defeatist," why should uplift necessarily be preferred in dramatic terms?

Joseph Wood Krutch—who defended Odets against the philistines throughout the thirties, and who was one of the very few critics to praise *Clash by Night*—likewise abandons good sense in his approach to *The Big Knife*. "Something, alas, is always preventing Odets from being what he ought to be," says Krutch, confusing Odets with the character in the play, ". . . like a woman might say, 'I always wanted a world in which I could be chaste; but the men just *will* go on asking me.'" But is Charlie's complaint—"Could you ever know that all my life I yearned for a world and people to call out the best in me?"—really so vulnerable? Is Krutch's witty analogy really unassailable? Recently a pope of the Roman Catholic Church told his followers that it was extremely difficult for a man to be "good" in the twentieth century. Was the pope going soft on sinners? Was he shifting the blame to society? Kappo Phelan asserts that Odets "is angry about his position in our society: a position which might be described as that of a man who thinks to the left at the same time as holding jobs as far to the right as possible. But in such a position, a man's ultimate anger ought only to be directed against himself. . . ." Note that Phelan also speaks of Odets instead of Charlie Castle. What dramatic law demands that a man's anger in this situation be directed *only* against himself? What moral law requires this one-sided approach? Why isn't it legitimate for a man to be angry about the circumstances that force creative people into such positions?

According to W. David Sievers: "We cannot empathize fully with Charlie, whose problem is that he sees life in a semantic 'either-or,' 'all or nothing' [way,]—either complete integrity and no Hollywood career, or complete concession and no integrity whatever. In a materialistic world, the characters of Odets seem unable to find the middle road toward self-realization." Charlie's conflict lies between a job in the movies that pays him well but denies him spiritual satisfaction and a job in the theater that pays poorly but provides some outlet for his artistic aspirations. Man is composed of body and soul, and both need to be satisfied. What exactly is "the middle road toward self-realization" in this context? Life at best is a matter of compromise; but are the terms of *this* conflict—the one posed by *The Big Knife*—inevitably in the nature of things? If the problem is lacking in "mature" treatment—why, as things are presently constituted, do the lives of so many creative people in America end badly? Is *every* "either-or" situation in life and art suspect? If so, why did Christ declare: "I would that thou wert cold or hot. But because thou art lukewarm, and neither cold nor hot, I am about to vomit thee out of My mouth"? Did Christ need a lesson in General Semantics? John Gassner suggests that a "mature" individual ought to be capable of dividing his time between Hollywood and Broadway. Is this happy adjustment to things as they are, an adjustment— which would seem to end in a kind of schizophrenia of the soul—

all that one might reasonably hope for in our time? The same critic also claims that Odets predicates "a prior innocence" in Charlie Castle. Not so. Odets merely affirms that Charlie was happier, more alive—but hungry—as a stage actor. This would not seem to make the protagonist a paragon of virtue, nor would it appear to stretch credibility to the breaking point.

Gerald Rabkin questions Charlie Castle's "act of faith." "Faith," the critic asks, "in what?" Although Odets does not stridently underscore the hero's motivation in all its complexity in the last scene, the answer to Rabkin's question is discernible if one reads the play with reasonable care. Charlie informs Marion: "Short of murder, we won't silence that girl" (p. 71). However, Charlie cannot acquiesce in Dixie Evans's murder; and he despairs of surrendering himself to a corrupt police force. Instead of offering himself as a penitent in the courts of a hypocritical and decadent society, then, Charlie Castle has recourse to a more primitive form of expiation in which he administers punishment to himself; that is, he destroys the self so that it can sin no more. At the same time, though, he hopes by this extreme action to prevent the murder of Dixie Evans. Charlie's "only way of saving her is suicide," Odets explained to Russell Rhodes. "That's his integrity—and act of faith, though it comes too late."

Rabkin also feels that "there are sufficient grounds for criticism [of Hollywood] without implying that producers and agents [sic] are would-be murderers." (It is interesting to note that F. Scott Fitzgerald's plot for The Last Tycoon also includes murder at the executive level of the film industry; and, like The Big Knife, Fitzgerald's unfinished novel has not infrequently been branded as a "melodrama.") Obviously, Odets was projecting a vision of life—he was seeking to highlight a tendency in modern society—and documentary accuracy was not his prime concern. Later I shall try to suggest, though, how close The Big Knife remains to the literal level. Suffice it here to note that one need not be a muckraker in order to point out that the history of many American industrial empires (including the motion picture business) does not encourage close scrutiny, for many companies engaged in practices during their formative years, say, or in the years of violent labor disputes, that do not make pleasant reading today. Some readers might feel that Odets goes too far by having the police involved in Dixie Evans' murder; but here again the evidence from urban life in America would lend more than a little support to Odets' vision. Rabkin also says: "The crucial fact is that *Golden Boy* presents a social alternative; *The Big Knife* does not." But how important is the "social alternative" in the earlier play? And is the presence of the union organizer, Frank Bonaparte, the quality that makes *Golden Boy* an effective play? (Odets seemed a trifle confused on this point himself. "No critic has hit the chief fault of this play," he told Rhodes. "Where is the actor going if he quits Hollywood?" It is difficult to see how this could be a "fault" *in the play*. More important, Odets is wrong in his contention that there is "no alternative choice" in *The Big Knife*, a point which has been sufficiently discussed above.) Finally, Rabkin feels that Odets fails to answer "the real question[, namely,] in what or in whom does the responsibility lie for the destruction of Charlie Castle? In society? In his own weakness?" Rabkin seems to want a simple "either-or" situation. Odets, however, suggests a complex answer: Charlie Castle suffers as a result of both his own weakness and the corrupting influence of society. In short, Odets makes *both* the hero *and* his world responsible for Charlie's plight.

John Mason Brown's review of *The Big Knife*, however, takes the prize for shallow sermonizing and irrelevance. After pointing out that Odets' play is "overwritten and turbulent" (which to some extent it is, but Mr. Brown does not add that turbulence is not always to be deplored), the reviewer betrays some hysteria himself when he speaks of Marion as "the actor's wife who is as liberal in her thinking as she is in her doses of sleeping pills"— and then lumps the "liberal" Mrs. Castle among "the scum of the earth." After devoting considerable space to Odets instead of the play, Brown piously concludes as follows: "There are plenty of self-respecting, intelligent, decent, and amusing people to be found [in Hollywood], Evelyn Waugh notwithstanding. They just happen to be utterly realistic about their jobs. Mr. Odets seems to have been not only unrealistic about his but strangely ungrateful, too." The reader should have little difficulty evaluating the cogency of Brown's remarks. The "biting-the-hand-that-feeds-you" note, it should be observed, appears in a number of reviews. In a commercial society such as ours, though, one fairly questions whether "gratitude" is precisely the appropriate word for employer-employee relations. There is a disconcertingly shrill note in the reviews of *The Big Knife* which is cause for wonder. Perhaps Odets' own "knife" penetrated some tender and vulnerable skins. If *Golden Boy* reflects the period in which it was written, the same might be said with equal justice of *The Big Knife*. Undoubtedly, however, the critics did not relish the latter reflection.

Although correspondence is not the most valuable element in a work of art, some degree of verisimilitude seems desirable. *The Big Knife*, as Frederick Lumley says, "may be unpleasant, it may seem excessive, but I am sure that for Odets it is an honest view of the way he felt in Hollywood." A year after *The Big Knife* appeared Hortense Powdermaker published *Hollywood, the Dream Factory*, a remarkable report which, as Lumley was the first to point out, verifies Odets' study of the film world. Powdermaker records how the actor in Hollywood is not respected, how he is treated as a child, or, what is worse, as a mere thing. "The executive attitude is a combination of cracking the whip to the tune of the contract and at the same time cuddling and wheedling with endearments," the author observes. "Terms of address are always 'darling' and 'sweetheart' between males as well as males and females, followed by the most exaggerated compliments." Like Charlie Castle, real actors "react with scorn" to these "endearments." Friendship is rare in Hollywood, notes the anthropologist, as a result of the competitive drive toward "success" and the impermanence of status once it is achieved. Sex often becomes "an outlet for frustration . . . a way of making life seem less empty." Powdermaker sees the actor faced with "two alternatives. One is to try to believe that the synthetic or phony role is a true one. The other is to accept that part realistically for what it is, but play it as well as possible. The second reaction seems the healthier." Charlie Castle employs the "second reaction." In Hollywood the agent is regarded, says Powdermaker, as a "necessary evil," as one who "would sell [the actor] down the river if that were profitable." Here Odets is actually somewhat more charitable toward the system than he might have been. Although Marion says: "I like Nat—he's very fatherly—but Hollywood agents aren't worth their weight in feathers" (p. 16), Odets treats the agent with considerable warmth and sympathy. Odets' picture of Castle's relations with his business manager— "All right! Then get tough and bossy!" says the actor (p. 17)— also reflects the Hollywood situation researched by Powdermaker. For the business agent is another model of paternalism, and one who often leads the actor to forget that it is actually his own money which is doled out to him. That financial considerations dominate thinking in Hollywood is clear from a reading of Powdermaker's book. The New York bankers "have an important voice in the decision on what kind of entertainment will be popular," she notes. When Marcus Hoff says: ". . . I am beholden to our stockholders. They control our every action—they are our invisible but ever-present monitors" (p. 68), Odets is merely underlining the economic realities of film making as a business. Odets' picture of life in Hollywood, then, is far from fanciful; and his portrait of the tormented star, Charlie Castle, is a haunting one. As Powdermaker puts it: "For all members of our species, not to be regarded as human is a severe threat."

The language in an Odets play is generally one of its strongest elements, and The Big Knife shows no loss of verbal power in the dramatist. Some memorable and moving lines from the piece have already been cited. Other striking expressions, however, are not difficult to find. Nat says of Hoff: "I know Marcus more than thirty years. Before he wore three-hundred dollar suits and put his old, dead mother's picture on his desk—that mother he got from Central Casting. He's stepped in the tar himself enough, but he always keeps his shoes clean" (p. 21). Charlie reflects: "California, think of it—a place where an honest apple tree won't grow . . ." (p. 40). "Life is a queer little man . . ." (p. 43), says Coy. "Try to be happy," Charlie urges Buddy Bliss, "—this isn't a Russian novel" (p. 55). Charlie informs a neighbor, Dr. Frary: "I'll bet you don't know why we all wear these beautiful, expensive ties in Hollywood. . . . It's a military tactic—we hope you won't notice our faces" (pp. 55–56). Charlie says of Nat Danziger: "Why did I add this burden to that grotesque, devoted soul? Did you ever notice? He moves his lips when he reads . . ." (p. 70). In 1939 Anita Block said: "In the half-articulate idiom of the street, spoken by the ordinary folk who constitute the throbbing characters of a Clifford Odets, their counterparts in the audience hear their own inarticulate cries; in the taut mono-syllables of frustration and longing, they hear their own eager and bursting hearts." A year earlier Grenville Vernon wrote: ". . . Odets' people are at once primitive and intelligent, and it is the antinomy which imparts to them their color and variety. Neither of these qualities are hurt by the fact that their emotion is not strong enough to conquer their intelligence nor their in-telligence deep or keen enough to kill their emotion. It is this struggle of emotion with intelligence which is the basis of much of the great drama of the world. . . ." Although the characters in *The Big Knife* are placed higher on the social and economic scale than the people in Odets' earlier plays, and though Charlie Castle is less "inarticulate" than, say, Ralph Berger, the substance of the critical opinions just cited applies to the playwright's later work, too. The language of *The Big Knife* is not only quotable: it is also functional, it springs naturally from character and situation, and it at once moves the action and reveals the theme. This is dramaturgy at its best.

It is interesting to note that Arthur Miller's *Death of a Sales-*

man was running on Broadway at the same time that Odet's *The Big Knife* was at the National. This fact occasioned Kappo Phelan to write: "It is no critical evasion to suggest that [Odets] walk four blocks up the town to learn how the American paradox (tragedy) is to be handled without social, ethical, or artistic pretensions. It is true Arthur Miller's *Salesman* is not angry, it's merely sure. Moreover, and which will perhaps most impress Mr. Odets, it is producing box-office records as well as discussion." Phelan's remarks are not merely uncharitable, they are also ignorant. More than one critic has been perceptive enough to see the influence of Odets on Miller. Take, for example, the climax of *Death of a Salesman*, where Willy Loman kills himself in order to provide his son Biff with insurance money and the chance for a new life. Certainly this feature of Miller's play has much in common with Odets' *Awake and Sing!*, where Grandfather Jacob kills himself in order to provide the young Ralph with the means for rebirth. As William Weigand has noted, there is a strong resemblance between Ben Gordon in *Paradise Lost* and Biff Loman in Miller's play. When Frenchy in *Rocket to the Moon* says: "In this day of stresses I don't see much normal life, myself included. The woman's not a wife. She's the dependent of a salesman who can't make sales and is ashamed to tell her so. . . ." (p. 404), one is again reminded of *Death of a Salesman*. Other examples would not be hard to discover.

The Big Knife is not one of Clifford Odets' "pleasant plays"; it is, like *Night Music* and *Clash by Night*, a very dark play indeed. Nor has Odets' treatment of Hollywood quickened either the intelligence or the sympathy of his critics. True, the piece is occasionally overwrought and crude, but most of Odets' plays suffer to some extent from these faults. As Joseph Wood Krutch pointed out years ago: "Odets, being a good writer, cannot be adequately described as the sum of his defects." *The Big Knife* is a powerful drama—disturbing, wild and unforgettable— something which comes when an artist has driven his vision to an extreme.

CHAPTER NINE

The Country Girl

The theater is mysterious . . .

—Georgie, *The Country Girl*,
p. 47

Unlike Odets' other plays written after the passing of the Group Theater, *The Country Girl* (1950) was a commercial and—to a large extent—a critical success. Nevertheless, Odets did not care very much for the piece, which, like *Golden Boy*, he had written for money. The dramatist informed Mendelsohn:

> I don't . . . think I would change my mind about *The Country Girl*. It's a good show; it's a theater piece. It does have about it a certain kind of psychological urgency, because if you are creative, things do creep in despite the conscious impulse. For instance, there crept into that play a central problem of my own life. And this did give a certain urgency and heat to much that went on in the script. I didn't *mean* for that problem to come out; I cannily and unconsciously disguised it. But that is unconsciously what came out in the writing of that play.

Harold Clurman believes that the biographical feature of *The Country Girl* involves Odets' expressed need for "a comrade in his craft, a friend who has a practical professional understanding of the actor's need and a faith in his talent which will enable the friend to overcome all the difficulties the actor's unsteady char-

acter sets in the way." No doubt, other, perhaps deeper, sound-
ings could be taken on this subject.

The Country Girl is a two-act play. (The title page of the
published text erroneously describes it as "A Play in Three Acts.")
There are five scenes in Act One and three scenes in Act Two.
The time-sequence covers about two months. In "How *The
Country Girl* Came About," Odets says: "I write fluently, but to
combine a certain linear drive of story with psychological drive is
the real problem. I don't know anyone who can do it, who ever
did it." This is a typical Odetsian exaggeration. Many plays combine "linear drive" and "psychological drive"—indeed *The Country Girl* itself combines the two drives. Which is to say that the
play, though not without its faults and limitations, is much better
than its creator believed.

In Act One, Scene One, Bernie Dodd, a young director, offers
the alcoholic actor Frank Elgin a role in a Broadway show.
Frank, who has a morbid lack of confidence in himself, is reluctant to accept the assignment. In Scene Two, Georgie, Frank's
wife, is prepared to leave her husband, but when Frank resolves
to take the part in the show she decides to give him one more
chance. The point of attack occurs, then, when Frank accepts
responsibility for himself. He informs Georgie of a dream he had
the previous night:

> A big sign—now get this—a big banner was stretched across
> the street: "Frank Elgin in . . ." I couldn't make out in
> what. . . . I'm going to take that part, Georgie! You don't
> have to tell me not to drink—haven't I been a good boy
> all summer? . . . This morning I got up early—that funny
> laughing dream. And I was thinking about our lives—
> everything—and now this chance! Don't you see that all
> those people in the dream, they wish me luck. I won't
> fail this time! Because that's what counts—if the world
> is with you—and your wife! (*He looks at her, earnest, boy-
> ish, and questioning, appealing for her support.*)
>
> (p. 35)

Several important dramatic questions are posed here: Will Frank stay sober and make a success of himself in the role? Will Georgie stay with Frank permanently? What is the nature of the bond that unites the couple?

Complications develop in the following scene. Frank is secretly dependent on Georgie, but he pretends to others that his wife is really the neurotic partner in the marriage. The early action of the play suggests that, in spite of Bernie's resentment and suspicion of Georgie, the two young people may eventually grow attracted to each other. Frank's two-faced attitude causes many problems; characteristically, however, he allows his wife to correct matters. One of these incidents occurs near the end of Act One, with the result that Frank and Georgie quarrel:

FRANK. Boy, I'll never understand your moods, and that's the truth! A man can't be right can he? Two strikes against him before he opens his mouth! (*Sullen and offended, he goes back to his dressing. She sits, stiff, cold, and wordless.*) Now my stomach's all in a whirl again. That's what you wanted, isn't it? (*He sits at the make-up shelf; there is silence and distance between them.*)

GEORGIE. One day soon . . . we'll see what I want. . . .

(p. 72)

Which line looks forward to the resolution of the play.

During Act Two Frank struggles with the demands of his role, and also with his increasing desire to escape anxiety by means of the bottle. Eventually Frank's neurotic inner pressure reaches an almost unbearable level of intensity—and he succumbs to temptation. When Georgie discovers that her mate has been furtively drinking there is another, more violent, quarrel:

GEORGIE. Oh, the hell with it! . . . I'm going back to the hotel— do what you want! Sometimes I think you're plain out of your head!

(*She exits without more ado, slamming the door hard.* FRANK *whirls around; he glowers bitterly, snorting and mimicking her tone, walking in circles before he snatches his tie off a hook.*)

FRANK. Out of your mind! Do what you want . . . plain out of your mind! . . . That's right walk out on me! Typical! Typical! (*He is down at the pier glass now, angrily snapping the tie into a knot, muttering to himself.*) Forget I'm alive. Take their part and forget I'm alive! Helpmate, real helpmate. . . . (*He dribbles off, his attitude abruptly changing. He stops and then tiptoes to the closed door and listens. Then he goes to the trunk and from the bottom drawer brings out a full bottle of cough syrup. He uncaps it, takes a swig, and throws the cap away over one shoulder. The bottle plopped down on the chest in front of him, he continues with the tie and collar. His tone is less intense but as bitter.*) Helpmate! Sweetheart! Country girl!

(pp. 95–96)

This is the turning point of the action because Frank's decision to get drunk will force Bernie to make a counter decision regarding the actor's part in the show. Similarly, Frank's action will compel Georgie to render a decision about the future of the Elgin marriage.

The crisis arrives in the next scene. Bernie finally discovers that Frank is a pathological liar, and that Georgie, far from being the villain of the piece, is the show's best hope in the joint effort to preserve the star's sobriety.

BERNIE. Dammit, listen to me! You're knocking all the apologies out of my head! (*He has pulled her in close to him and is holding her by both arms.*) Now, *listen*, Lady Brilliance: you have to stay—he doesn't play unless you stay! It's a time for promotion, not more execution! But I can't take the chance *if you don't stay!*

(*A quick tense moment follows.* GEORGIE *is frozen in his arms, her hands against his chest.*)

GEORGIE. Why are you holding me? (*Pushing*) I said you are holding me!

(*Abruptly, not releasing her, he kisses her fully on the mouth . . .*)

. . .

BERNIE. . . . I deserve anything you say—no excuses, no excuses. . . . (*His manner changes.*) Now I need your answer. For Frank's sake, I want you to stay.

GEORGIE. Wanting, wanting, always wanting!

BERNIE (*humbly for him*). I'm asking . . . Will you stay?

GEORGIE (*after a pause*). Yes.

(*He starts for the door, his face rigid. She stops him.*)

GEORGIE. You kissed me—don't let it give you any ideas, Mr. Dodd.

BERNIE (*quietly*). No, Mrs. Elgin.

(*He walks out, quietly closing the door.* GEORGIE *stands for a full moment, as if listening, an air of impenetrable unreality about her. Her hand slowly moves up to her face. Her fingers touch her lips.*)

(pp. 108–110, italics in original)

The scene ends with Georgie's final decision suspended, with Frank's success in the show still uncertain, and with the future of Bernie and Georgie in doubt.

The climax, which Odets skillfully plays down in order to avoid the appearance of melodramatic contrivance, follows in the final scene of the play. Frank's success in his role prompts a new self-confidence in him, and as a result he asks Georgie for her decision:

FRANK. . . . Don't leave me, darling. Give me a chance. I love you. . . .

GEORGIE. Frank . . . I married you for happiness. . . . And, if necessary, I'll leave you for the same reason. Right now I don't know where I stand.

FRANK (*humbly*). You don't . . . ?

GEORGIE. . . . No. Because neither of us has really changed. And yet I'm sure that both our lives are at some sort of turning point. There's some real new element of hope here—I don't know what. But I'm certain . . . and you, Frank, have to be strong enough to bear that uncertainty.

FRANK (*hushed*). I think I know what you mean. . . . I—I don't know how to say this, but no matter what happens, you have saved me, Georgie—you and Bernie. . . . I think I have a chance.

(pp. 121–122)

But it remains for Bernie Dodd to reveal the future better than Georgie herself knows: "You'll never leave him," he informs her. Then—after kissing her "lightly on the lips"—he exits. The play concludes as Georgie *slowly walks out of the room with* FRANK's *robe across one arm*" (p. 124).

As the title of the play suggests, Georgie, not Frank, is the protagonist. True, Frank's decision launches the point of attack; and it is again Frank's action that brings about the turning point. Thereafter, however, the resolution largely depends on Georgie. Actually, it might be argued that the play is not as "well made" as most critics would have it. The reviewers—Margaret Marshall, Walter Kerr, Harold Clurman and others—all commented on the "smooth" craftsmanship of the piece. Similarly, in *American Drama Since World War II*, Gerald Weales says that Odets' play is, "extremely well structured (*slick* is the word that comes to mind, but it would have to be used as a compliment). . . ." In "How *The Country Girl* Came About," Odets remarks that the play went through various drafts, and that Georgie evolved from a "destructive bitch" dying from cancer to the much more admirable woman of the final version. According to Odets, Georgie is the main character. It seems possible that in his final treatment of the play Odets failed to unify the structure completely, for analysis suggests some confusion of focus in motivation. Certain details in the play reveal that the dramatist, consciously or unconsciously, was aware of problems in construction.

The point of attack, for example, is framed by Georgie's decision to leave Frank and by her later postponement of that leave-taking. Although Frank is responsible for the turning point, Georgie is made the innocent cause of his decision to get drunk. Which is to say that Odets seeks to make Georgie the active force, or protagonist. For the remainder of the play the focus is steadily on Georgie. In the last scene Frank is a success in his part, but the action takes place off-stage and the spotlight is on Georgie. As already noted, there are no fireworks in the last scene; Odets plays down the climax. The first question—will Frank be a success?—is answered almost at once. The second question—Will Georgie marry Bernie?—is not left in much doubt, for the crisis ends with Bernie kissing Georgia but calling her "Mrs. Elgin." In spite of what Georgie says at the climax, the audience is made to feel that she will stay with her husband, and consequently there can be little surprise in store when, at the conclusion, Bernie confirms the permanence of the Elgin marriage. It seems a fact worth noting that Odets had a tendency to shift the focus from his male protagonists to his female leads late in the action of some of his best plays; witness the displacement of interest from Ralph to Hennie in *Awake and Sing!*, from Ben to Cleo in *Rocket to the Moon* and from Frank to Georgie in *The Country Girl*. (This inclination was perhaps rooted in psychological conflicts in Odets, a problem which lies outside the scope of the present study.)

In order to show how *The Country Girl* is much more complex than a discussion of its logical structure suggests, it is necessary to discuss "the play-within-the-play" device in Act One, Scene One, and also to analyze some of the "external" techniques Odets employs to unify the action. One critic objected to the use of "the play-within-the-play," but investigation reveals that this rather long enactment of Frank's reading for the role is far from inconsequential. The dialogue of "the play-within-the-play"

foreshadows subsequent developments in the "real" play and
exposes the character traits of Frank and Bernie. Thus, Frank
enacts the role of the rather corrupt Judge Murray; Bernie reads
the part of the young "reformer" who wants to marry the Judge's
grandchild, Ellen. The two characters struggle over Ellen, as
Frank and Bernie are later to struggle over Georgie. The Judge's
moral decline parallels Frank's alcoholism and emotional sickness. Bernie, who calls himself an Italian-American (p. 31), is
identified with the "Wop bastard" who aspires to Ellen's hand
(p. 16). During this audition Bernie is guilty of a "slip of the
tongue"—a slip that is not without its Freudian significance—
and calls the Judge "Frank." Similarly, Frank calls Bernie "son"
(p. 18). When Bernie taunts the Judge that Ellen has already
deserted him, the older man proudly proclaims his former and
future greatness, and stresses the belief that he is a long way from
being beaten. The younger man, however, is unrelenting in his
attack. "*Soon* [BERNIE] *is pacing around* FRANK, *like a bull fighter
around a helpless animal, which is the impression* FRANK *gives
for the moment*" (pp. 17–18). Clearly then, the opening sequence
has an integral function in the dramatic action and casts much
light on both character and theme.

In his short story "The Gambler, the Nun, and the Radio"
(1933), Hemingway deals with some "opiates of the people."
Each of the opiates mentioned in the piece is a form of escape
from the self; thus the protagonist plays his radio all night long
in an effort to forget his pain. Odets employs the same device in
The Country Girl. In the opening sequence, for example, Bernie
is disturbed by a radio blaring while he is talking to Frank:

> BERNIE (*abruptly calling off to the left*). Hey, "Props"! Shut
> off that radio or close the door! (*Gently, to* FRANK) Read the
> part, Frank.
>
> (p. 15)

There are a couple more references to sound in this scene
(p. 13 and p. 17). When Scene Two opens Odets says: "*Loud*

music comes out of a small radio" in the Elgin apartment. Bernie knocks on the door, but Georgie mistakenly thinks it is a neighbor complaining about the music. After turning off the radio, Georgie finally opens the door for Bernie (p. 25). The radio, then, is identified with Georgie. In the first scene Bernie's anger at the radio noise and his gentle approach to Frank prepares the audience for the coming struggle between Georgie and the director over the alcoholic actor. Georgie's listening to the radio, like her voracious reading, underlines her loneliness and sexual frustration. "When you think about it—so many plays and books, so much reading in the stillness of the night," Georgie remarks at one point, "—and for all of it, what?" (p. 74). In Act One, Scene Five, Georgie and Bernie have one of their numerous arguments over Frank:

> [BERNIE] *looks at* [GEORGIE] *carefully, with a polite charm masking a certain scorn, then leaves. Despite her awareness of his good sense,* GEORGIE *is somewhat disturbed by him. Thinking, she turns on a small radio. She looks up as* FRANK *enters.*
>
> (p. 61)

After a brief exchange, Frank barks: "Shut the radio off!" (p. 62). In other words, both Bernie and Frank "turn off" Georgie, which is to say, they frustrate her need for love.

When Act Two opens Georgie is once again listening to the radio and talking to the playwright, Unger. After the latter praises Bernie to Georgie, he asks: "Does my typing bother you?"; to which Georgie replies: "No. Does the music?" (p. 75). Georgie's radio and Bernie, then, are again juxtaposed. Later in the same scene Georgie indulges in some revealing play acting:

> *She takes off her glasses and looks at herself* [*in a mirror*]. *Something poignant reaches out from image to reality. The radio has begun playing a waltz.* GEORGIE *begins to sway to its rhythm, and in another moment she is waltzing alone, almost as if it were possible to waltz herself back to a better time.*

*What she is murmuring to herself we cannot hear. Then she
stops abruptly. A sardonic* BERNIE *stands in the doorway.*

(pp. 82–83)

Immediately Georgie dons her glasses again—and shortly
afterward snaps off the radio (p. 84). When Bernie later remarks
that Georgie is "as phony . . . as an opera soprano," she slaps his
face (p. 87). However, when Bernie finally kisses Georgie, Odets
says: "*She seems to come out of sleep*"—and then the hostility
vanishes (p. 109). Bernie, instead of continuing to "turn off"
Georgie, now loves her and hence "turns on" the woman. There
are no more references in the play to the radio.

Off-stage noises become identified with Frank's success in the
show, and with the new sense of command he exercises. In the
last scene, for example, he barks: "Close that window!" (p.
117), and his resemblance to the Bernie of the first scene is plain.
Finally, the director realizes that he "can't escape [Frank's]
voice" (p. 114), and decides to give up his hope to possess
Georgie. It is interesting to note that the image of Bernie as a
bull-fighter stalking Frank, the "helpless animal" at the start,
merges with the radio device I have just analyzed. When the
opening curtain goes up a radio is playing "*a popular Mexican
song. . . . [And]* BERNIE *. . . is softly whistling with the song*" (p.
11). The reference to Bernie's "whistling" foreshadows his loneliness and his openness to Georgie's charm, which will persist
beneath the cynical crust of his opposition to her. The Mexican
motif is carried through when, right before the crisis, Georgie
informs Bernie: "I'm going back to New York, to the fiesta of
a quiet room" (p. 108). Bernie then kisses her, and the "fiesta"
explodes in the dressing room in Boston.

The most impressive feature of *The Country Girl*, however, is
Odets' brilliant psychological characterization. Critics seem not
to have noticed how deeply the dramatist probes into Georgie,
Bernie and Frank. For one thing, it is quite apparent that Odets
has depicted a symbolic oedipal triangle in *The Country Girl*.

Frank is fifty years old (p. 14), Georgie is over thirty (p. 82), and Bernie is thirty-five (p. 14). Indeed, Frank openly refers to himself as "Poppa" (p. 71), and calls Bernie and Unger his "sons" (pp. 30, 46 and 76). The first time Bernie sees Georgie he exclaims: "You're even younger than I thought . . . you act like an old lady and you're not" (p. 27). Later Georgie informs Bernie: "Frank's brought out the mother in me" (p. 47). There is not, it should be noted, much sexual life in the Elgin marriage. Although Georgie stands for the "mother" her age would seem to make her more ideally suited to Bernie than to Frank. In Scene Two, Georgie complains of a toothache and a chill: "It's cold out," she tells Bernie. "The summer collapsed so abruptly, didn't it? You could fall asleep here and not wake up till they called you for the Judgment Day . . . I have a bad toothache. All of autumn's in this tooth. . . . My hands are numb. . . . What time is it? . . . Three clocks, a radio, and never know the time" (pp. 26–27). This theme is repeated later in the play in an exchange between Georgie and Frank:

GEORGIE. I haven't felt like a woman in ten years.
FRANK. . . . I suppose that's my fault.
GEORGIE (*lightly*). Summer dies, autumn comes, a fact of nature —nobody's fault.

(pp. 52–53)

Directly before the curtain falls ending Act One, Georgie declares: "I really must . . . get these teeth fixed" (p. 71). Clearly, Georgie's "toothache" is Frank and the unsatisfactory life he has given her. The "cold autumn rain" represents Georgie's premature sexlessness. Georgie is half-dead; she doesn't know "what time it is"; even her hands are "numb." She is like a fairy princess asleep in the midst of life. In *The Big Knife* Marion Castle says: "I believe the fairy tale is a lie. In real life no one ever comes to wake us up" (p. 34). In *The Country Girl*, however, Bernie Dodd kisses Georgie, and she comes "*out of her sleep*" (p. 109). Viewed in these terms the crisis of the play is "the Judgment

Day," and the verdict rendered is that Georgie is renewed and
ready to go on with Frank: "*For a moment* [GEORGIE] *wears a sad
and yearning look* [*after* BERNIE]; *finally a towel in her hand
calls her back to reality*" (p. 124).

Why did Georgie marry Frank? Evidently she was lonely, even
as a child. "My father was always away on tour," she informs
Unger. "My mother was off with gardening and hobbies" (p.
73). As a result, Georgie read a lot of books—"too many," she
says—and became excessively romantic (p. 105). Note that
Georgie's father, like Frank, was in show business. Which suggests that Frank is a father image to Georgie. Moreover, Georgie
believed that Elgin, like her father, was a strong man:

GEORGIE. You mystify me, Frank, your sense of guilt and inse-
    curity. Take a lesson from my father, the late Delaney the
    Great. He didn't care what people thought of him, no matter
    what he did. Played every vaudeville house in the world.
    Didn't show up at home but twice a year—and those two
    times he was down in the cellar perfecting new magic tricks.
FRANK. Oh, sure, you'd love that—seeing me only twice a year!
GEORGIE (*whimsically*). My mother didn't mind it as much as I
    did—it orphaned me. Might not have married you if I'd had
    a father. But he *believed* in himself, I mean—you don't. That's
    cost you plenty . . . it's cost me as much. . . .

                                        (p. 53, italics in original)

Georgie later explains to Bernie that she "had such a naïve
belief in Frank's worldliness and competence" (p. 105). It
is certainly worthy of note that Georgie refers to Bernie as
"Bernardo the Great" (p. 54). Like "Delaney the Great," Bernie
is a "magician" to both Georgie and Frank (p. 113). Part of
Bernie's attraction for Georgie, then, derives from his image as
a strong father figure.

But Bernie, like Frank, is not as strong as he pretends. "I
don't know," he admits to Georgie at the end of the play, "maybe
a magician *does* live in this frail, foolish body, but he certainly

can't work wonders for himself!" (p. 124, italics in original). Bernie calls himself "frail" here, a word which Georgie previously used to describe Frank (p. 105). Much of the psychological motivation in the piece involves the problem of whether Frank or Bernie will assume the final father role. Although Bernie, like Frank, refers to himself as "Poppa" (p. 59), the older man retains possession of Georgie. Furthermore, the "magic" associated with Georgie's father appears to be left in Frank's keeping: "A man like Elgin, giving his best performance," says Bernie, "—he has the magic to transform a mere show to theater with a capital T!" (p. 103). Bernie's interest in Frank, however, seems to depend on more than merely a business arrangement.

Like Elgin, the elder Dodd was an alcoholic (p. 22). Whereas Frank simply attempted suicide in the past, though, Bernie's father succeeded in destroying himself (p. 90). For Bernie then—as for Georgie—Frank stands in the place of the father. There is a strong element of latent homosexuality in Bernie's attitude toward Frank. From the opening of the play, Bernie reveals a hostility toward women. For example, he barks: "Don't come in here, Nancy—we're busy" (p. 12)—a line which reflects Bernie's contempt for women, and his desire to keep them out of his life. "Does he like women?" Georgie asks Frank after meeting Dodd (p. 51). Bernie is recently divorced, and consequently he is extremely bitter toward women: "*My* wife was so twisted"— says Bernie, apparently identifying himself with Frank and the former Mrs. Dodd with Georgie—" 'I hope your next play's a big flop!' she says. 'So the whole world can see I love you even if you're a failure!' " (p. 45, italics in original). During the play a number of references are made to Georgie's knitting, and at one point Georgie sews a loose button on Frank's coat (p. 53). Later in the action Bernie informs Georgie: "I was married to one like you. . . . It took her two years—she sewed me up!" (p. 85). If Odets is presenting a "negative oedipus complex" here, the roles in the original relationship are reversed; for Bernie is

the more active and aggressive one, Frank is the more passive
and dependent one. At the end of the play, of course, Frank
steals the "magic" and becomes "Poppa" again. On one level
then, *The Country Girl* represents a struggle between Georgie
(the wife-mother) and Bernie (the friend-son) for possession of
Frank (the husband-father). Thus, Bernie warns Georgie: "I'm
going to fight you as hard as I can for this man!" (p. 85). "I'll
think about you," Bernie tells Frank, "if you take this job. I'll
commit myself to you—we'll work and worry together—it's a
marriage!" (p. 31). (The reader will recall that Odets used the
same approach in *Golden Boy*, where homosexual symbolism
underlined Joe Bonaparte's loss of his true nature. In *The Country Girl*, however, Odets fails to extend the symbolism beyond
the psychological realm.) "Nobody wants to get your goat,
Mrs. Dodd," Bernie assures Georgie (p. 32)—which in the light
of the present analysis takes on significance when Frank remarks:
"You know Poppa—walks like a mountain goat—never slips" (p.
77). Bernie is convinced that Georgie is "jealous" of him (p.
91), and the reader may feel that she has good reason for her
jealousy.

Bernie's unconscious attraction to Frank originated in the past.
At the beginning of the play he says: "Twelve years ago I saw
[Frank] give two performances that made my hair stand up—
(*Abruptly he calls offstage*:) Close that door and keep it closed!"
(p. 13). Here we see Bernie's admiration for Frank juxtaposed to
the radio noise outside, which symbolizes Georgie. (Since "hair"
represents male potency—witness, for example, the Samson and
Delilah story—the reference to Bernie's "hair" standing up is
suggestive.) The unconscious sexual symbolism is rationalized,
however, into mere hero worship: "You and Lunt and Walter
Huston," Bernie tells Frank, "—you were my heroes" (p. 30).
That Bernie regards Frank as a father is plain from Odets'
manipulation of the word "kid." In the audition scene Bernie,
reading the play with Frank, says: "Look at me! I'm a fresh

kid—I wanna marry your grandchild and you don't want me to"
(p. 17). The following exchange occurs in Act Two between
Frank and Bernie:

FRANK. . . . Why kid around? It's all my fault—I'm no good.

. . .

BERNIE. You're guilty as hell! But I want you to do something
for the kid—
FRANK. What kid?
BERNIE. *This* kid! Stop being naïve: stop protecting her!

. . .

BERNIE. . . . If we go on together, you move in with me for the
duration!

(p. 102)

There is an element of irony here, for in the audition scene
Bernie played the "kid" who wanted the mother surrogate (the
"virginal" Nancy-Ellen seems to be a disguised maternal imago),
but now his desire is fixed on the father figure, Frank. After
"marrying" Frank, however, Bernie, like Georgie before him, is
rudely jolted into seeing the truth about the man. As a result of
his disillusionment, Bernie's love for the mother in Georgie returns and Frank becomes a rival for the woman's affection. Actually, the negative oedipus complex was only a smokescreen
concealing Bernie's deeper desire for the mother.

Twice in the play Bernie calls Georgie "Mrs. Dodd" (p. 104
and p. 107). The form of address is ambiguous. Is Bernie unconsciously confusing Georgie with his ex-wife whom he detests?
Or is he expressing an unconscious desire to make Georgie "Mrs.
Dodd"? It is also possible, considering the symbolic triangles of
the play, that Bernie is transforming Georgie into his mother,
for the latter would also be "Mrs. Dodd." After Bernie kisses
Georgie, however, he calls her "Mrs. Elgin" (p. 110). Why?
Is Odets suggesting that Georgie is no longer, for Bernie, either
an ex-wife or mother? Or is the playwright merely foreshadowing
Bernie's final renunciation of the forbidden woman? Perhaps

we do not have an "either-or" situation here but a "both-and"
construction.

Bernie Dodd is one of a long line of characters in Odets' plays
who are in search of a "home." It is part of Bernie's grudge against
modern women that they "don't want a home: the only piece
of furniture they'll touch is the psychoanalyst's couch!" (p. 44).
At the end of the piece, Bernie bemoans his fate: "A job is a
home to a homeless man. Now the job is finished—where do I
go from here?" (p. 113). Georgie's character, though, has im-
pressed itself upon Bernie, and as a result he is no longer a
misogynist. The good mother in Georgie has inspired a new
appreciation in the director for women. Hence, he informs
Georgie: "You are . . . steadfast. And loyal . . . reliable. I like that
in a woman!" (p. 124). Odets suggests, by the way, that Bernie
may not be entirely homeless in the future. At one point in the
play, Georgie and Nancy gaze together into a mirror and Nancy
remarks: "Look at you—we could be sisters!" Immediately
Georgie begins to dance, and then Bernie enters (p. 82). If
Georgie and Nancy "could be sisters," perhaps the one could be
replaced by the other in Bernie's affections. After Frank strikes
Nancy during a performance in the final scene, Bernie soothes
the girl with a kiss (p. 116). It seems quite possible, then, that
Bernie may eventually find a home with the "virginal, which is to
say untried and initiatory" Nancy (p. 37).

In his characterization of Frank Elgin, Odets projects an
accurate portrait of an orally regressed neurotic. Some recent
psychoanalytic theory places an increasing emphasis on the oral
level of development, and regards disturbances in this area as
being the decisive factor in neurosis. The oedipus complex, in
this view, is merely a later "rescue station" from a basic oral
regression. Such an explanation of neurotic motivation seems
especially meaningful in the case of an alcoholic, who clearly sub-
stitutes a bottle for a breast, but whose solution to the infantile
conflict is ultimately self-destructive. For the oral neurotic is a
psychic masochist inwardly fixated on the bad cruel mother that

he has himself imaginatively, and unconsciously, constructed. Significantly, the oral neurotic spends his life denying his neurotic attachment by erecting a number of defenses, such as pseudo-aggression, displacement of blame for his allegedly unprovoked suffering onto a mother-surrogate, and alcoholism. Originally, so the theory goes, the infant believes that the mother's breast is part of his own organism; and when the infant is in any way frustrated during breast feeding he is consumed by intense aggressive feelings. He comes to feel that bad Mother, whose independent existence he slowly awakens to, is sadistically refusing him. Since the infant cannot act out his rage, however, the aggression boomerangs, and in the process produces severe guilt feelings in the infant. Furthermore, since every organism seeks pleasure and avoids pain, the unpleasant guilt feelings and aggression become "libidinized," that is, they are converted into "pleasurable pain." The alcoholic, according to this approach, denies that he wants to be refused by the mother, and consequently he seeks to establish what the late Edmund Bergler called a "liquid pseudo autarchy." By drinking excessively the alcoholic proves that he can take care of himself with "milk" (alcohol), but in addition he indicates—unfortunately with self-destructive results—that all one can get from Mother is "poison." This intrapsychic process is further complicated by the alcoholic's identification with the mother. Thus, he not only "poisons" himself—an expression of masochism—but he also incurs guilt by "poisoning" Mother. Marriages involving oral neurotics are distinguished by defensive pseudo-aggression, self-provoked suffering, and general "injustice collecting." My description of the oral neurotic is necessarily sketchy, but perhaps enough has been said in order to analyze and interpret Frank Elgin.

That Frank represents what the psychoanalyst would call an oral neurotic seems clear. Whenever Frank feels expansive, for example, he turns to food. "Let the wind blow down the street," he informs Georgie happily, "—the oysters and lobsters are delicious!" (p. 51). "Guess what I'm in the mood for?" he asks his wife later. "One of those one dozen oyster stews. . . . Oh, boy, what that'll do for my stomach!" (p. 70). Whenever Frank's unconsciously provocative behavior prompts Georgie to react with resentment toward him, however, the neurotic actor at once assumes a conscious self-pitying pose: "Now my stomach's all in a whirl again. That's what you wanted, isn't it?" (p. 72). And he then commences to drink with a vengeance. Georgie tells Bernie that Frank "has to be nursed, guarded, and coddled!" (p. 107). At one point Odets refers to Frank as a "child" (p. 92). Even Frank's acting is described in oral terms by Bernie: "my problem," the director informs Georgie, "is to keep him going—overflowing. The longer I keep him fluid and open, the more gold we mine" (p. 60). *Consciously*, Frank wants people to like him (p. 67); *unconsciously*, though, he prompts rejection through his drinking and lying. In order to appease his unconscious conscience, however, Frank must vociferously deny that he wants to fail; he must place the blame elsewhere: "They all want me to fail!" he tells Georgie. "And you want me to fail, too! You don't love me!" (p. 95).

There are times in the play when one feels that Georgie is a psychic masochist, too. Her consciously expressed reason for marrying Frank—namely, that he resembled her father—may have been merely a rationalization for a deeper orality. For Georgie knew that Frank was a drunkard when she married him. And there is something masochistic in Georgie's remaining with Frank over the years. "I don't know who's punishing who anymore!" she tells Frank in one scene (p. 92). The Elgin marriage appears to thrive on quarrels. Numerous references are made to Georgie's oral propensities. When Frank asks her why she married him, Georgie replies: "That's easy: you always had a box of Chiclets in your pocket" (p. 79). And she informs Bernie that her one aim in life is "to buy the sugar for my coffee!" (p. 108). Georgie, like Frank, consciously maintains that she wants to get "milk" (gum, sugar), and not be refused; yet her capacity for suffering seems suspiciously inexhaustible. (There are like-

wise repeated references to Bernie's overindulgence in smoking
—another oral practice.)

In "How *The Country Girl* Came About," Odets says: "I
never wrote a play that didn't tell a story. The only thing is that
I usually verbalized the implications. It may be that in *The
Country Girl* I didn't verbalize them—things like what makes
a man like Frank Elgin a drunkard." When *The Country Girl*
was filmed a scene was added which showed the Elgins' child
killed by an automobile, supposedly as a result of Frank's carelessness. In the play, however, Georgie tells Bernie:

> There's no one reason [for Frank's drinking]. . . . I'd say
> bad judgment started him off. He had some money once,
> but you don't know my Frank—he wanted to be his own
> producer—eighty thousand went in fifteen months, most
> of it on two bad shows. . . . A year later we lost our little
> girl. It was awesome how he went for the bottle. He just
> didn't stop after that.
>
> (p. 74)

Earlier in the piece, though, Frank traces his difficulties back to
the couple's days in California: "I knew it then—on the coast—
I lost my nerve! And then, when we lost the money, in '39, after
those lousy Federal Theater jobs—! . . . Whatever the hell I did,
I don't know what!" (p. 33). As noted, however, Frank drank
before he met Georgie; consequently, the basic motivation for his
self-destructive tendencies must be said to lie farther back in his
past.

One might note that psychic masochists, not surprisingly, are
notoriously prone to "bad judgment" (p. 74). Similarly, oral
neurotics unconsciously create their mates in the image of the
bad cruel mother of the nursery. As previously noted, Odets
started with the idea of making Georgie a "bitch," but later he
changed his mind and transformed her into the "good mother."
The original conception of Georgie as the "bitch" (that is, the
bad mother) has existence in the finished play solely as a fan-

tasy creation of Frank and Bernie. "Lady," Bernie tells Georgie, "you ride [Frank] like a broom! You're a bitch!" (p. 69). Georgie accuses Frank: "You have a real conviction of woman's perfidy, don't you?" (p. 52). When Georgie threatens to leave her husband and return to New York, Frank fumes: "Who's in New York? What pair of pants are you looking for?" (p. 95). Frank is capable of casting Bernie in the role of the bad mother, too. At the crisis of the play, for example, Bernie says to Frank: "Sit up! Don't act as if I'm beating you up! Don't make me the victimizer! Sit up!" (p. 102). Unconsciously, Bernie seems to be saying: "Don't cast *me* in Georgie's role; that is, the role of the bad cruel mother—the role, incidentally, that I myself cast women in. Let me play the good mother to you, Frank!"

Although Odets did not, as he put it, "verbalize" the reasons for Frank Elgin's alcoholism, he would seem to have presented sufficient material on which a psychological interpretation could be established. With its conscious motivation, unconscious oedipal symbolism and unconscious oral symbolism, *The Country Girl* surely represents Odets' most complex approach to character. It might be objected that the ending is unsatisfactory. Thus, Gerald Rabkin asserts that Frank "might well have gone on another bender and failed to achieve his theatrical triumph," that the "element of hope" for the future is unconvincing, and that "Frank's theatrical triumph does not arise out of the fact of his coming to terms with himself." In 1949 Odets told Russell Rhodes: "Chekhov was the ideal playwright—all character and nothing happens. But people crave excitement and movement." And somewhere Chekhov says that the beginning and end of plays are almost always dishonest. Given the depth and complexity of Frank's neurotic illness, it would be extremely difficult for a dramatist to solve the man's character problems in an entirely satisfactory fashion in the last scene. Here, if not elsewhere in the play, the "linear drive of story" tends to some extent to clash with "psychological drive." Yet Odets has included certain details in the last scene that might serve to lessen the weight of critical censure. Frank Elgin is a man who functions chiefly on the affective, rather than the intellectual, level. Acting is a form of sublimation for Frank. Early in the final scene Bernie, listening to the performance off-stage, remarks: "[Frank's] erratic, in and out—the bursts aren't coming! We'll see . . ." (p. 112). Frank succeeds in the play because he fully identifies with the role. When Frank slaps Nancy-Ellen during the performance he is of course symbolically asserting himself against Georgie— hence the importance of the audition scene in the opening act, where Frank, Bernie and Georgie are identified with the characters in Unger's play—and thus establishing his marriage on a more normal, if perhaps only temporary, basis. The actor informs Bernie:

> I'm sorry, kid, forgive me—it just came out that way! That's what he should do there, the Judge—no one wants him, not even his grandchild! And suddenly I got the image—they're caging a lion—like you shove him in the face! Like they do in the circus, with chairs and brooms! And I couldn't hold it back. . . .
>
> (p. 117)

Notice too that Odets is not inclined to stress Georgie's "hope" for the future in a strident fashion. *The Country Girl* is a long way from *Awake and Sing!*. Under the circumstances of a successful first night performance, one might, like Georgie, feel a mingling of "hope" and "uncertainty."

It is not difficult to locate the faults in *The Country Girl*. One might point out, as suggested earlier, the problem of focal unity in the logical structure of the play. In *Group Psychology*, Freud maintains that individual and social psychology are the same. One might argue that in *The Country Girl* Odets shows three characters in a determined effort to make marriage, which is a *social* institution, a "home." In addition, the playwright takes the audience backstage and reveals the economic instability of the acting profession. Nevertheless, one cannot help but feel that

The Country Girl lacks the social extension of, say, *Golden Boy* or *The Big Knife*. Furthermore, one might be disposed to agree with E. V. R. Wyatt, who says: ". . . Odets has written [*The Country Girl*] with the same conviction that he showed in *Awake and Sing!* but without the sardonic humor." Finally, one might concur with Walter Kerr that "*The Country Girl* is an infinitely better constructed play [than *Night Music*], but its language is somewhat flat alongside the earlier flair for earthy imagery." Once made, these criticisms may be put a little to the side. For all its limitations, *The Country Girl* can unashamedly assume its place among the better plays of the American drama. And it can do this mainly on the strength of its character portrayal. As W. David Sievers has rightly observed: "*The Country Girl* reflects Odets' most mature understanding of human psychology." Indeed, it is entirely possible that *The Country Girl* will still be playing in revivals long after more "profound" and "socially conscious" plays of the present moment have been consigned to oblivion. As Odets said on this point: "It may be that limitation is the beginning of wisdom." Which recalls Nietzche's remark: "One must be narrow to penetrate."

CHAPTER TEN

The Flowering Peach

*Thank you, Lord above, thank you. . . . But what I learned
on the trip, dear God, you can't take it away from me. To
walk in humility, I learned. And listen, even to myself . . .
and to speak softly, with the voices of consolation. Yes,
I hear You, God—Now it's in man's hands to make or destroy the world . . . I'll tell you a mystery. . . .*

—Noah, *The Flowering Peach*

In his last produced play, *The Flowering Peach* (1954), Clifford Odets went to Genesis and wrote what might be called a
modern morality play based on the legend of Noah. During the
Boston try-out of the piece, Odets was interviewed by Herbert
Mitgang of *The New York Times* (December 25, 1954), and said
of his new work:

> This play began about a year and a half ago but I
> didn't intend it as a play. I wanted to do this story of
> Noah and his family as an opera with Aaron Copland. . . .
> But he's a very busy man and somehow we never did get
> together to do it. Then the story began to take shape as
> a play. I have a favorite aunt and uncle in Philadelphia.
> This uncle of mine is very voluble, very human. It occurred
> to me that here was a man of flesh and blood who was the
> Noah of the play. It's important for me to know how

my people speak. I said to myself, wait a minute, Noah had three sons, it was a family life, I know family life. There are children and parents, with ambitions, with disappointments, with anger and love. In the play, these people think like us, speak like us, they're a distillation of modern and biblical. Noah's wife became my Aunt Esther.

The meaning of the play is personal to me and it has whatever meaning anyone in the audience wants to give it. The play came together in my mind with certain feelings about war, which we all have, and some big changes in my personal life. Also, I'm not a kid any more, I'm 47. And at this age I began to ask myself, what happened? Do you want to begin all over again? Who are you and where are you? I went through an examination of personal resources while doing this play. From all this came something, I think, that is very affirmative.

Encouraged by Odets' biographical approach, perhaps, Harold Clurman saw a parallel between Noah and the playwright: "Noah was once a man of great gifts. . . . But somehow in the hectic and sinful times he has suffered for his dreams—dreams of universal comradeship in which all beings were to be sacred to one another. . . ." Malcolm Goldstein and Mordecai Gorelik both follow Clurman in search of biographical details in *The Flowering Peach*. According to Goldstein, Noah's comfort-seeking decision at the end of the play to spend his remaining days with "his obsessively materialistic second [*sic*] son," Shem, corresponds to Odets' "willingness to comply with the House Un-American Activities Committee in Washington." Gorelik, referring to what he calls "the Saroyanesque love-conquers-all theme of redemption" in *The Flowering Peach*, says: "Odets' appearance before the House Committee may have had some influence on his philosophy. Whether it improved his work is open to debate."

It takes no great sagacity to discern that the "personal mean-

ing" approach and the "whatever-meaning-anyone-in-the-audi-
ence-wants-to-give-it" approach both threaten to end in critical
chaos. The first approach runs the risk of falling into the biographical fallacy and the intentional fallacy; the second approach
offers the play as some kind of inkblot test for the audience.
Clurman, of course, goes beyond biography to the play itself.
Goldstein and Gorelik settle for sarcasm and generalization. As
H. D. F. Kitto says: "Criticism is of two kinds: the critic may tell
the reader what he so beautifully thinks about it all, or he may
try to explain the form in which the literature is written." Perhaps it is time, then, to discuss the form of *The Flowering
Peach*.

The play is arranged into nine scenes. (During the New
York run at the Belasco Theater the structure was divided into
two acts.) The time is "Then, not now"—but that description, as
is true of all allegory, remains valid only in a special sense. About
a year passes in the course of the action. When the play opens,
Noah has just had a dream in which God informed him that the
"world's gonna be destroyed!" Esther, Noah's wife, cannot understand why God would choose to save Noah and his family from
the world's fate. Actually, Noah is not happy with God's assignment for him. For one thing, Noah feels too old and weak for the
burden; for another, he knows nothing about boats. Esther remains scornful; indeed, she accuses her husband of sick fantasies,
prompted by senility and overindulgence in alcohol. At times,
Noah himself doubts whether God really communicated with
him. In short, Noah is one of "God's lonely men." Esther, how-
over, argues that her husband's loneliness mainly stems from his
rigid moral code. "Only *you* know God and His command-
ments," she taunts him, "—that's how you used to speak. An'
the people they didn't like it." Yet, curiously enough, Esther
also grudgingly admires her husband's "absolutism," a trait of
Noah's which is extremely vital in the thematic development of
the action. Although Noah and Esther wrangle constantly they
remain very fond of each other, for Odets refers to their quarrels

as "harmless." Nevertheless, within the bipolar tensions of the piece Noah represents abstract morality and Esther stands for concrete "realism." "We'll eat supper," Esther says at one point, "that's real."

This is not to suggest, however, that Noah is merely a cardboard symbol in a lifeless allegory, for he is a complex and engaging creation. "Is Poppa a saint or a fool?" asks Japheth, Noah's youngest son. "Now I know he's half of each . . . but I never know which half is operating." Indeed, for all his absolutism Noah remains a basically humble man. "You are All and Everything an' I'm unworthy," he confesses to God. "You see me—what am I good for? . . . Pass me by—pass me by. Please. . . ." The conflict between Noah and Japheth is even greater in importance and intensity than the one between Noah and Esther. Although Japheth is seemingly mild-mannered and shy, he possesses a stubborn quality in his proud personality. The young man's frequent stammering suggests the presence of buried resentment and hostility toward his father's authoritarian ways. "Perhaps it is because Noah makes unconscious identification with Japheth," Odets says in the directions, "that the boy has always panged the old man's heart; they are two outcasts in the more competent and fluent world."

The point of attack occurs in Scene Two:

NOAH. At least I got one son he believes me, a boy clean as rain. He'll go with me to the end of the way, won't you, sonny?

JAPHETH (uneasily). Poppa, I see your dream . . . but it would be a bitter dose to take—

NOAH (answers in his most lucid and naïve tone). Oh, yeh, it's bitter gall. So many poor people is bound to suffer.

. . .

SHEM [to JAPHETH]. . . . . Who are you? I suppose if God really ordered us to build an ark, you'd think about it!

JAPHETH. I'm thinking about it right now. . . .

SHEM. I'm curious—You would or you wouldn't build the ark?

JAPHETH. Maybe I wouldn't . . . I might decide to die with the others. . . . What's funny? Someone, it seems to me, would have to protest such an avenging, destructive God!

Thus, the struggle between Noah and Japheth is clearly presented, and the major dramatic question—Which man will circumstances prove right?—is projected. Before the scene ends, God sends Noah a gitka ("an olden time creature"), who sings a wordless song in a falsetto voice. The creature's song lures animals to Noah's house, and the family—seeing the gitka as a message from God—is united behind the patriarch. "And only Japheth, alone and horror-struck," says Odets, "stands outside of the tight family scene."

In Scene Three, Japheth works moodily on the ark. Noah, who is too old to do any work himself, grumbles constantly about his son's "disrespect" for authority. Esther—always the "realist" —suggests that Japheth needs a wife. The son, however, protests that he cannot take a wife in such evil times. Nor is this a mere pose on Japheth's part—for Esther has heard her youngest son weeping brokenly in the night and pleading with God to spare the world. Increasingly, Japheth doubts God's goodness. "This son is no longer a boy," Odets says; ". . . there is a responsible and mature air about him, but he is also very tired, distracted and even a little dazed; he is 'marching to the sound of another drum' it would seem." Noah, to be sure, stoutly defends the wisdom and providence of God: "The Lord is good for anybody an' everybody, at all times! He was a wonderful for the world in the old days an', blessed be His name, He will be for the new days to come!" As might be suspected, Esther tends to take Japheth's part against Noah's dogmatic position:

ESTHER. A better son than Japheth you don't have . . . you should tell him we can't get along without him.
NOAH. What, I'll lie to him?
ESTHER. Lie? Try for a week to build the ark without him! You big fool, you!

As Noah sees it, it is God—not Japheth or any other man—
"who does all the work!" For Noah, man's fate is completely
in the hands of God; for Japheth, man's fate is his own
responsibility.

NOAH. . . . [Y]ou've changed, Japheth, in different ways.
JAPHETH. Because I insist upon a rudder? I can't help it—a rud-
    der is vital to the health of the Ark. Would you want me to lie?
ESTHER (*to* NOAH). You want him to lie?

The verbal echoes here plainly underline how much Japheth
is his father's son, and how tight the unity of opposites is between the two characters. Finally, Scene Three ends with Japheth
quitting the ark in protest against God's punishment of man.

Japheth returns, however, in the next scene. And it is worthy
of observation that the young man's motives for returning are
prompted, not by love for or obedience to God, but by regard
for the family. Furthermore, a woman, Goldie, has been instru-
mental in saving Japheth's life and persuading him to rejoin
Noah. For the town has turned against the old man and his
family—"People hold grudges," the woman tells Noah, ". . . and
they're superstitious—they don't like this flood business"—with
the result that some men tried to set fire to Japheth. Thus Goldie,
a woman of loose morals, had to come to the young man's rescue.
Odets is foreshadowing in a skillful way here, for it is to be
through another woman—Rachel, the unhappy wife of Japheth's
brother, Ham—that Noah's favorite son will eventually arrive at
self-realization in love. Tension develops among the members
of the family again in Scene Four, but God intervenes by touch-
ing Noah and the old man is miraculously made young and strong
again.

Esther, in the following scene, pleads with Japheth to join
the family on the ark. The young man, however, remains ada-
mant in his refusal. Desperate now, the mother turns to Rachel
and begs the girl to leave Ham, who has never appreciated her,
and marry the man she truly loves—namely, Japheth. According

to Esther, Japheth and Rachel need to express their mutual love in order to realize themselves fully. Noah, though, stands inflexibly opposed to such an arrangement.

NOAH (*emphatically*). Where marriage an' divorce is concerned, it says in the rules an' regulations, from way back—!

ESTHER (*impatiently*). But since "way back" people are changing, Noah!

NOAH (*writhing*). No, girlie, He didn't destroy the whole world, the Awmighty, to find all the sins on the ark! (*Exploding*) Esther, you don't see—you're blind? *They don't stop acting like human beings*!!

JAPHETH. God had to pick human beings to help Him, didn't He? Now, if He doesn't like it that human beings act like human beings, He's out of luck!

For his part, Noah insists that Japheth marry Goldie: "The world," the old man argues, "needs babies!" At the moment, though, Japheth is not in favor of marrying any woman. He informs Rachel: "Those roads down there! The patterns they make! They're not cobwebs, those roads, the work of a foolish spider, to be brushed away by a peevish boy! Those roads were made by men, men crazy not to be alone or apart! Men, crazy to reach others!" Although Rachel is sympathetic toward Japheth's agony of conscience, she is, like Esther, also "practical" and "realistic" in her appraisal of the situation. Thus, she says: "Japheth, I beg you to think! There is idealism now in just survival!" And with penetrating feminine intuition, she adds: "You're not inspired by your love for your mother or me. You're inspired by your pain, and it's vile." When the flood finally comes, Noah and Esther have a last determined confrontation with their recalcitrant son:

NOAH. You go right in the ark! I'll tell you once again it's God's orders—!

JAPHETH. I'm not obeying orders!

ESTHER (*anger arriving*). But then you'll die in the water!
   What're you talking about?

JAPHETH. I'd rather die in protest, Mamma, than live.

ESTHER. Protest—that's foolish! You think you know what's
   right? So have your own sons an' teach them!

Losing patience, Noah suddenly strikes Japheth and knocks
him unconscious. As the young man is carried to the ark, the
scene ends in an "appalling atmosphere."

Throughout Scene Six, Noah is increasingly beset by the con-
tentions of his family. The chief difficulty is Japheth's desire to
marry Rachel. According to Noah, his son must marry Goldie
because God wants it that way. "He's Boss over me," says Noah,
"an' I'm boss over you. . . ." Shem, Noah's oldest son, agrees: "In
unstable times respect for authority must prevail." Noah's view
of God and morality remains unyielding. When the old man
continues to encounter opposition to his views, he grows in-
censed—and, finally, he disappears, in order to get drunk. And
he remains drunk for nine weeks. Meanwhile Japheth steers the
ark and, in Noah's absence, assumes leadership on the vessel.

In addition to Noah's other difficulties, Esther is dying. Yet
the old man will not be persuaded that he is in any manner responsible for the troubles on the ark. Consequently, he asks God:
"Why don't you tell the boys they're wrong?" When Noah discovers Japheth employing a rudder, he is angry. Shem tries to
function as a mediator: "You must learn to work together—the
ark needs you both." Noah remains stubborn, however, and the
turning point in the action arrives in Scene Seven when the old
man forces the issue regarding Japheth's use of the rudder.
"Poppa claims," says the youngest son, "the ark is in Divine
Hands only? Well, I'm ready to agree. . . . We'll throw off the
rudder." As the ark begins to fill with water, the family panics,
and even Noah is visibly disturbed:

NOAH. Japhie knows about such things . . . he'll use his own
   judgment. . . .

JAPHETH (*simply*). To use my own judgment, Poppa, I'd have to trust myself.

NOAH (*poignantly*). So, really . . . *why* don't you trust yourself?

JAPHETH. Because you don't permit that!

. . .

SHEM. Japheth, the fate of every living thing depends on you. . . .

JAPHETH (*to* SHEM *or himself*). I have a strange feeling that God changed today. . . . I'll go . . . but I never want to talk to Poppa again. . . .

SHEM [*to* NOAH]. Go down and stay with Mamma. And make no mistake she's very sick. Don't get in our way today. (*Then voice trembling*) I'm very ashamed to say it . . . but your youngest son is a better man of God than you!

. . .

NOAH. The oldest day of my life. . . . What did I done, God . . . ? I'll let the boys run things. I'll be the janitor on the ark . . . it fits to me. . . . Oh, gitka. My Esther is sick? Maybe dying? I'm ashamed to face her. God is far away, children . . . we're lonely people.

This is the turning point because it focuses the problem raised at the point of attack—that is, What will be the result of the clash between Noah and Japheth?—and, with Noah's apparent defeat here, it prepares the audience for the resolution, where the final meaning of the play shall stand revealed.

The crisis and climax occur in Scene Eight. As was also evident in *The Country Girl*, Odets tends to play down the resolution. The pivotal points are approached slowly and the effects are rather muted. When Noah first appears in this scene, Odets describes him as "a sad, wistful and somewhat purged man, almost as old as he was before God transformed him. . . ." Esther still pleads with Noah to marry Japheth and Rachel, but the old man persists in his refusal. "[God] won't permit such marriages," Noah claims. ". . . And secondly, He won't let nothing happen to you, the God I know"; to which Esther replies: "Maybe you don't know Him . . . any more. . . ." This is the crisis, for if Noah does not "know" God, then he must agree that Esther and Japheth have been right and that he, in his authoritarianism and utter dependence on God, has been wrong. "The children," says Esther, placing a hat on her head to shade her eyes from the sun, "their happiness . . . is my promised land." The end is near for Esther, however, and her final words to her husband are: "Noah, I'll tell you a mystery—." When the dove returns to the ark to signal that land is near, Noah discovers that his wife is dead. "Children," Noah says, realizing at last the folly of his uncompromising rigidity, "the whole night is ahead to give thanks to Heaven. Go better now every husband should kiss each wife, as Mother wanted. And I'll go kiss mine and close her eyes. . . ." This is the climax of the play.

When Noah appears in the final scene, he is clearly a changed man:

Here he is, old NOAH, *humorous, gentle and affable, very affectionate with here and there a lost, wistful touch; there is nowhere a trace of his old impatient and authoritarian attitudes. He is wearing a strange little hat on the back of his head; his arms are filled with* ESTHER'S *one-leafed plant and Becky, the dove, in a wicker cage.*

The hat, of course, is a traditional symbol of authority; consequently, the significance of Odets' directions is clear. For events have transformed Noah into the image of his late wife; in other words, Noah is now a humanist. Thus Odets returns to the resurrection theme first delineated in *Awake and Sing!*; however, Noah, unlike Ralph Berger, is an old man who will soon die. "I cannot see any future without Mother!" Noah remarks in Scene Eight. "If she dies, I will go right with her . . . so help me, God, which is true."

In *The Flowering Peach*, as in *Awake and Sing!*, though, the future belongs to youth. For at the conclusion of Odets' last play all the women are pregnant with new life, and the presence of love is everywhere in evidence. "The world looks washed," Rachel says; and to confirm her hopeful view "a young peach tree grows in profuse and handsome bloom." A warm, kindly Noah says: "Go now, children, an' be fruitful and multiply. . . . An' everywhere and in all things replenish the earth." The world is beautiful again, and Noah feels that the experience on the boat forced all of the members of the family to change, to appreciate this new-found treasure. "Maybe," says Japheth diplomatically, "God changes when men change." As the younger people exit happily to work out their destinies, Noah remains alone on stage:

> Right here I could sleep out my remaining years . . . till my Esther wants me. . . . (*Then he cocks his head, for like us he hears the returning presence of God*) (*Dreamily*) You're hanging around, Lord? That's just how I feel. (*Listening*) No, I *won't* get off the ark. Forgive me, Sir, excuse me . . . first a little guarantee, a covenant, an' then I'll go . . . (*Watchful and waiting*) You know what I want, Lord. Just like you guarantee each month, with a woman's blood, that men will be born . . . give such a sign that you won't destroy the world again. . . . (*He waits tensely until the music hum relaxes into a quality of benevolence, and relaxing and smiling, asks:*) Where shall I look? Where? (*Anyone who would be watching sees the rainbow in the sky before* NOAH *turns and sees it with an awed happiness*) Thank you, Lord above, thank you . . . But what I learned on the trip, dear God, you can't take it away from me. To walk in humility, I learned. . . . And listen, even to *myself* . . . and to speak softly, with the voices of consolation. Yes, I hear You, God— Now it's in man's hands to make or destroy the world. —I'll tell you a mystery. . . .

Harold Clurman claims that in the course of action Japheth "learns that his idealism is too absolute, that forbearance is necessary." There is, however, no evidence in the play to support this interpretation. True, Japheth declares in the final scene that "we've all changed"; but the youngest son has not moved in the direction indicated by Clurman. In Scene Five, the reader will recall, Noah is forced to knock Japheth unconscious in order to get his son on the ark. Nor is there any suggestion in the rest of the play that Japheth has altered his thinking about God's treatment of man. Quite the contrary—for he affirms, as my analysis of the structure brings out, an evolving conception of God. Japheth changes into a more self-confident individual, it would seem, for two reasons: one, he establishes his sense of identity through the struggle with his father; two, he is made to feel more secure—and hence better able to trust himself—through the agency of Rachel's love for him. Like Noah, Japheth is humanized to a large extent by a woman. The turning point and resolution of the play both pivot on the conflict between Noah and Japheth—a conflict which, as I have shown, ends in Noah's defeat. Perhaps Odets, as some critics have suggested, came to feel that "There is idealism now in just survival," but it is far from clear that Japheth shares this alleged conviction.

Some reviewers complained about what they considered to be the "gratuitous" and "pointless" quarrels of the family, and a few registered the opinion that the "wife swapping" was equally irrelevant. Both these criticisms, of course, miss the whole point of Odets' arrangement of the action. The many arguments between the members of Noah's family underlines the radical imperfection of man. In Scene Six, as I have previously pointed out, Noah complains that his family continues to act human; and Japheth declares that man cannot help but act according to the nature God gave him. Nor does Odets despair over man's lack of perfection. *The Flowering Peach* does not posit an absurd universe; there is no waiting for Godot . . . or for Lefty. Similarly, the "wife swapping" action is integrally related to the structure and theme of the play, for here again man—not God—is the measure of things; the heart—not law—is man's most reliable guide in life.

In his review of *The Flowering Peach*, Maurice Zolotow accuses Odets of religiosity—that is, of using the Noah legend when it is not at all certain, according to the reviewer, that the playwright believes in God or Noah. Zolotow also attacks Odets on the score of historical carelessness, citing the dramatist's employment of anachronistic religious rituals. Aesthetically, the historical question is irrelevant, for the rituals that Odets uses do not impair either the coherence or the significance of the action. Odets is not the only important modern writer to employ "myth" as a symbolic scaffolding for his work. Joyce, Faulkner, O'Neill, Hemingway, Eliot, Fitzgerald, Obey, Yeats, Tennessee Williams and others have all drawn on one or another available "myth"—Homeric, Christian, Freudian, Marxist, Horatio Alger—to meet the challenge of an age in which a community of shared beliefs is lacking. The Bible, as Faulkner put it, is simply a "tool that will make a better chicken-house." The story of Noah lends Odets' play a necessary universality. Nevertheless, there is no rigid one-for-one correspondence between the Old Testament and *The Flowering Peach*. Odets, in fact, treats the legend imaginatively and ironically; for instance, he "argues" for an end to authoritarianism—both religious and, by logical extension, political—and an adoption of humanism. Which is not exactly the style of an Old Testament prophet.

Yet *The Flowering Peach* is a "religious" play. As Eric Bentley (not noted for his enthusiasm for American drama) says: "If religion is to be found, not in creeds and avowals but in reverence for life, in humility before the mystery of things, in a man's spontaneous and pervasive spirituality, then this Noah is a religious man, and so is his author. In fact, Mr. Odets has shown our fumbling theological playwrights how to put religion —or rather, religiousness—on stage." And Richard Hayes adds: "How wonderful . . . to find in this time of noisy commitments and harassing coercion a serious statement about human life which never says *must* or *should*, never imposes, sets up programs, announces, prescribes—only draws from the neglected

well of our common pieties the small, permanent manifestations
of tenderness and affection, of pleasure and reverence and a faith
rich enough to nourish the seeds of the word."

Although much of *The Flowering Peach* is vintage Odets, it
is also plain that there is something new under the sun in this
last play. For one thing, as Michael J. Mendelsohn has suggested,
The Flowering Peach—unlike *Awake and Sing!*—clearly emphasizes the importance of family unity. For another thing, there is
the question of money. "On the ark," says Noah, "nothing will
be for sale, no investments, hear me? Money is unholy dirt on
the ark—." When Noah learns that Shem, the businessman, has
been saving dried manure briquettes for fuel, the old man cries:
"On the holy ark he's makin' business! Manure! With manure
you want to begin a new world?" Esther, however, rushes to
Shem's aid: "If you made it to sell, Shem, you're a low dog! But
if you made it for the family . . . why throw it overboard . . . ?"
According to Clurman, Esther's statement suggests that Shem's
"canniness may be useful if he will employ it for the family,
the community." Since Esther knows the truth about Shem's
motives—namely, that he *is* thinking of business (Odets says:
"Esther begins to navigate a little" here)—it would appear that
Clurman is in error in his interpretation of the scene. Man is,
once again, a very imperfect being; and there is something almost
too pure about Noah's stance on the money question. In Eugene
O'Neill's *The Iceman Cometh*, the disillusioned ex-radical Larry
Slade says: "The material the ideal free society must be constructed from is men themselves and you can't build a marble
temple out of a mixture of mud and manure." Odets seems to
say, however, that the "free society" has no choice but to build
on "mud and manure"—that there can be no flowering peach
without manure. Man, in other words, must bring his ideals
into harmony with reality. Only those who suffer from Noah's
own earlier purity of purpose (from what the theologian refers
to as "angelism") would reject Odets' approach here as necessarily evidence of a "loss of standards."

The Flowering Peach, Barry Hyams points out, suggests a playwright who "sees life in three dimensions, in which saints and lunatics must be arbitrated into moderation and compassion; where evil can be part of good, and the opposite can possibly be true." An analysis of Odets' early plays, however, reveals a dramatist who is occasionally guilty of "either-or" thinking. (As I pointed out in my opening chapter, evidence of such thinking is revealed in the rhetoric, if not always in the actions, of many representative figures of the thirties.) And if there is intensity and power in the early plays there is also in them a certain naïveté. Odets told Herbert Mitgang:

> When you start out, you have to champion something. . . . But if you still feel that way after ten or fifteen years, you're nuts. No young writer is broad. I couldn't have written *The Flowering Peach* twenty years ago. As you grow older, you mature. The danger is that in broadening, as you mature, you may dilute your art. A growing writer always walks that tightrope.

Odets would seem to have walked the "tightrope" successfully in *The Flowering Peach*, which is both "broad" and largely "undiluted." True, *some* of the old anger, drive and passion has disappeared; that, however (as Odets himself suggested to Mitgang), is to be expected in any writer. The characteristics of youth are not the only values to be looked for in a play. Balance, restraint, wisdom—these are virtues, too.

The Flowering Peach is, then, one of the most impressive plays in the American theater. Yet, one regrets to say, it has never been published in its complete version. Why not? "All I know," Odets informed Bob Thomas in 1959, "is that my last play, *The Flowering Peach*, contained some of the best writing I have ever done. No, it wasn't a commercial success. But that doesn't matter in the long analysis." And—"in the long analysis"—Odets was, of course, correct.

SUMMING UP

Clifford Odets was a complex man, nurtured in a complicated age, but out of his intense struggles with self and society were born six plays of continuing importance. The stock picture of Odets as the radical author of *Waiting For Lefty*, who later abased himself before the Un-American Activities Committee and sold out to the Establishment, makes classification easy for criticism at a gallop. Such a view fails to do justice, however, to the depth, intensity and relevance of Odets' plays. It is simply untrue, for example, that the later work of Odets is uniformly poor. *The Big Knife, The Country Girl* and *The Flowering Peach* can stand comparison with *Awake and Sing!, Golden Boy* and *Rocket to the Moon.* Indeed, the early *Golden Boy* and the late *The Flowering Peach* are probably—all parts considered—the two best plays Odets wrote in his twenty years as a major American dramatist.

Although *Waiting for Lefty* will continue, no doubt, to be required reading in college survey courses (it fits so snugly into an anthology and it is, moreover, so conveniently pigeonholed!), Odets was moving away from "proletarian drama" by 1936. (Even *Awake and Sing!* has a rich personal, or psychological, dimension and a level of thematic concern which resists glib labels). Like every play that has ever been written, *Golden Boy* bears the stamp of its decade. Nevertheless, this fine play also transcends the narrow interests of the thirties, for in Odets' depiction of a young man's struggle between self-realization and self-destruction, between idealism and materialism, *Golden Boy* persists in being meaningful. Similarly, the later plays project specific pre-occupations of the post-Second World War period; yet *The Big Knife, The Country Girl*—and, especially, *The Flowering Peach*—also reveal themes that have obsessed imaginative writers in every decade since, at least, the First World War. Odets, in other words, is very much in the mainstream of modern theater and literature.

In the past critics have frequently tended to confuse Odets with the protagonists of his plays. Too many commentators, for instance, speak of Joe Bonaparte, Charlie Castle and old Noah as though these characters were identical with their creator and not formal elements in a dramaturgical design. To be sure, Joe Bonaparte, say, or Charlie Castle possesses enormous vitality on the stage (as John Gassner says somewhere: ". . . Odets could galvanize a corpse into providing an illusion of life") but the "life" such characters possess is an *artistic* "life"; such characters do not have a one-for-one correspondence with Odets himself. Biographical criticism of Odets has too often substituted intrusive preachment and irrelevant backstage gossip for rigorous analysis of the plays. At times, Odets encouraged the biographical fallacy— his press interviews offer abundant proof for this assertion; not infrequently, Odets was guilty of the intentional fallacy. The playwright's own evaluations of his work, although generally interesting and often illuminating, are sometimes misleading, which is to say that Odets was capable of writing better than he knew or intended. Only by patient scrutiny of each play—with detailed attention to structure, character, dialogue and theme— can one hope to arrive at a reasonably objective estimate of Odets' achievement.

The structure of an Odets play—critical clichés about Chekhov and the dramatist's own erroneous remarks notwithstanding— is Ibsenite. There are times, it is true, when the Russian master's influence appears discernible in certain *surface* Odetsian techniques—those tragi-comic juxtapositions, for example, in *Awake and Sing!* and in some other pieces. The *basic* form of each play, built up from individual but causally related scene units, however, reveals a single-action development. And analysis of this logical structure in Odets' best plays refutes the charge that he was merely a "scenewright." There is much more unity and coherence in *Awake and Sing!*, *Rocket to the Moon* and *The Big Knife* than is usually allowed. *Golden Boy* and *The Flowering Peach* are perfect in structure, as I tried to show in my chapters devoted to these two plays.

"Every human being has his own gallery of characters which he himself is," Odets explained to Mendelsohn. "The more gifted the human being, the larger his gallery of characters. . . . If you are really creative, you can only write out of this gallery of characters. You're lucky if you have six or seven of them." Odets himself created a memorable "gallery of characters": young Ralph Berger, Jacob, Bessie, Myron, Morty, Moe Axelrod, Joe Bonaparte, Eddie Fuseli, Ben Stark, Cleo Singer, Prince, Charlie Castle, Frank and Georgie Elgin, Bernie Dodd, Japheth and old Noah; these and others are unforgettable creations. Though such characters derive, as Odets put it, from "psychological character-istics or trends" in the playwright and though they are part of a pattern in the totality of a play, they somehow manage to assume a life of their own. One does not easily forget the Ralph Berger who complains: "It's crazy—all my life I want a pair of black and white shoes and I can't get them. It's crazy!" (p. 42). One re-mains haunted by the Charlie Castle who, just before killing himself, says: "Could you ever know that all my life I yearned for a world and people to call out the best in me?" (p. 72). Nor does one quickly lose the memory of Cleo Singer as she says: "It's getting late to play at life; I want to *live* it. . . . You see? I don't ask for much . . ." (p. 416, italics in original). Such char-acters, once encountered, continue to exist in one's imagination. How many other contemporary playwrights can claim an equiv-alent "gallery of characters"?

Even unsympathetic critics of Odets have acknowledged his verbal gifts. This talent has little to do with the accuracy of a tape-recorder, or with the ability to write stunning curtain lines.

The Odets canon is full of quotable dialogue (in the present study I have given many examples), but no line in the best plays is there for its own sake. Odets told Wagner "there are playwrights who don't know their punctuation isn't very important in the recreation of the character they've written, or that, as we used to say in the Group Theater, their script is only a series of stenographic notes." Analysis of Odets' plays nevertheless reveals a highly sophisticated use of dramatic language, an employment of words that can bear close reading and analytical criticism. Dialogue in the best work of Odets performs a number of simultaneous functions: it expresses character; it forwards action; it creates mood; and it exposes theme. But in addition, Odets' language also possesses color, power and variety—that is, it has distinction aside from its service to character, structure and theme. Imagery in some plays—*Golden Boy*, for instance—is especially noteworthy. In short, Odets is one of the rare "poets" of the modern drama.

Throughout this book a number of Odetsian themes have been explored and analyzed. Here I should like to review a couple of them, to point up and trace a pattern of thematic development in Odets' work. For example, in *Awake and Sing!* Jacob says: "A woman insults a man's soul like no other thing in the whole world" (p. 48). Bessie is the head of the family in that play because natural relations have been reversed as a result of socioeconomic dislocations. Joe Bonaparte in *Golden Boy* and Ben Stark in *Rocket to the Moon* are "half men" because they have compromised with their true nature. In *Night Music,* Fay is much more active and aggressive than the vociferous hero, Steve Takis; whereas in *Clash by Night*, Odets again portrays a world in which men fail to be wholly masculine, a world in which women are left unfulfilled and unhappy in their dominant role. Similarly, *The Big Knife* and *The Country Girl* both project male leads who are "half men." Charlie Castle in the first play has, like the earlier Joe Bonaparte, compromised with his better self; Frank Elgin in the second play has regressed, as my analysis of his neurotic

personality suggests, even further into the past than the childish
Jerry Wilenski of *Clash by Night*. Psychological and social factors appear in most of these plays, although the degree of emphasis in them shifts from play to play. Sometimes there is a
split between the two levels of motivation—as in *Night Music*
and *Clash by Night*; at least once—in *The Country Girl*—social
causation almost disappears from view.

The Flowering Peach represents a development in Odets' thematic concerns. Although Noah is strong and aggressive (he is,
one might say, a "real man"), he also needs the help of a strong
woman in order to realize his full humanity. Although Noah
wears his wife's hat at the conclusion of the play, unlike previous
Odetsian protagonists, he has not been symbolically emasculated.
At the conclusion to *Awake and Sing!*, according to Odets, Ralph
"stands full and strong in the doorway" (p. 101); there is some
doubt, however, about the young man's newly acquired manhood. Noah, in his conflict with Esther and Japheth, is tempo-
rarily "castrated": "I'll be the janitor on the ark," the old man
says at the turning point (and one is reminded here of Schlosser,
the janitor who "lost his identity twenty years before," in *Awake
and Sing!* [p. 39]); but the Noah who, at the end of the play,
stands before the audience bargaining with God Himself is a
character in complete possession of his manhood. Male and
female, Odets seems to be saying in his last play, should comple-
ment one another. Consequently, *The Flowering Peach* represents Odets' most mature picture of life and human relations,
including sexual relations. If the Group Theater had once led
Odets to confuse drama with religion and if the Group, together
with the Marxists, had encouraged him to expect eventual perfection from man, *The Flowering Peach* reveals a wiser playwright, one who is able to treat a religious theme dramatically,
one who is able to accept the ineradicable imperfections of man
with charity and understanding. If Odets' early play *910 Eden
Street* (and note the ironic Biblical reference) "gave evidence
of internal injury in the writer" (Clurman), *The Flowering*

Peach suggests a writer who has come, at least in the act of creation, to terms with himself and his world. One could argue that Odets' last play transcends such distinctions as "personal" and "social" and achieves a level of universality lacking perhaps in even the best of his other plays.

Finally, the work of Odets gives expression, in part, to a characteristic vision of our time—a vision of disgust, fear, emptiness and melancholy. As noted earlier, Odets told Mendelsohn: " . . . I have shown as much of the seamy side of life as any other playwright of the twentieth century, if not more." Unlike a number of favored dramatists today, however, Odets never rests ultimately in negation; he never degrades man; he never confuses the normal and the abnormal; he never reduces life to a dry abstraction; he never withholds hope. Love, anger, ecstasy, power, "belief" ("I would say," Odets also informed Mendelsohn, "that I have a *belief* in man and his possibilities as the measure of things")—these are the hallmarks of Odets' art. In Odets' first play, *Waiting for Lefty*, Agate cries: "Put fruit trees where our ashes are!" (p. 31). In *Paradise Lost*, Leo Gordon says: "Oh, if you could only see with me the greatness of men. . . . I tell you the whole world is for men to possess. Heartbreak and terror are not the heritage of mankind! The world is beautiful. No fruit tree wears a lock and key" (p. 230). At the conclusion of his last play, Odets has Noah—who holds a branch of the young peach tree in his hands—exclaim: "*This* is ahead . . . a fruitful world . . . the people need happiness" (italics in original). Have we contemplated the Valley of Ashes for so long that we can no longer behold the rainbow that appears before the curtain falls on *The Flowering Peach*? Have we wandered through so many dreary contemporary Waste Lands that we can no longer believe in the "fruit tree"? Perhaps, as someone has suggested, we have come to love our vision of the Valley of Ashes and the Waste Land; perhaps we have come to cherish, in some masochistic fashion, our self-pity and unhappiness. If so, the fault would seem to lie in us—and not in the plays of Clifford Odets.

REFERENCES

Aaron, Daniel. *Writers on the Left.* New York, 1961.

Adamic, Louis. *My America.* New York, 1938.

Agee, James. *Agee on Film.* Boston, 1964.

Allen, Frederick Lewis. *Since Yesterday 1929-1939.* New York, 1940.

Anon. "White Hope," *Time* [cover story on Odets], XXXII (December 5, 1938), 44–47.

Aulicino, Armand. "How *The Country Girl* Came About," *Theater Arts,* XXXVI (May 1952), 54–57.

Bell, Daniel. *The End of Ideology.* Glencoe, 1960.

Bentley, Eric. "Ibsen, Pro and Con," *In Search of Theater* (New York, 1954), 344–356.

———— "Poetry of the Theater" [Rev. of *The Flowering Peach*], *What Is Theater?* (Boston, 1956), 34–38.

Bernanos, Georges. *The Diary of a Country Priest.* New York, 1954.

Bergler, Edmund. *The Basic Neurosis.* New York, 1949.

Block, Anita. *The Changing World in Plays and Theater.* Boston, 1939.

Bradley, A. C. *Shakespearean Tragedy.* Cleveland, 1955.

Brown, John Mason. "Biting the Hand" [Rev. of *The Big Knife*], *Saturday Review,* XXXII (March 19, 1949), 34–35.

Brustein, Robert. "America's New Culture Hero," *Commentary,* XXV (February 1958), 123–129.

Burke, Kenneth. *The Philosophy of Literary Form.* New York, 1957.

Clurman, Harold. *The Fervent Years.* New York, 1945.

———— *Lies Like Truth.* New York, 1958.

———— "Introduction," *Famous American Plays of the 1930's* (New York, 1959), 7–17.

Communist Infiltration of the Hollywood Motion-Picture Industry, Part 8. Hearings Before the Committee on Un-American Activities, House of Representatives, Eighty-Second Congress, Second Session (May 19 and 20, 1952). U. S. Govt. Printing Office. Washington, 1952.

Corbett, James J. *The Roar of the Crowd.* New York, 1924.

Cowley, Malcolm. "A Remembrance of the Red Romance," *Esquire,* LXI (March 1964), 124–130.

——— "While They Waited for Lefty," *Saturday Review,* XLVII (June 6, 1964), 16–19, 61.

——— "The 1930's Were an Age of Faith," *The New York Times Book Review* (December 13, 1964), 4–5, 14–17.

Downer, Alan S. *Fifty Years of American Drama 1900–1950.* Chicago, 1951.

Dusenbury, Winifred. *The Theme of Loneliness in Modern American Drama.* Gainesville, 1960.

Eisinger, Chester E. *Fiction of the Forties.* Chicago, 1963.

Farrell, James T. [Rev. of *Paradise Lost*], *Partisan Review and Anvil,* III (February 1936), 28–29.

Ferguson, Otis. "Pay-off on Odets," *New Republic,* C (September 27, and October 4, 1939), 216–217, 242–243.

Fiedler, Leslie. "The Search for the 30's," *Commentary,* XX (September 1955), 285–289.

——— "John Peale Bishop and the Other Thirties," *Commentary,* XLIII (April 1967), 74–82.

Fitzgerald, F. Scott. *The Crack Up.* New York, 1956.

Flexner, Eleanor. *American Playwrights: 1918–1938.* New York, 1938.

Freud, Sigmund. *Group Psychology and the Analysis of the Ego.* London, 1922.

Gagey, Edmond M. *Revolution in American Drama.* New York, 1947.

Gassner, John. "The Long Journey of a Talent," *Theater Arts,* XXXIII (July 1949), 25–30.

——— "Anton Chekhov," *A Treasury of the Theater* (New York, 1960), 205–206.

——— "Introduction," *Play-Making* by William Archer (New York, 1960), v–xxxi.

Gibson, William. "Preface: A Momento," *Golden Boy: the Book of a Musical* (New York, 1966), 11–24.

Gilder, Rosamond. [Rev. of *Rocket to the Moon*], *Theater Arts,* XXXIII (January 1939), 12–13.

——— [Rev. of *Clash by Night*], *Theater Arts,* XXVI (March 1942), 150–152.

Gold, Michael. *Jews Without Money.* New York, 1930.

Goldman, Eric. *The Crucial Decade—and After: America, 1945–1960.* New York, 1960.

Goldstein, Malcolm. "Clifford Odets and the Found Generation," *American Drama and Its Critics*, ed. Alan S. Downer (Chicago, 1965), 133–146.

Gorelik, Mordecai. *New Theaters for Old*. New York, 1962.

——— "Legacy of the New Deal Drama," *Drama Survey*, IV (Spring 1965), 38–43.

Gurko, Leo. *The Angry Decade*. New York, 1947.

Gwynn, Frederick L., and Joseph L. Blotner (eds.). *Faulkner in the University*. New York, 1958.

Hauser, Arnold. *The Social History of Art*. New York, 1958.

Hayes, Richard. [Rev. of *The Flowering Peach*], *Commonweal*, LXI (February 11, 1955), 502–503.

Hebbel, Friedrich. "Journals," *Playwrights on Playwriting*, ed. Toby Cole (New York, 1961), 285–288.

Heinz, W. C., ed. "Drama" [A Note on *Golden Boy*], *The Fireside Book of Boxing* (New York, 1961), 305.

Hemingway, Ernest. *The Green Hills of Africa*. New York, 1935.

——— "The Gambler, the Nun, and the Radio," *The Snows of Kilimanjaro and Other Stories*. New York, n. d.

——— *For Whom the Bell Tolls*. New York, 1940.

Hewes, Henry. "American Playwrights Self-Appraised," *Saturday Review*, XXXVIII (September 3, 1955), 18–19.

Hicks, Granville. *The Great Tradition*. New York, 1935.

Himelstein, Morgan Y. *Drama was a Weapon*. New Brunswick, 1963.

Howells, William Dean. *Criticism and Fiction*. Cambridge, 1962.

Hughes, Catharine. "Odets: the Price of Success," *Commonweal*, LXXVIII (September 20, 1963), 558–560.

Hyams, Barry. "Twenty Years on a Tightrope," *Theater Arts*, XXXIX (April 1955), 68–70, 86.

Kael, Pauline. "Tourist in the City of Youth," *New Republic*, CLVI (February 11, 1967), 30–35.

Kaplan, Charles. "Two Depression Plays and Broadway's Popular Idealism," *American Quarterly*, XV (Winter 1963), 579–585.

Kazin, Alfred. *Starting Out in the Thirties*. Boston, 1962.

Kempton, Murray. *Part of Our Time*. New York, 1955.

Kernodle, George K. "Patterns of Belief in Contemporary Drama," *Spiritual Problems in Contemporary Literature*, ed. Stanley R. Hopper (New York, 1957), 187–206.

Kerr, Walter. [Rev. of *Night Music* revival], *Commonweal*, LIV (April 27, 1951), 58–59.

Kitto, H. D. F. *Greek Tragedy*. New York, 1954.

Koestler, Arthur. *The God That Failed*, ed. Richard Crossman (New York, 1950), 11–66.

Kostelanetz, Richard. "Men of the 30's," *Commonweal*, LXXXIII (December 3, 1965), 266–269.

Krutch, Joseph W. [Rev. of *Golden Boy*], *Nation*, CXLV (November 13, 1937), 540.

———— "The Theater," *America Now*, ed. Harold E. Stearns (New York, 1938), 72–81.

———— [Rev. of *Night Music*], *Nation*, CL (March 2, 1940), 316–317.

———— [Rev. of *Clash by Night*], *Nation*, CLIV (January 10, 1942), 45–46.

———— [Rev. of *The Big Knife*], *Nation*, CLXVIII (March 19, 1949), 340–341.

Lawson, John Howard. *Theory and Technique of Playwriting*. New York, 1960.

Lumley, Frederick. *Trends in 20th Century Drama*. Fair Lawn, 1960.

Marshall, Margaret. [Rev. of *The Country Girl*], *Nation*, CLXXI (November 25, 1950), 493.

McCarten, John. "Revolution's Number One Boy," *New Yorker*, XIV (January 22, 1938), 21–27.

Mendelsohn, Michael J. "Odets at Center Stage," *Theater Arts*, XLVII (May and June, 1963), 16–19, 74–75; 28–30, 78–80.

———— "Clifford Odets and the American Family," *Drama Survey*, III (Fall 1963), 238–243.

Meserve, Walter J. *An Outline History of American Drama*. Totowa, 1965.

Moravia, Alberto. *The Empty Canvas*. New York, 1961.

Nathan, George Jean. [Rev. of *Night Music*], *Newsweek*, XV (March 4, 1940), 42.

O'Hara, John. [Rev. of *Clash by Night*], *Newsweek*, XIX (January 12, 1942), 46.

O'Neill, Eugene. *The Iceman Cometh*. New York ,1946.

Patterson, Floyd. *Victory Over Myself*. New York, 1962.

Phelan, Kappo. [Rev. of *The Big Knife*], *Commonweal*, XLIX (March 25, 1949), 590–591.

Phillips, William. "What Happened in the 30's," *Commentary*, XXXIV (September 1962), 204–212.

Powdermaker, Hortense. *Hollywood, the Dream Factory*. Boston, 1950.

Rabkin, Gerald. *Drama and Commitment*. Bloomington, 1964.

Rahv, Philip. "Proletarian Literature: A Political Autopsy," *Southern Review* (Winter 1939), 616–628.

Richler, Mordecai. "A Hero of Our Time," *New York Review*, VIII (February 23, 1967), 28–30.

Rideout, Walter. *The Radical Novel in the United States 1900–1954.* New York, 1956.

Shuman, R. Baird. *Clifford Odets.* New York, 1962.

Sievers, W. David. *Freud on Broadway.* New York, 1955.

Stanton, Stephen S. "The Well Made Play and the Modern Theater," *Camille and Other Plays* (New York, 1957), vii–xxxix.

Stein, Jean. "William Faulkner," *Paris Review*, IV (Spring 1956), 28–52.

Steinbeck, John. *The Grapes of Wrath.* New York, 1939.

Swados, Harvey, ed. *The American Writer and the Great Depression.* Indianapolis, 1966.

Troy, William. "F. Scott Fitzgerald—The Authority of Failure," *Accent*, VI (Autumn 1945), 56–60.

Tunney, Gene. *Arms for Living.* New York, 1941.

Vernon, Grenville. "The Stage and Screen," *Commonweal*, XXIX (December 16, 1938), 215.

Wagner, Arthur. "How a Playwright Triumphs," *Harper's*, CCXXXIII (September 1966), 64–74.

Weales, Gerald. *American Drama Since World War II.* New York, 1962.

———— *A Play and Its Parts.* New York, 1964.

Wecter, Dixon. *The Age of the Great Depression.* New York, 1948.

Wiegand, William. "Arthur Miller and the Man Who Knows," *The Western Review*, XXI (Winter 1957), 85–102.

Wright, Richard. *The God That Failed,* ed. Richard Crossman (New York, 1950), 103–146.

Wyatt, E. V. R. [Rev. of *Clash by Night*], *Catholic World*, CLIV (February 1942), 601.

———— [Rev. of *The Country Girl*], *Catholic World*, CLXXII (January 1951), 310.

Young, Stark. [Rev. of *Golden Boy*], *New Republic*, LXXXXIII (November 17, 1937), 44–45.

Zolotow, Maurice. [Rev. of *The Flowering Peach*], *Theater Arts*, XXXIX (March 1955), 23, 90.